Elections in 18th-Century England:
Polling, Politics and Participation

Elections in 18th-Century England: Polling, Politics and Participation

Edited by

M. O. GRENBY

and

ELAINE CHALUS

WILEY

for

THE PARLIAMENTARY HISTORY YEARBOOK TRUST

John Wiley & Sons

Registered Office
John Wiley & Sons Ltd, The Atrium, Southern Gate, Chichester, West Sussex, PO19 8SQ, UK

Editorial Offices
101 Station Landing, Medford, MA 02155, USA
9600 Garsington Road, Oxford, OX4 2DQ, UK
The Atrium, Southern Gate, Chichester, West Sussex, PO19 8SQ, UK

For details of our global editorial offices, for customer services, and for information about how to apply for permission to reuse the copyright material in this book please see our website at https://www.wiley.com/WileyCDA/Brand/id-35.html.

Library of Congress Cataloging-in-Publication data is available for this book

ISBN 9781394279098

A catalogue record for this title is available from the British Library
Set in 10/12pt Bembo
by Aptara Inc., India
Printed and bound in Singapore
by Markono Print Media Pte Ltd

1   2024

CONTENTS

Parliamentary History, Vol. 43, pt. 1 (2024), pp. 3–4

NOTES ON CONTRIBUTORS

Nigel Aston is Emeritus Reader in the School of History, Politics, and International Relations at the University of Leicester where he taught for two decades and is currently Research Associate at the University of York. Aston has written and published widely on British and French religious, political, and intellectual history in the long 18th century, and his latest book, *Enlightened Oxford: The University in the Cultural and Political Life of Britain and Beyond, 1680–1820*, was published by OUP in 2023.

Elaine Chalus is Professor of British History at the University of Liverpool. An expert on gender and political culture, Elaine's numerous publications recover 18th-century women's political activities and pay serious attention to the social, cultural and local dynamics of politics in 18th-century England. Her research interests extend to studies of political fashion, sociability and spa culture, as well as to late 18th-century English cosmopolitanism and the experiences of the political/naval family. She was a Co-Investigator on the AHRC-funded 'Eighteenth-Century Political Participation and Electoral Culture' project (ECPPEC).

David Cowan is a PhD candidate in history at the University of Cambridge. He previously worked as a researcher and staffer in the House of Commons and received a BA in history and MPhil in political thought and intellectual history from the University of Cambridge. His research focuses on the development of political party identities in late 18th- and early 19th-century Britain.

Chris Dudley is a scholar of early 18th-century British politics. He has published several articles and chapters on topics in that field, most recently in *The Hanoverian Succession in Great Britain and its Empire*, edited by Brent S. Sirota and Allan I. Maccinnes. His current project is on voting and elections from 1710 to 1742. He received his PhD from the University of Chicago in 2010 and has taught history at East Stroudsburg University in Pennsylvania since 2011.

Ben Gilding is the Don King Junior Research Fellow at New College, Oxford. He completed his PhD on the British state's attempts to reform the East India Company between 1773 and 1784, which is currently under preparation as a monograph. He has published several articles and chapters on the intersections between domestic and imperial politics in 18th- and 19th-century Britain and its empire.

M.O. Grenby is Pro-Vice-Chancellor for Research and Innovation at Newcastle University, and Professor of 18th-Century Studies in Newcastle's School of English Literature, Language and Linguistics. He has published on 18th-century political fiction, book history, children's literature and culture, and the history of heritage. He was the Principal

Investigator of the AHRC-funded 'Eighteenth-Century Political Participation and Electoral Culture' project (ECPPEC).

Joshua J. Smith is a third-year Scottish Graduate School for Arts & Humanities-funded PhD candidate at the University of Stirling. His research examines political readers, reading and membership in early-19th century subscription libraries across the Atlantic world, with a focus on the records of the Bristol Library Society and the Leighton Library, Dunblane. He is a team member on the AHRC-funded project, 'Books and Borrowing: An Analysis of Scottish Borrowers' Registers, 1750–1850', jointly based at the universities of Stirling and Glasgow, which examines the borrowing records of 18 historic libraries in Scotland over the course of the long 18th century.

Robert D. Tree is double graduate of the University of Glasgow and currently a final-year PhD researcher at the University of Stirling. His thesis is focused on the Scottish Privy Council's role in church and civil government between 1689 and 1708. It is funded by the Leverhulme Trust as part of the Scottish Privy Council Project across the universities of Stirling and Dundee. His main interests lie in the politics, religion and government administration of 17th-century Scotland, in addition to the social and cultural implications of coal mine workers' bound labour in the 17th and 18th centuries.

Kevin Tuffnell has returned to the study of history following a 30-year career as a corporate finance lawyer in the City. His principal interest is in the politics of the reign of Queen Anne. His PhD, completed in 2022, considered how public and political discourse were used to influence, and to articulate, British policy in the making of the treaty of Utrecht.

Parliamentary History, Vol. 43, pt. 1 (2024), pp. 5–19

Elections in 18th-Century England: Polling, Politics and Participation

M.O. GRENBY (iD) AND ELAINE CHALUS (iD)

Introduction

This special issue of *Parliamentary History* is one product of 'Eighteenth-Century Political Participation and Electoral Culture' (ECPPEC), a research project funded from January 2020 to June 2023 by the UK's Arts and Humanities Research Council.[1] ECPPEC was designed to shed new light on participation in parliamentary elections in England in the long 18th century, from about 1695 to the Reform Act of 1832. It was concerned with 'participation' interpreted broadly, both in the sense of voting, and also through other means: for instance, by attending – or being an active part of – the rituals of parliamentary elections, or by consuming – or creating – electoral print, song, dress, or other artefacts. ECPPEC thus had a dual focus on polling data and electoral culture, and an ambition to discover how these two aspects of elections worked together, with electoral culture potentially affecting election results.

The principal output of the project is its sophisticated website, which is available online at https://ecppec.ncl.ac.uk/. This is a vast resource. It includes a directory of all surviving poll books from the period; new information on how many parliamentary elections took place between 1695 and 1832 (the count at the time of writing this being 11,676, of which 3,312 were contested); and a record of voting behaviour at parliamentary elections in twenty case-study constituencies, carefully selected to be as representative as possible of different kinds of constituencies in different parts of England. This case-study constituency data comprises 483,060 individuals, casting 797,105 votes. The data is presented in ways designed to be visually appealing and accessible. It also aims to enable new kinds of analysis and understanding of 18th-century elections: for instance, it will allow researchers to explore poll book data in detail, to look at voting patterns across the duration of a multi-day election, to map voters geographically, and to reveal their voting tactics. In addition to this data, the website includes a wide selection of electoral print and artefacts, which have been found,

[1] ECPPEC was supported by the Arts and Humanities Research Council (grant number AH/S01098X/1). The Principal Investigator was Matthew Grenby, Professor of 18th-Century Studies at Newcastle University, with Co-Investigators Dr Tom Schofield, Senior Lecturer in Digital Cultures also at Newcastle, and Elaine Chalus, Professor of British History at Liverpool University. Three postdoctoral research associates worked on the project: Dr James Harris, Dr Kendra Packham and Dr Hillary Burlock; along with two Research Software Engineers, Dan Foster-Smith and Dr John Schoneboom. Many other scholars have contributed to the project in various ways, for instance by contributing polling data or writing material for the project website. ECPPEC benefitted in particular from the work undertaken by Penelope J. Corfield, Edmund Green and Charles Harvey for the pioneering London Electoral History project, beginning in 1992; and from the support of History of Parliament.

collected and photographed. These range from ceramics to cockades, fans to furniture, weapons to watercolours. Electoral songs have been arranged and recorded, engravings have been analysed, and several online 'exhibitions' of electoral material have been curated. All of this material is accompanied by contextualising text for each constituency and each election, and by many 'Feature' essays (currently 36) explaining different aspects of electoral history, as well as election processes, practices and behaviours. These Features are informative and purposefully accessible, aimed at different kinds of audiences, from those coming to the site with close to no knowledge of 18th-century elections to experts in the field. Some are interactive, allowing readers to manipulate data, learn about who could vote in a fun way, or investigate an image in great depth to see, for example, how it tells the story of a particular election. Many of the elements of the website are discussed in more detail below. But our aim in this introduction has been to show how the ECPPEC project, with its new data and new means of accessing that data, can encourage and facilitate new kinds of research.

During its 42-month lifespan, the ECPPEC project convened a number of events to explore aspects of 18th-century electoral history, although the Covid-19 pandemic had a very limiting effect on initial plans. A workshop on election songs, for example, brought together political historians, print specialists, musicologists and practising folk singers to consider the composition, motivation, traditions, contexts, practicalities and likely effects of election ballads, as well as their textual and musical formats and contents. It resulted in experimental (and rather wonderful) recordings by celebrated folk musicians, now available on the ECPPEC site. The project's main conference, held at Newcastle upon Tyne in July 2022, invited papers considering any aspect of political participation and electoral culture in the long 18th century in England, Scotland, Wales or Ireland. Over forty scholars presented their work, giving a good indication of the vibrancy of the field. Many papers presented at the conference examined visual, aural, print and material culture relating to elections, and a selection of these are being prepared for publication elsewhere. A number of other presentations focused on polling data, voting behaviour and electoral practice, and it is a selection of these papers that has been collected for this special issue of *Parliamentary History*. They stretch across the long 18th century and encompass different kinds of electoral activity, from the activities of the Scottish Privy Council in the late 17th century to the reading habits of voters in early 19th-century Bristol, and from the politics of the often-neglected English university constituencies to the relationships between stockholders and elections in the East India Company's Court of Proprietors. Together, these essays give a good idea of the use that historians can make of polling data when it survives. The rest of this introductory essay follows that lead, considering what the data collected by the ECPPEC project – as opposed to the electoral culture – is able to tell us.

Elections and Contests

As already mentioned, one fundamental statistic that the ECPPEC project has endeavoured to pin down is the number of parliamentary elections that took place in England during the long 18th century. Notionally, this is an easy thing to calculate, since each of England's 203 borough constituencies, 40 county constituencies, plus the 2 university constituencies, was

Table 1: *By-election causes for England 1695–1832*

Reason	Number	Percentage
Deceased	1301	33.9
Vacated seat	543	14.2
MP chose to sit for a different constituency	337	8.8
Re-elected after vacating seat	19	0.5
Re-elected after appointment to office	1152	30.0
Called to House of Lords	340	8.9
Granted pension	3	0.1
Refused to take the oaths	1	0
Declared ineligible to sit	6	0.2
Expelled	39	1.0
No return made	1	0
One seat declared vacant	4	0.1
Previous election declared void	90	2.3
Total	**3836**	**100**

required to elect its MPs each time parliament was dissolved. This was legally required at least every three years under the Triennial Act from 1694, and then at least every seven years following the passage of the Septennial Act in 1716. The picture is complicated, however, because of by-elections that were required in individual constituencies when a seat in the House of Commons became vacant. Of course, the existence of these by-elections has long been known, being recorded chiefly in the indispensable History of Parliament Trust constituency surveys as well as other published sources.[2] What ECPPEC has done is to collect and consolidate this information in one database. But new elections periodically turn up, their existence gleaned from long-buried references in newspapers or perhaps manuscript records of the poll. The diligent work of Edmund Green, for instance, has unearthed previously unknown poll books, even if sometimes these are simply the bare result of the poll or a record of it having taken place. We are grateful to Dr Green for sharing this ongoing research, including discoveries as yet unpublished, and allowing ECPPEC to incorporate this new information into our database. The result is that we can now produce a fuller count of the overall number of elections in 18th-century England. At the time of writing, the count for the period from the Triennial Act in 1695 to the eve of the Reform Act in 1832 is 11,676 elections. Of these 3,836 were by-elections.

One simple but interesting analysis that we can perform with this data is to tally the causes of by-elections (see Table 1). The most common cause was the death of a sitting MP, which accounted for just over a third of by-elections. Promotion to the House of Lords also required a by-election, as did expulsion from the Commons. It was not unusual for an individual to stand for election in more than one constituency, either concurrently at the time of a general election (to maximise his chances), or in an attempt to 'trade

[2]In addition, see, for instance, John Cannon, 'Polls Supplementary to the History of Parliament Volumes 1715–90', *HR*, xlvii (1974), 110–16.

© *2024 The Authors.* Parliamentary History *published by John Wiley & Sons Ltd on behalf of Parliamentary History Yearbook Trust.*

up' his seat at a by-election. If he was successful, he would have to relinquish one of his seats. This circumstance resulted in 337 by-elections over the course of the century. After death in office, however, the next most common cause of by-elections was appointment to government office, as a judge, or to a commission in the army. This was the consequence of legislation passed in 1706 that attempted to limit governmental corruption; it required any MP who received an office of profit from the crown to seek re-election if he wished to continue sitting in the Commons. These appointments accounted for almost a third of by-elections. Equally, a by-election could be required not as a result of something that had happened to the MP, but because something was deemed to have been amiss with the constituency's return. An MP could be declared ineligible to sit or, most commonly, an election could be declared void. This was usually based on complaints or petitions from the constituency, citing corrupt practices or voting irregularities.

It is vital to remember, of course, that not all elections were contested. For a contest to happen there had to be more candidates than the number of seats available within the constituency, which is to say three or more for a two-member constituency, or two or more when a constituency had only one seat, or in a typical by-election. When this was the case, the election would proceed to a poll, although it should be noted that would-be candidates often dropped out before a poll actually took place. Clearly the question of how many elections were contested is crucial to our understanding of 18th-century politics and particularly relevant to the issue of popular participation. It shows how often electors were able to choose between different candidates, parties and ideologies, or different local and national interests, and thus to influence government at a national level. The constitution might outwardly seem, or be claimed to be, representative, but if few elections were actually contested, the right of large numbers of men to vote (at least in some places) would be largely moot.

The ECPPEC database has assembled this information in one place and facilitates detailed analysis, either through the website's 'Data Explorer' facility or by downloading the data for offline analysis. As a headline, we can see that (at the time of writing) of the 11,676 elections we have identified, 3,312 (or 28.4 per cent) were contested. For general elections this rises to 33.7 per cent (2,640 of 7,840), whereas by-elections were substantially less likely to be contested at 17.5 per cent (672 of 3,836).[3] Doubtless one factor that influenced whether an election was contested was the predictability of general elections: this gave challengers time to prepare for a contest, whereas by-elections tended to occur with much less warning, which prevented candidates from securing support and fixing their funding. The election data we have collected facilitates much more nuanced analysis, too. It enables searches within specific date ranges, for instance, or filtering by the cause of a by-election, or the constituency franchise type.

Table 2 shows the proportion of all contested elections and by-elections, comparing counties, universities and boroughs, and dividing the boroughs up into the main franchise types. County elections were contested less than borough election, although from 1695–1710 the reverse had been true. Also interesting is that the university constituencies (whose

[3] These figures are complicated by a few elections where it cannot definitively be determined whether a contest took place, which have been counted here as non-contests. There are 11 such examples (one county and 10 borough seats: Berkshire 1701; Weobley 1708 [the second of that year]; Lostwithiel 1695; Dover 1698; Rye 1698; Wycombe 1699; Dover 1701; Hertford 1702; East Retford 1722; Wendover 1695; and Wallingford 1698).

Elections in 18th-Century England　　9

Table 2: *Number of contested elections and by-elections*

Constituency	No. of elections	No. of contested elections*	% elections contested	No. of by-elections	No. by-elections contested	% By-elections contested
Counties	1700	422	24.8	419	71	16.9
Universities	103	35	34.0	39	15	38.5
Boroughs (total)	9873	2855	28.9	3378	586	17.3
Burgage	1546	211	13.6	614	46	7.5
Corporation	1331	249	18.7	523	54	10.3
Disputed**	22	7	31.8	8	3	37.5
Freeholder	394	98	24.9	147	19	12.9
Freeman	4286	1473	34.7	1324	285	21.5
Householder	608	237	39.0	196	54	27.6
Scot and Lot	1686	580	34.4	566	125	22.1
Totals	**11676**	**3312**		**3836**	**672**	

* See footnote 3.

** The town of Callington in Cornwall had a disputed franchise for much of the 18th century: either householders resident for a year or inhabitants paying scot and lot. Since the number of voters was so small the difference between the franchises was minimal, so the matter was never settled.

© *2024 The Authors.* Parliamentary History *published by John Wiley & Sons Ltd on behalf of Parliamentary History Yearbook Trust.*

Table 3: *By-election cause as determinant of contestation*

Reason	Number	Contested	Percentage contested
Deceased	1301	316	24.3
Vacated seat	543	45	8.3
MP chose to sit for a different constituency	337	56	16.6
Re-elected after vacating seat	19	2	10.5
Re-elected after appointment to office	1152	94	8.2
Called to House of Lords	340	70	20.6
Granted pension	3	0	0
Refused to take the oaths	1	0	0
Declared ineligible to sit	6	1	16.7
Expelled	39	13	33.3
No return made	1	0	0
One seat declared vacant	4	4	100
Previous election declared void	90	71	78.9
Total	**3836**	**672**	

workings are explained in Nigel Aston's and David Cowan's essays in this volume) were proportionally more often contested than either counties or boroughs. Another oddity is that, at the universities, by-elections were more likely to be contested than general elections (although since there were only two university constituencies, this does not affect the overall statistics much). As for franchise types, elections were far more likely to be contested – about a third of the time, overall – in relatively open boroughs such as freeman, household, and scot and lot, than in burgage (13.6 per cent) or corporation (18.7 per cent) boroughs which were relatively closed and easier to control. By-elections, as already noted, were less likely to be contested in any kind of borough, but we can dig down into this too to show major disparities between the reason for a by-election and its likelihood of being contested (see Table 3). Perhaps unsurprisingly, by-election contests always, or almost always, ensued when a seat was declared vacant (100 per cent) or when a previous election was declared void (79 per cent). They were much less common when the MP had died, had been appointed to office, or called to the House of Lords. Perhaps this is an indication that seats where MPs were likely to be promoted were often under close control by a strong patron or by the government; or, perhaps we might deduce that there had been no particular dissatisfaction with the MP and so no pressure to contest his replacement. We also need to remember, however, that contests could be so expensive and divisive that constituents and candidates generally preferred to avoid them. It is notable that even the expulsion of an MP led to a by-election only about a third of the time.

These explorations of the electoral data are only some relatively straightforward examples of the kinds of analyses that ECPPEC enables, and much more highly tailored analyses are possible. A researcher might wish to look, for instance, at how many sitting MPs were forced to seek re-election after appointment to office during the Walpole ministry; or, by selecting particular constituencies, how many by-elections took place in Cornish boroughs;

or whether northern or southern counties went to the polls more frequently; or, indeed, if the tendency of MPs to die in office changed over time or place; or even in what month most 18th-century elections took place (it was May by some distance, followed by March, April, June and July; the least popular month for elections being September and then August, perhaps on account of harvesting).

A good place to see this kind analysis in action is the interactive 'Feature' essay on 'Contested Elections' written by James Harris for the ECPPEC website. Harris uses the data to tell − and visualise − several stories. One is about how the frequency of general elections changed over the course of the long 18th century, with a phase of stability being bookended by two phases of frantic electoral activity at each end of the period. A second is about changes in the number of contested general elections, with a high proportion between 1695 and 1734 before a significant drop-off in the mid-century, followed by recovery from 1774, although not to the levels of the beginning of the century. The data supports long-standing interpretations of the period's politics − about the 'rage of party', the growth of a crushing Whig hegemony, and increasing patronal dominance − made by historians from Lewis Namier to Geoffrey Holmes and Frank O'Gorman. Harris's interrogation of the data allows more nuance. In the largest boroughs, he notes, the proportion of contested elections never fell below 39 per cent and averaged 57 per cent across the whole of the period.[4] Since, between them, these boroughs contained two-thirds of the total borough electorate, Harris argues that we need to rethink our view of electoral activity, understanding that electoral contestation was, in terms of numbers of people participating in elections, more consistently spread across the century than in any particular 'age of party'. Finding the most useful and appealing ways to visualise this data was an important part of the ECPPEC project. Harris's final graph, designed by Tom Schofield, who led the digital design element of the project (Fig. 1), offers a representation of the relationship between the number of elections in each English constituency (x axis) and the percentage of these that were contested (y axis).

Naturally, small 'pocket' boroughs with restrictive franchises that were under the domination of local landowners were almost never contested. These can be found at the bottom of the graph, such as St Germans or Castle Rising, neither of which saw a contest during the period. At the top of the graph, by contrast, are boroughs such as Maidstone and Southwark, where 87 per cent and 82 per cent of elections were contested. Probably more surprising, however, is the spread of the numbers of elections. Furthest to the left on the graph is Newcastle upon Tyne with only 35 elections between 1695 and 1832 (28 per cent of which were contested), while furthest to the right is Weymouth and Melcombe Regis with 72 elections (31 per cent contested). The explanation is that these 'pocket' boroughs could be used either by aspiring politicians with major patronage, or by Government for their supporters. When the men who had been elected to these safe seats inevitably moved on to a more prestigious constituency, or gained government office, a by-election was required, though it would seldom be contested.

---

[4]Harris counts boroughs with electorates of more than 1,000 in the late 18th century as 'large'. They are: Bedford, Beverley, Bridgnorth, Bristol, Canterbury, Carlisle, Chester, Colchester, Coventry, Cricklade, Dover, Durham City, Evesham, Exeter, Gloucester, Hereford, Kingston-upon-Hull, Lancaster, Leicester, Lincoln, Liverpool, London, Maidstone, Newark, Newcastle upon Tyne, Northampton, Norwich, Nottingham, Oxford, Southwark, Westminster, Worcester and York.

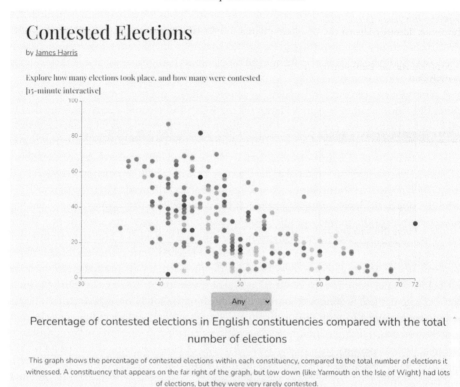

Contested Elections

by James Harris

Explore how many elections took place, and how many were contested
[15-minute interactive]

Percentage of contested elections in English constituencies compared with the total
number of elections

This graph shows the percentage of contested elections within each constituency, compared to the total number of elections it
witnessed. A constituency that appears on the far right of the graph, but low down (like Yarmouth on the Isle of Wight) had lots
of elections, but they were very rarely contested.

go back   next

read more

Figure 1: Screenshot of visualisation from ECPPEC 'Contested Elections' Feature, showing number of elections in each English constituency (x axis) and percentage of these contested (y axis). Design by Tom Schofield.

Poll Books and Voters

If one aim of the ECPPEC project has been to consolidate information about the number of elections, another has been to provide data and facilitate analysis on individual voters. For this information, we need to turn to poll books. Poll books are a characteristic feature of 18th-century English elections. Records of voting were kept before, but were regulated by parliament from the 1690s onwards. By 1711 a series of acts of parliament required sheriffs to deposit poll books for county elections with the clerk of the peace within twenty days of the poll declaration and to make copies of poll books available to anyone who wished to view them. This did not apply to boroughs, however; it was not until 1843 that the permanent preservation of poll books was made mandatory for all constituencies. As a result, the creation and preservation of poll books was uneven and sporadic during the 18th century. So too was their format.

Poll books are, in essence, simply lists of voters' names, recording the name of the candidate or candidates for whom they polled. This was sometimes accompanied by other details, such as the voter's occupation or residence, or even by notes added by whoever made the list. Some poll books had an official status; others were commercially printed as a record of the election. The latter could serve as a kind of public service, and were often compiled, printed and sold by local booksellers or newspaper editors. These might be kept and updated by election agents, who annotated them with details of voting intentions as well as actual votes, or the means by which a vote could be bought, or a voter's qualification challenged. A Norwich poll book of 1734, for instance, made this purpose explicit; its stated intention was to 'be of great service both in taking and scrutinizing future polls'.[5] Poll books could, however, also operate as the last action in a vituperative campaign, celebrating election success or deliberately denigrating political opponents. This can be seen in two rival poll books for the 1741 York election, in which, Richard Wallis argues, voters' listed professions were changed either for purposes of ridicule or insult.[6]

Other polling records are more difficult to track down. They might be lists published in local newspapers as the poll was progressing, or one person's handwritten record of voting – perhaps the actual minute-by-minute record of the poll kept by the official polling clerks as it progressed – that survive by chance in a set of family papers. Furthermore, the survival of poll books is erratic, not least because of the deliberate destruction of the entire collection of poll books held by the Crown Office in 1907. Those poll books that do survive are consequently now widely dispersed in national and local archives. Great work has been done to find and record their locations, notably by John Sims, whose *Handlist of British Parliamentary Poll Books* was published in 1984, and by Jeremy Gibson and Colin Rogers, whose *Poll Books 1696–1872: A Directory to Holdings in Great Britain* first appeared in 1989. Since then, more work has been done to identify other extant poll books, especially by Edmund Green, whose article 'New Discoveries of Poll Books' appeared in this journal in 2005, and who has continued to locate other survivals.[7] One of the foundational objectives of the ECPPEC project was to unite these disparate sources in a single online, open access, expandable database. This is now available at https://ecppec.ncl.ac.uk/pollbook-directory/. It currently lists 1,929 surviving poll books for the period 1695 to 1832. It is fully searchable, and can be filtered according to date, name of constituency, type of constituency, type of franchise, and type (general or by-election) and cause of election. It also provides the location details for the physical copies of the poll books.

Readers of *Parliamentary History* will hardly have to be told what the polling data contained in poll books can be used for, nor be warned that the information they contain, because it was so often partisan in nature, has to be treated with a certain amount of

---

[5] Quoted in John Cannon, 'Short Guides to Records: Poll Books', *History*, xlvii (1962), 166. For much more detail on poll books, see a series of 'Feature' articles on the ECPPEC site, including 'What is a Poll Book?' and 'Poll Books and the Reading Public' both by James Harris, from which the account presented here draws, and Edmund Green's new long essay 'Poll Books: A History', which gives a definitive guide to their varieties and formats.

[6] Richard Wallis, 'Fake News in Eighteenth-Century York', *The Shandean*, xxix (2018), 61–77.

[7] *A Handlist of British Parliamentary Poll Books*, ed. John Sims (Leicester, 1984); *Poll Books 1696–1872: A Directory to Holdings in Great Britain*, ed. Jeremy Gibson and Colin Rogers (4th edn, Bury, 2008); E.M. Green, 'New Discoveries of Poll Books', *Parliamentary History*, xxiv (2005), 332–67. See also Cannon, 'Short Guides', 166–9; S.W. Baskerville, Peter Adman and K.F. Beedham, 'Manuscript Poll Books and English County Elections in the First Age of Party: A Reconsideration of their Provenance and Purpose', *Archives*, xix (1991), 384–403.

caution. At the most basic level, the ECPPEC database, with its almost half a million voters in 20 constituencies, is a directory of names, of interest to anyone keen to discover the existence, and voting record, of known individuals. Genealogists will find this useful data; so too will biographers and historians. The 'Data Explorer' facility allows searches of the whole database by surname. It easily locates, just for example, the author Laurence Sterne, listed as a 'Clerk' of Sutton on the Forest (where he was then vicar), who voted in the 1742 Yorkshire by-election for the Whig Cholmley Turner, as of course (a separate search shows) did his uncle in York, the Whig politician Jacques Sterne. (Laurence Sterne had written pro-Walpole material for his uncle's *York Gazetteer*, but in July 1742 publicly renounced 'the abusive Gazetteers I wrote during the late contested election', causing a lifelong estrangement from his uncle.)[8] It is similarly easy to find the writer, composer and abolitionist Ignatius Sancho, listed as a tea dealer and then grocer of Charles Street, Westminster, who voted in the 1774 and 1780 elections. Other black voters will doubtless be present in the database, though locating them is difficult, since one has to be able to search for them by name. One might, however, make educated guesses about certain categories of voter. For example, if one were searching for Jewish voters, who were allowed to vote if they met the various franchise qualifications but could not hold public office, then the database includes five men surnamed 'Cohen' (in Westminster and Middlesex), six surnamed 'Levi' (in Westminster, Northampton and Coventry) and two 'Israels' (in Westminster) – although the existence of well over a hundred voters with 'Isaac' as first or second name counsels caution.

Beyond providing information on individual voters, poll books offer historians unique and invaluable insights into voting behaviour, both personal and collective. Just how voters used their two votes has long been a matter of historical interest: to what extent did they vote 'straight' (supporting two complementary candidates typically from the same party), or 'split' their votes (giving one vote each to two apparent rivals), or 'plump' (supporting just one candidate, throwing the other vote away)? The ability to trace voting behaviour can shed light on the importance of political ideology or of party in specific constituencies at particular points in time. This is a question discussed in this volume by Kevin Tuffnell in relation to Wareham and Dorchester in the early years of the century. He finds that political principle seems to have trumped expediency in the minds of many voters.

The data assembled by ECPPEC allows similar kinds of analysis for the case study constituencies. We include an interactive visualisation of voting tactics on each election page, which shows at a glance how voters for each candidate used (or did not use) their other vote. The 1780 Cambridge University election, discussed in detail by David Cowan in this volume, provides a nice example. Our chart (see Fig. 2) shows the complicated alliances between the five candidates (as actualised by voters' choices) and the significant power of even a few plumpers in a constituency where only 500 voted.

Indeed, it can be surprising to see how plumping sometimes determined results, which helps to explain why campaigns were so keen to encourage it. Among the items included in the ECPPEC cultural artefact explorer is a decorated earthenware jug produced for the 1807 Yorkshire election, now held in the Fitzwilliam Museum, Cambridge. It is inscribed: 'He that calls here / Shall have this full of Beer / That gave Milton / A Plumper'. After a

---

[8] *Letters of Laurence Sterne*, ed. Lewis Perry Curtis (Oxford, 1935), 21.

Figure 2: Screenshot of visualisation from ECPPEC's page for the Cambridge University 1780 election, showing how voters for each candidate deployed (or discarded) their second vote. Design by Dan Foster-Smith.

fervent campaign and the polling of more than 23,000 voters, Viscount Milton was indeed narrowly returned, along with the frontrunner, William Wilberforce. A study of the polling data makes it clear that it was his 9,061 plumpers (81 per cent of the 11,177 total votes cast for him) that carried the day.[9]

---

[9]The full story of this election, with further analysis of the tactical voting, is set out in Kendra Packham's ECPPEC Feature article: https://ecppec.ncl.ac.uk/features/yorkshire-1807/ (accessed 29 Aug. 2023).

Alternatively, poll book data makes it possible to trace individuals across a run of elections. In his essay in this volume, Chris Dudley uses data from 28 Sussex poll books for the period 1710–35. His focus is on non-voting as much as voting, and he is able to demonstrate a surprisingly low level of consistency in voting from one election to the next. Moreover, even when a definite promise to vote a certain way was made, the pledge was not necessarily kept. Dudley's argument is that voters could not be relied upon, but needed to be mobilised if their votes were to be secured. This helps to explain the nature of 18th-century electoral propaganda, which was designed not so much to persuade opponents as to muster pre-existing but dormant support. Work like Dudley's relies on record linkage across different poll books. This has been the goal of computer-based polling analysis since at least 1970 when W.A. Speck and W.A. Gray published an 'Initial Report' on 'Computer Analysis of Poll Books'.[10] Even now, it remains challenging, in part because names were often inconsistently recorded in the 18th century. And if this is true of tracing names from one poll book to the next, it is all the more problematic when we try to link names across different data sets. It should, for instance, be possible to trace many of the London, Westminster and Middlesex voters recorded in the ECPPEC database into the 'London Lives' project database, which has mined and amalgamated the records of many plebeian Londoners in the period 1690 to 1800. As yet, this integration has not been attempted, a smaller-scale attempt to link data sets is to be found in Joshua Smith's essay in this volume, where the borrowing records of the Bristol Library Society are matched with contemporary polling data. Smith finds that the Bristol Library Society members were certainly interested in politics, but not in political change: their reading choices matched, and perhaps underpinned, their opposition to reformist candidates.

These are just some of the possible uses for polling data. What ECPPEC provides, in today's terms, is a cache of 'big data': thousands of names and voting choices; but also often other information such as order of voting, place of residence, and profession or trade guild membership. All sorts of enquiries therefore become possible. ECPPEC has mapped voter abodes for some elections, thus visualising the geographies of a constituency. We might interrogate this data to ask which areas within constituencies polled most heavily for particular candidates. Or we might find out much more about 'outvoters': those voters who owned property in a constituency, or qualified to vote because they were freemen, but lived beyond – sometimes far beyond – the boundaries of the constituency.[11] In extreme cases, these outvoters might make up as much as 70 per cent of the turnout in an election, as they did in late 18th-century Lancaster.[12] Moreover, in times of crisis, outvoters could be particularly crucial to an outcome: in Gloucester, in 1830, as many of two-thirds of the new

---

[10] W.A. Speck and W.A. Gray, 'Computer Analysis of Poll Books: An Initial Report', *BIHR*, xliii (1970), 105–12. See also W.A. Speck, W.A. Gray and R. Hopkinson, 'Computer Analysis of Poll Books: A Further Report', *BIHR*, xlviii (1975), 64–90.

[11] In the English counties, the original act of 1430 that established the 40-shilling freeholder franchise had stipulated that voters should be resident, but this requirement quite quickly become obsolete: Edward Porritt, 'Barriers Against Democracy in the British Electoral System', *Political Science Quarterly*, xxvi (1911), 3. In the English boroughs, only a few constituencies had residence requirements, although some boroughs had a stipulation that one had to be resident for a set number of days before the election. For example, in Bedwin (Wiltshire) it was the custom to let burgage houses four or five days before an election: Edward Porritt and Annie G. Porritt, *The Unreformed House of Commons: Parliamentary Representation Before 1832* (2 vols, Cambridge, [1903] 1963), i, 35.

[12] Frank O'Gorman, *Voters, Patrons, and Parties. The Unreformed Electoral System of Hanoverian England, 1734–1832* (Oxford, 1989), 191 and notes.

freemen created were non-residents.[13] With its linked data, the ECPPEC database enables us to see quickly what outvoters' allegiances were; it can show us when these voters arrived in a contest and what effect they had on results. In the 1761 Liverpool election, for instance, we can see at a glance that of the 36 voters who gave their residence as London, all but five voted for the challenger candidate, William Meredith, 30 of them plumping for him alone. Contrast that with Bristol in 1774, where 416 voters gave their address as London but split their votes evenly between the main three candidates. In the closely fought Newcastle upon Tyne election of the same year, the burgesses' party, who were neck-and-neck in the race until the last two days of polling, complained about the influence of outvoters. The 157 Londoners who voted were in fact only narrowly more supportive of the magistrates' candidates (Matthew White Ridley and Walter Calverley Blackett). They cast 94 votes for each, as opposed to the 63 votes cast for each of the burgesses' candidates (Constantine Phipps and Thomas Delaval). None of these outvoters split their support.

Rather, in order to understand the pattern of voting in this election, it is probably most revealing to look at the voting preferences of Newcastle's trade guilds. Membership of a guild entitled a man to vote. The 172 merchants cast 157 and 155 votes for Blackett and Ridley respectively, and only 22 and 15 for Phipps and Delaval. A similar pattern emerges by filtering the results for the 201 mariners and 136 barber surgeons. Support for Phipps and Deleval tended to come from the smaller guilds associated with the building trade, such as the 58 bricklayers and 92 joiners. The 235 butchers were more evenly divided. Clearly this kind of poll book analysis has much to tell us about localised social, economic and ideological history: it can also give us insights into the socio-political identity of rapidly developing industries, the political aspirations of particular occupational groups, and the dissolution and re-formation of local and national loyalties.

Voter Practices and Behaviours

Poll books can tell us much about the practices of voting, too. Some poll books are written in the order in which votes were cast, or allow this to be deduced by numbers assigned to each voter. This can tell us about the formation of the tallies in which voters came to the poll. Voters might be grouped, for instance, by their place of residence, profession or guild membership, as well as by who they were supporting. As election turnout and the deployment of tallies of voters was often carefully managed over the course of a multi-day election in order to rally support, or even to prolong a poll and make the election costlier for the opposition, this information is valuable.

Marginalia features on some poll books, particularly if a previous poll book was used as part of the canvass. These comments can reveal much about voter intention and the personal factors that influenced votes, or the arguments that were brought to bear on voters to secure their votes. Comments on poll books about what happened on the hustings are particularly revealing of the practice of challenging would-be voters about their right to vote. The complications of the franchise, which varied from borough to bor-

---

[13] *The History of Parliament: The House of Commons, 1820–1832*, ed. D.R. Fisher (7 vols, Cambridge, 2009), ii, 408.

ough and might well even be contested within a borough if it was open to contending historical interpretations, gave election agents plenty of scope to question the qualification of anyone likely to vote against their wishes. Was the would-be voter resident in the borough? Did he meet the property qualification? Was he a freeman or a legitimate householder? Was he in receipt of alms? Did he pay his rates? Could all this be proved, either by documents he had brought with him, or by the testimony of respected members of the community, who could perhaps cite precedent from previous elections? These manuscript notes are included in the ECPPEC database and can be searched for using the 'Data Explorer'.

Since the Parliamentary Elections Act of 1695/6, the legal minimum voting age had been set at 21, and the poll books show that this too could be a cause for challenge. Terms like 'age' or 'minor' can be searched in the 'notes' field of our database. This denotes a challenge, either intended or made, the success or failure of which is sometimes also recorded. At the 1734 Bedfordshire election, for example, we can find a John Sperrey listed as 'refus'd being under age' and, in the same constituency in 1831, a William Turner appears with the note 'Not of age'. A voter at the 1734 Coventry election was marked 'not of age'; similarly, nine would-be voters in the 1727 Northampton election have the note 'Q[uery] Age' listed by their names, and there are comparable annotations in the poll book of the Yorkshire 1727 election. Even at Cambridge University, where only those who (alongside the other standard criteria) had obtained an MA degree were entitled to vote, one voter in 1727 attracted the remark 'Under Age'. The question we have to ask is whether these instances should be taken as an indication that underage voting was common in 18th-century England. It is certainly possible to read these challenges as an indication that election agents *expected* minors to attempt to vote and were on the watch for it. There were, after all, underage MPs. Some corroboration comes from post-poll attempts to challenge election results. The result of the 1768 Northampton election, for example, was so close that scrutinies of voters' qualifications began almost immediately. Attempts were made to have certain votes rejected, chiefly on the grounds that the voters were 'Lodgers & Boarders, or Under Age'.[14] Indeed, when an election was controverted (which is to say, legally challenged, with the petition to overturn the result coming before the Committee of Privileges and Elections of the House of Commons), allegations of underage voting were not infrequent. A glance at the petitions lodged for just a few mid-century years shows that retrospective discounting of votes cast by 'Minors' was urged for elections for Northampton and Southampton in 1734, Yorkshire in 1736, Denbigh and Ruthin in 1740, and Gloucester in 1741.[15] These allegations could be made against specific individuals or larger groups. Even if the numbers of underage voters brought to the Committee were quite small overall, these claims (however tendentious they might have been) suggest that underage voting was something that people imagined was happening – and which probably did.

[14]See Zoe Dyndor, 'Widows, Wives and Witnesses: Women and their Involvement in the 1768 Northampton Borough Parliamentary Election', *Parliamentary History*, xxx (2011), 309–23. An annotated pollbook used to challenge the result gives more detail but does not distinguish further between the specific reasons for disputing voters' qualifications (BL, Add. MS 75752).

[15]*CJ*, xxii (1732–1737), 334, 345, 506, 696; *CJ*, xxiv (1741–1745), 32, 566, 579.

Conclusion

The essays that make up this special issue all draw upon, or have been inspired by, the work on polling, politics and participation that was the focus of the ECPPEC project. They go some way to demonstrating the wide variety of ways that the information that the project has made openly available to researchers can be used to enrich our understanding of the 18th-century political world. Not only do they serve to identify individual voters, illuminate voting patterns and highlight electoral strategies, but they also remind us forcefully of the political importance of individual agency, and of the range of factors – personal, cultural, associational and institutional – that shaped and determined political choice.

ECPPEC sought to expand our understandings of electoral participation beyond the act of polling, and the wider culture of elections will be the subject of other project publications. However, many electoral artefacts and texts, exhibitions and songs, as well as accompanying essays, are already available on the ECPPEC website, and we invite you to take a look (and a listen). Your responses to the site will be very welcome, and will be able to inform its further development. In the meantime, we hope you find the many types of data we have compiled valuable and that you will be able to use them in your own work. We thank the many people who have contributed to the development of the website, and of course the authors of the essays collected in this volume. It was a pleasant surprise to find such a large community of historians working in this field, and keen to engage with the ECPPEC project. Reports of the demise of political history seem to have been exaggerated; the study of 18th-century electoral politics evidently remains in rude health. New technologies, new ways of presenting data, and new ways of understanding political participation more broadly seem likely to sustain this interest for years to come.

Parliamentary History, Vol. 43, pt. 1 (2024), pp. 20–35

Voting and Not Voting in Early 18th-Century English Parliamentary Elections

CHRIS DUDLEY

East Stroudsburg University

This article uses data from 28 poll books to explore voter behaviour over time in early 18th-century English parliamentary elections (from 1710 to 1735). Voters in this period exhibited a high degree of partisan loyalty from one election to the next. But voters were also quite likely to drop out of the electorate between elections. As a case study of Sussex elections in 1734 shows, even among voters who made a definite promise to vote for a given candidate or set of candidates, there was a significant proportion who did not vote. While some non-voting can be explained as an attempt to avoid disobliging powerful patrons, this article argues that voters needed to be motivated to appear at the polls. The electoral culture of the early 18th century – treats, balls, public appearances by the candidates, etc. – should be understood as attempts to mobilise rather than to persuade potential voters.

Keywords: elections; political participation; poll books; Tory; voter behaviour; Whig

William Acton lived in the market town of Kingston in Surrey in the second decade of the 18th century. As a freeholder, he was entitled to vote in county elections for members of parliament, which were unusually frequent. Acton voted in general elections in 1710 and 1713 and in by-elections in 1717 and 1719. He was a loyal Tory, voting for the candidates of that party at every opportunity. Acton was just one of thousands of Surrey freeholders whose votes were recorded in poll books of those parliamentary elections.

How typical was William Acton as a voter? What explains his voting record, both in terms of loyalty to the Tories and his participation? While it might be possible to investigate William Acton further as an individual, this article approaches these questions in aggregate terms, using voting data from surviving early 18th-century poll books. Based on that data, particularly from constituencies with poll books from multiple elections, it appears that Acton's loyalty was fairly typical. As Part I of this essay shows, the majority of partisan voters in one election continued to support the same party in subsequent elections. But the data also shows that Acton's participation in four consecutive elections was not as common. Many voters from the first election, often as much as half the voterate, cannot be identified as having voted in the next election. Voters on the whole were very consistent about whom they supported, but much less so about whether they voted at all.

The second part of this article explores why voters behaved that way, with particular emphasis on those who did not participate in the subsequent election. Part II is a case study on two Sussex constituencies in the 1734 election, made possible by combining poll books for the county and the borough of Lewes with extensive political correspondence in the papers of the Whig grandee Thomas Pelham-Holles, duke of Newcastle. Based on that correspondence, cross-referenced with information from the poll books about what voters did, it appears that the many campaign events – balls, treats, public appearances by the candidates, etc. – were primarily intended to motivate rather than to persuade voters.

The argument of this article, therefore, is twofold. First, voters in the early 18th century were highly partisan. The polarisation of the 'divided society' that historians describe at the beginning of the century continued past 1715. For the most part, potential voters did not have to be persuaded to vote for the Tories or the Whigs because they were already inclined towards one of the two parties and so, secondly, the purpose of campaigning was to turn them into actual voters. The voting process posed challenges for potential voters, starting with the time and effort required to appear at the poll. Voters needed to be sufficiently invested in the process to overcome those challenges. The political pageantry surrounding early 18th-century elections was what we would today call an effort to 'get out the vote'. Electoral success was achieved, not by flipping the votes of the opposition, but by getting supportive voters to the polls.

Scholarship on voting in the early 18th century is tied to broader narratives about the nature of politics. Despite a large number of important revisions, those narratives continue to be driven by J.H. Plumb's 1967 account, *The Growth of Political Stability in England*. Plumb argues that political stability, in the form of the 'Venetian oligarchy' of the Whigs, depended on two political developments after 1714: the virtual disappearance of the Tory opposition as an effective political force, and the Whigs' turn under Robert Walpole away from principle to government based on 'the fundamental temptations that beset 18th-century politics – power and profit'.[1] Because ideological disagreement disappeared, in this account, the key to 18th-century politics and elections was patronage by the aristocracy and gentry.

Since Plumb, a number of historians have challenged the first of his two main conclusions. Historians have uncovered the importance of Jacobitism and the Whig opposition, while in the most direct refutations of Plumb have shown that the Tories retained more ideological and electoral vigour than he allowed.[2] For most of these historians, the fact that Plumb underestimated the strength of the opposition serves to highlight the importance of his second factor, bribery and patronage.[3]

The literature on elections, including especially 1734 elections like the ones described in Part II of this article, makes similar arguments. Over a century ago, Basil Williams explored the same Newcastle correspondence and concluded that it revealed a political system defined by an alliance between leading politicians like Walpole and 'the great organizers of

---

[1]J.H. Plumb, *The Growth of Political Stability in England, 1675–1725* (Harmondsworth, 1967), 168. See also J.C.D. Clark, *English Society, 1688–1832: Ideology, Social Structure, and Political Practice during the Ancien Regime* (Cambridge, 1985). It is worth mentioning that both Plumb and Clark included a substantial discussion of the socio-economic foundations of this oligarchy.

[2]For Jacobites, see P.K. Monod, *Jacobitism and the English People, 1688–1788* (Cambridge, 1989); Eveline Cruickshanks and Howard Erskine-Hill, *The Atterbury Plot* (New York, 2004); Daniel Szechi, *1715: The Great Jacobite Rebellion* (New Haven, 2006). For opposition Whigs, see Nicholas Rogers, *Whigs and Cities: Popular Politics in the Age of Pitt and Walpole* (Oxford, 1989); Kathleen Wilson, *The Sense of the People: Politics, Culture, and Imperialism in England, 1715–1785* (Cambridge, 1995). For Tories, see Linda Colley, *In Defiance of Oligarchy: The Tory Party, 1714–1760* (Cambridge, 1982).

[3]For example, Colley, *In Defiance of Oligarchy*, 120–4. Others go further, even arguing (based on legislation like the Riot Act of 1714) that Whig political hegemony was based on 'state-sponsored terrorism and physical coercion': Wilson, *Sense of the People*, 98. See also Monod, *Jacobitism and the English People*, 347.

"influence" or corruption, at the head of whom stood Newcastle'.[4] More recently, Paul Langford argued that in the hostile political climate of 1734, Whigs primarily held power by holding 'smaller, close constituencies', and that when they did win larger ones it was due to 'the almost frighteningly thorough commitment' of men like Newcastle, whose 'private, not ministerial' influence carried the day.[5]

My argument is most similar to that of Frank O'Gorman, who highlights the limitations of patronage and the exhaustive effort patrons had to put into persuading voters in the unreformed electoral system. The Newcastle correspondence, which documents campaign activity for months leading up to the election, certainly supports this point. But O'Gorman also argues that 'the source of electoral activity was overwhelmingly local' and that national political issues were relatively unimportant.[6] The partisan, rather than personal, loyalty of voters demonstrated in Part I suggests that national partisanship continued to be an important factor.

There are two methodological points that need to be mentioned before moving on. The voting data in this essay comes from a selection of available poll books for English parliamentary elections from 1710 to 1735, mostly for general elections but including several by-elections as well. The first methodological point concerns the nature of those poll books and partisanship. In a general election, most constituencies in England returned two MPs and voters were allowed to vote for up to two candidates. As a result, parties, almost always Tories and Whigs in this period, typically stood two candidates for each constituency. It was also relatively common for the party that was weaker in a given constituency to stand a single candidate and hope to pick off one of the two opposing candidates. Compared with a single-member, single-vote constituency, therefore, it is much easier to identify partisan voters than voters who gave their support for different reasons. A person who voted for two candidates of the same party, or who plumped for a single candidate of a party (declining to use his second vote), was probably a supporter of that party. These are called 'partisan voters' in this article. For by-elections, there was only one MP elected, voters had a single vote, and the parties ran a single candidate. In those cases, therefore, partisanship cannot be separated from other factors as cleanly. To allow for comparisons of partisanship from a general election to a by-election, however, the data in Part I classifies by-election voters as partisan according to which candidate they voted for.

The second methodological point relates to tracking individual voters across elections, which is the core of Part I. The poll books generally include the first and last name of the voter, the freehold or parish that qualified them to vote and the place they lived if those were different, a title such as 'gent.' or 'clerk' if they had one, and sometimes – especially in boroughs – their occupation. In principle, therefore, once the voters are entered into a database, it is a tedious but conceptually simple process to sort the dataset and match up voters from two different elections. In practice, however, there are two problems. Eighteenth-century

[4]Basil Williams, 'The Duke of Newcastle and the Election of 1734', *EHR*, xii (1897), 449. Importantly, Williams considered the correspondence but not the poll book. His conclusions, like those of many of scholars, were based on taking at face value some of the claims made by Newcastle's correspondents about the extent of their electoral influence. See *The History of Parliament: The House of Commons, 1715–1754*, ed. Romney Sedgwick (2 vols, 1970), i, 332.

[5]Paul Langford, *The Excise Crisis* (Oxford, 1975), 133–7.

[6]Frank O'Gorman, *Voters, Patrons, and Parties: The Unreformed Electoral System of Hanoverian England, 1734–1832* (Oxford, 1989), 9, 106–71, 224–59.

English people were not very creative when it came to names, especially first names, but were extremely creative in the field of orthography. In the 1710 Surrey poll book, for example, there were 11 voters with the surname 'Billinghurst'. Three were 'John', three were 'William' and two were 'Thomas'. Billinghurst was not a particularly common last name. In the same poll book, there were 13 men called 'John Smith', three called 'John Smither', and one called 'John Smythes'. Surrey's multiple men called 'John Smith' point to the second problem: 'Smith' could be spelled as we commonly do today, or with an 'e' at the end, or with a 'y', or with or without a second 's' – all potentially referring to the same person. Since those spellings could also vary across time, the process of matching voters in two different poll books involves some unavoidable uncertainty.

In compiling the data found in Part I, I was fairly conservative about identifying repeat voters. Not every field in the database had to be identical, but if there was reasonable doubt that two voters were the same person, or if there was no way to distinguish between voters with similar names, those voters were omitted. Almost certainly, then, there were more repeat voters than could be included. In addition, some number of voters from the first election died, relocated or otherwise became ineligible to vote by the time of the subsequent contest. This also introduces uncertainty, since those people cannot be said to have chosen not to vote in the second election. Neither factor should systematically affect the data about partisan loyalty across elections but, as discussed further below, it does mean the evidence about turnover in the electorate needs to be treated with some caution. The data in Part II about promised voters in Sussex largely avoids this problem. Because the number of voters named in the correspondence was much lower than in a poll book, there were only a few ambiguous cases. As with the Part I data, those were eliminated from the sample. But for the voters categorised as 'not voting', I have a high degree of confidence that they did not vote: neither they nor anyone with a similar name, freehold or other identifier appears in the poll book.

I: Votes over Time

This section presents the bulk of the data from poll books related to voter behaviour over time and highlights two results. First, partisan voters tended to stick with their party from election to election. This was, in most cases, party rather than personal loyalty to an individual candidate. Secondly, voters were relatively likely to drop out of the voterate from one election to the next. These two results paint a contradictory picture of voter behaviour. From the perspective of partisan loyalty, voters were very consistent, but from the perspective of participation, they were more volatile. Part II of the article will expand on and attempt to explain that contradiction.

Tory and Whig voters as a group were strongly loyal across multiple elections. Table 1 shows pairs of elections in the same constituency. The percentage of loyal voters represent the proportion of partisan voters who appeared in both poll books and who voted for the same party in both elections. By-elections are indicated by the letter 'b'. With a few exceptions, two-thirds or more of partisan voters from the first election who also participated in the second election voted for the same party. Although not the focus here, it is worth noting that Whigs usually (in 9 of 13 cases) had an advantage over Tories in voter loyalty. That this was true before and after the consolidation of the Whig supremacy between 1715

Table 1: *Tory and Whig voter loyalty*

Constituency	Percentage of Tory voters loyal	Percentage of Whig voters loyal
Hampshire 1710 and 1713	84.5%	86.1%
Surrey 1710 and 1713	82.8%	82.5%
Essex 1710 and 1715b	89.5%	92.3%
Northumberland 1710 and 1716b	54.6%	61.0%
Surrey 1713 and 1717b	80.1%	90.7%
Surrey 1713 and 1719b	80.7%	80.4%
Bedfordshire 1715 and 1722	59.3%	64.4%
Essex 1722 and 1734	78.6%	73.1%
Bristol 1722 and 1734	58.7%	73.6%
Newcastle upon Tyne 1722 and 1734	76.7%	31.9%
Bedfordshire 1727 and 1734	62.5%	80.9%
Derby 1727 and 1734	76.2%	79.1%
Norwich 1734 and 1735b	90.9%	95.2%

and 1722 suggests that Whig voter loyalty was not solely due to the oligarchic elements that feature so heavily in the literature.

Although the two can be hard to disentangle, this was clearly loyalty to the party rather than loyalty to individual candidates. The ability to identify partisan voters, explained in the discussion of methodology, is one indication of this. More direct evidence can be found in two cases where the same candidate crossed party lines between elections. The first of these cases was Sir Francis Vincent, who stood as a Tory candidate for Surrey in 1710 and 1713 before joining the Whigs and standing unsuccessfully in the 1719 by-election. Tory partisans who supported him in 1710 and 1713 largely declined to follow his switch in 1719: 82.2 per cent of them voted for his Tory opponent (almost exactly the same percentage who had remained loyal Tories from 1710 to 1713). Even the non-partisan voters who put Vincent on a split ballot in 1713 were not strongly loyal to him, voting for him in 1719 by the relatively small margin of 56.8 per cent to 43.2 per cent against.

The second such case, Charles Caesar in Hertfordshire, featured a more complicated candidate and constituency. Caesar had been a member of the Tory October Club and was probably a Jacobite, but some of the Hertfordshire Whig elites supported his successful campaign against two Tories in 1727.[7] In 1734, county leaders of the two parties agreed to compromise the election. Caesar ran against the compromise, leading to the odd spectacle of a Tory and Whig campaigning jointly against a Jacobite Tory who was believed to be tied to the ministry. Despite the absence of the typical Tory/Whig divide, Caesar's personal loyalty from voters was little different than a coin toss. Those whose 1727 votes included Caesar (either alone or in conjunction with one of the other candidates) were only slightly more

---

[7] The general speculation was that Caesar had been bought off by the Whig ministry, but while in parliament he voted against the government. *HPC, 1715–1754*, i, 517.

Table 2: *Repeat voters*

Constituency and years	Percentage of identifiable repeat voters
Hampshire 1710 and 1713	56.7%
Surrey 1710 and 1713	51.8%
Essex 1710 and 1715b	41.1%
Northumberland 1710 and 1716b	60.1%
Surrey 1713 and 1717b	41.8%
Surrey 1713 and 1719b	51.6%
Bedfordshire 1715 and 1722	41.5%
Hertfordshire 1722 and 1727	57.0%
Essex 1722 and 1734	31.2%
Bristol 1722 and 1734	33.5%
Newcastle upon Tyne 1722 and 1734	45.1%
Bedfordshire 1727 and 1734	53.3%
Hertfordshire 1727 and 1734	49.6%
Derby 1727 and 1734	43.2%
Norwich 1734 and 1735b	98.1%

likely to include him on their 1734 ballot (50.4 per cent) than not to include him (49.6 per cent). The examples of Caesar and Vincent show that in the absence of strong partisanship voters were only moderately loyal to persons, while partisan loyalty overwhelmed personal loyalty when relevant.

Of course, personal loyalty and influence played a role in voter behaviour. The comparison of the Newcastle elections of 1722 and 1734 is an example of this. Both elections featured the Whig William Carr standing against a member of the locally influential Blackett family allied with another Tory. Each election featured a significant amount of cross-party voting, with 21 per cent of voters picking Carr and Sir William Blackett in 1722 and 15.6 per cent opting for Carr and Walter C. Blackett in 1734. From the first election to the second, voters changed their preferences significantly, particularly Whigs switching to Blackett and Carr or a straight Tory ticket. But Blackett family loyalty was high: 85.1 per cent of voters who included Sir William on their 1722 ballot voted for his nephew Walter in 1734. As Table 1 shows, Carr lost a very high percentage of his partisan voters in 1734 (those who plumped for Carr), but most (43.3 per cent of 1722 Carr plumpers) abandoned him entirely rather than adding Blackett (15.8 per cent). While the Blackett family almost certainly had something to do with it, these voters were switching parties rather than solely acting out of loyalty to the family.

Voters who voted in a subsequent election were very loyal to their party, but the percentages who voted at all in the subsequent election were considerably lower. There was very high turnover in the voterate between elections (see Table 2). Although we should bear in mind the caveat from the introduction that the number of identifiable repeated voters is less than the actual number of repeat voters, in most cases half or fewer of voters in the first election could be identified as participating in the subsequent election.

The last row in Table 2 highlights the fact that the rest of these numbers are undercounts. It is likely that there really were more repeat voters from the 1734 general election to the 1735 by-election than in the other cases, since they were the closest pair chronologically in the dataset. But the reason the percentage of identifiable repeat voters in Norwich was so dramatically higher is that the two polls were printed in the same poll book, meaning that the identification of voters was done by contemporaries who knew them rather than by my trying to match names in two different poll books. Had the other pairs of elections been recorded in the same way, the numbers listed here would certainly be higher, perhaps much higher.

But even assuming a significant undercount on the order of 20 percentage points, these figures still show a high level of turnover from election to election. The figures on promised votes in Sussex presented in Part II, where a significant percentage of people who promised their vote just before the election do not appear in the poll book, also support the conclusion that a good deal of this turnover was real and not just a result of problems with the data. It should not be surprising that voter participation was irregular because, as discussed more fully in the conclusion, voting in the 18th century was difficult.

Based on the data from these election pairs, voter behaviour over time in the early 18th century was characterised by the combination of a high level of partisan loyalty as well as a high level of eligible voters dropping out of, or joining, the voterate from one election to the next. Part II offers additional context for that behaviour using two Sussex elections from 1734 as a case study for the ways campaigns motivated and mobilised potential voters.

II: Sussex 1734

The Sussex and Lewes elections in 1734 are excellent case studies through which to look more deeply at voter behaviour. This is not because they were especially representative of early 18th-century elections. While no elections were 'typical', the time and place of these Sussex elections deserve notice. Sussex was the political home of the Whig grandee Thomas Pelham-Holles, duke of Newcastle, the pre-eminent electioneer of the early 18th century.[8] Newcastle's brother, Henry Pelham, was one of two Whig candidates for the county, alongside James Butler. Two other Pelhams, Thomas Pelham of Lewes and Thomas Pelham of Stanmer, stood for the borough of Lewes.

The elections of 1734 were also hotly contested. The successful opposition to the government's proposed excise taxes the previous year gave Tories and opposition Whigs the potential for electoral success, especially as they hoped to combine their forces under a unified Patriot banner. In Sussex, the Tory John Fuller stood with the opposition Whig Sir Cecil Bishop, while in Lewes the opposition consisted of the Tory Thomas Sergison and the Whig Nathaniel Garland. Finally, because of Newcastle's prominence and personal involvement,

---

[8] While assessments of Newcastle vary, there is unanimity on this point. For Basil Williams, his capacity to control elections was the only quality that justified the high offices he held: Basil Williams, *Carteret and Newcastle: A Contrast in Contemporaries* (Cambridge, 1943), 1. Reed Browning takes a more generous view of Newcastle's overall ability but concurs about his role as an electioneer: Reed Browning, *The Duke of Newcastle* (New Haven, 1975), xi–xiii.

both sides viewed Sussex as symbolically important.[9] In short, these two elections featured an unusually high degree of engagement compared to other 18th-century elections.

What makes these elections such valuable case studies is the combination of sources available. The Newcastle Papers in the British Library contain extensive correspondence between the duke and his allies and agents in the county, describing how they wooed voters, often mentioning individual voters by name. Those names can be cross-referenced with the poll books for the county and Lewes to evaluate how successful Newcastle's campaign was. In particular, the correspondents were very concerned to obtain 'promises' from voters. Using the poll books, we can see whether named voters kept their promises, broke their promises, or did not vote.

The two constituencies stood near the extremes of the size spectrum. Sussex was a large county, in which almost 3,800 people voted in 1734. Lewes, on the other hand, was a 'scot and lot' borough with 156 voters in 1734. Despite this, many of the campaign practices were similar. The main difference, discussed further below, was that the small size of Lewes made it more feasible to exert pressure on voters and to retaliate for non-compliance.

Campaigning began early. On 9 July 1733, ten months before the county election, Robert Burnett, Newcastle's most active agent, reported visiting several freeholders 'in ye out scarts [outskirts] of Waldron' and that 'all promised for Mr. Pelham and Mr. Butler'.[10] The opposition was equally assiduous. In the same letter, Burnett informed Newcastle that 'Mr. John Fuller sayd he would shake every freeholder by Hand in the County. & kiss their wives before Christmas Day'. The following months were punctuated by visits, ales, bonfires and other election activities, some of which are described below. The promised vote was the prize both sides sought. Most common and most valuable was the promise of both votes, but some freeholders promised a single vote. There could be other caveats, such as the case of Mr Chillys, 'who is very zealous for your Grace', but was also old and unsure if he would live to see the poll.[11]

From the perspective of the historian, Burnett and other correspondents were often frustratingly vague about who promised. As with the letter quoted in the previous paragraph, they reported visiting unnamed freeholders and obtaining their promise. But in a number of cases they did record the name of the promised voter, which can then be compared to the poll book. For Sussex, there were 150 voters who made some kind of promise (133 promised to vote for both Whig candidates; 15 promised a single vote; and 2 promised not to vote against). For Lewes, there were 60 (57 promised both votes and 3 promised single votes). The relationship between a promised vote and an actual vote is presented in tables 3–5. In addition to the data in tables 3–5, the two Sussex voters who promised not to vote against Newcastle's candidates did not vote at all. The three Lewes voters who promised a single vote all gave a single vote.

To summarise in reverse order: for the smaller constituency of Lewes, extracting a promise was very effective. Only a few voters broke their promise or even declined to appear at the poll, perhaps because they feared the repercussions. On the other hand, in the county, getting

---

[9]BL, Add. MS 32688, f. 510: duke of Newcastle to gentlemen at Lewes, Claremont, 16 Oct. 1733.

[10]BL, Add. MS 32688, f. 19: Robert Burnett to duke of Newcastle, 9 July 1733. Sussex voted on 9 and 10 May 1734, while the Lewes poll was held on 27 April.

[11]BL, Add. MS 32688, f. 183: James Hargreaves to duke of Newcastle, East Hoadly, 25 Aug. [1733]. Chillys' name does not appear in the poll book.

Table 3: *Sussex voters who promised both votes to Newcastle's agents (n = 133)*

Voted both	67	50.4%
Voted split	10	7.5%
Voted against	18	13.5%
No vote*	38	28.6%

*This category includes the aforementioned Mr Chillys, as well as another voter whose promise was conditional on his ability to go to the poll.

Table 4: *Sussex voters who promised a single vote to Newcastle's agents (n = 15)*

Voted both	3	20.0%
Voted split (single)	4	26.7%
Voted against*	6	40.0%
No vote	2	13.3%

*That is, voted for both opposition candidates.

Table 5: *Lewes Voters who Promised Both Votes to Newcastle's Agents (n = 57)*

Voted both	47	82.5%
Voted split	0	0%
Voted against	7	12.3%
No vote	3	5.3%

the promise of a single vote was almost worthless. Almost as many voted against Newcastle's Whig candidates entirely as voted for one or both of them.

For the county, a promised double vote was almost as effective at preventing the freeholder from becoming an opposition voter as it was in Lewes (only 13.5 per cent of county voters, compared with 12.3 per cent of voters in Lewes, used both votes against their promise), although there was more vote splitting. But a very significant proportion of the promised voters did not vote at all. Even if the two voters with a conditional promise are removed, over a quarter of those who promised both votes did not cast a vote for any candidate.

It is also significant that the obtaining of promises happened early in the campaign calendar. All but two of the reported promises came before the end of October 1733, over six months before the election.[12] For the county, the bulk of the recorded promises were collected by August. For Lewes, most were collected in October. As discussed more fully below, the promise was the beginning of the campaign process rather than its culmination.

The experience of another Sussex magnate, Charles Seymour, duke of Somerset, illustrated the dangers of waiting to extract promises. Throughout the campaign, both sides eagerly courted Somerset's reportedly prodigious influence in the neighbourhood of his

[12]One promise each for the county and for Lewes was recorded in November.

Petworth estate. Perhaps because he was truly indecisive, or perhaps because he was holding out for a better offer, Somerset delayed declaring until just days before the election, when on 1 May 1734 he asked voters 'about Petworth' for a split vote of Henry Pelham and Sir Cecil Bishop.[13] Of the 69 voters from Petworth, 42 (60.9 per cent) voted for the Whig candidates Pelham and Butler, and another 9 (13.0 per cent) for the opposition Bishop and Fuller. Just 15 (21.7 per cent) voted according to Somerset's wishes.[14] Clearly waiting until the last minute was not an effective electoral strategy, although of course other factors could have been at play.

The timing of the promises suggests that the many public campaign activities in Sussex were intended to motivate rather than persuade. Specifically, the campaigns sought to make potential voters invested enough in the process to overcome challenges associated with voting. Almost all of the recorded promises preceded public events. In fact, when they started collecting promises in July 1733, Newcastle specifically instructed his agents not to act openly. Burnett went so far as to pay a crown to stop the ringing of bells, 'for that we did not come in that manner amongst them'.[15] The opposition was also reported to 'go on more silently' in August.[16] In the first months of campaigning, agents and candidates met voters individually or in small groups.

In these small meetings, the electioneers attempted to persuade voters. Their purpose was to remind voters of their stake in the election's outcome. The excise scheme was a major topic of conversation. William Hay, for instance, reported to Newcastle that an opposition agent 'has been trumpeting the Excise in their Ears', but that Hay attempted to placate the freeholders. Hay also reported that he had 'mentioned the Schism Bill to the Dissenters', to remind them of the dangers of a Tory government and that voters such as Mr. Blacklock were 'frightened with the Excise, but more with the Schism Bill'.[17] Ideally these meetings ended with the voter agreeing to promise for the Newcastle candidates.

Both the Whigs and the opposition held election treats starting in August – in most cases after the promise of votes. J. Board explicitly made that connection, reporting to Newcastle that most of the freeholders he had met had promised both their votes and 'to take part of a piece of Venison and a bowl of punch with me'.[18] That event served as a pep rally for the upcoming election, as the voters and the wives in attendance 'resolv'd to proclaim, in the most Publick manner they could, their confidence in & affection for their present representatives, & their Resolution ever firmly to adhere to & support the same'.[19] Lady Shelley, Newcastle's sister, hosted a breakfast at Arundel for 'all ye Women' in September, which seemed to serve a similar purpose.[20] Treats functioned to seal the promised vote by

---

[13]BL, Add. MS 32689, f. 216: James Butler to duke of Newcastle, Warminghurst Park, 2 May 1734.

[14]Somerset's influence extended beyond the immediate confines of Petworth, but it is doubtful he was more successful elsewhere. Only 169 voters in the whole county chose his preferred option of Pelham and Bishop.

[15]BL, Add. MS 32688, f. 19: Robert Burnett to duke of Newcastle, 9 July 1733.

[16]BL, Add. MS 32688, f. 169: Thomas Hurdis to duke of Newcastle, 23 Aug. 1733.

[17]BL, Add. MS 32688, f. 56: William Hay to duke of Newcastle, Glynbourn, 9 Aug. 1733. The Schism Act, passed under the earl of Oxford's Tory ministry in 1714, was an attack on dissenting schools. The Whigs repealed it in 1718. Hay clearly felt this was a winning issue for the Whigs, since he raised it on several other occasions. See BL, Add. MS 32688, f. 121: William Hay to duke of Newcastle, Glynbourn, 16 Aug. 1733.

[18]BL, Add. MS 32688, f. 226: J. Board to duke of Newcastle, Paxhill, 30 Aug. 1733.

[19]BL, Add. MS 32688, f. 228: J. Board to duke of Newcastle, Paxhill, 1 Sept. 1733.

[20]BL, Add. MS 32688, f. 249: Lady Shelley to duke of Newcastle, 4 Sept. 1733.

creating a social obligation that the vote would repay. As Henry Pelham wrote, he dined after church with some supporters, 'which it is very necessary to do … to oblige such very hearty friends'.[21] Another illustration that an obligation was created by an invitation to dine is a report by James Hargraves in October that several freeholders who intended to split their vote refused an invitation to dine at Newcastle's Haland estate due to 'an unwillingness to refuse any thing to you in your own house'.[22] In Lewes, William Hay criticised the Whig candidates for failing to secure promised voters, writing to Newcastle that, 'as soon as a man has promised, no more notice is taken of him', which the people of the town considered to be 'ill Usage'.[23] As one of the most common types of campaign activity, treats served to maintain and solidify promised votes.

The scale of public events grew as the election drew closer. In August and September the campaigns descended on places where voters were already likely to be present. Agents of the Whig and opposition campaigns attended the Stenning races on 15 August, for example, where the latter 'were very busy among the people who cried out, no excise'.[24] Fairs, such as the Cliff fair in late September, were another opportunity to meet voters.[25] Sir William Gage, a cricket player, used neighbourhood matches as an opportunity to speak to freeholders on at least one occasion.[26] Also around this time Newcastle's agents began distributing copies of a circular letter written by Henry Pelham. As Robert Burnett put it, these were less intended to persuade voters than 'to whet up their memory'.[27] Having obtained a promise, it was necessary to keep the upcoming election in voters' attention and to maintain their enthusiasm for voting.

By late 1733 Newcastle was organising large public gatherings independent of races, fairs, or other pre-existing events. In Hastings he organised a spectacular celebration of King George II's birthday, with drinking, a bonfire, illuminations and a ball.[28] Lewes, as a smaller constituency, was suitable to more sustained events. Starting in late October, the two Pelham candidates started a weekly club 'to see our friends' as a way of one-upping the opposition, who had announced they would be holding monthly meetings.[29] The largest event occurred in December, when Newcastle hosted a stag hunt attended by between 1,000 and 1,500 people, which reassured him that support in the county was strong.[30] Like smaller treats and appearances tied to pre-existing events, the campaign sought to keep voters mobilised and engaged as the election neared.

[21]BL, Add. MS 32688, f. 307: Henry Pelham to duke of Newcastle, Ashburnham, 10 Sept. [1733].

[22]BL, Add. MS 32688, f. 435: James Hargraves to duke of Newcastle, East Hoadly, 1 Oct. 1733.

[23]BL, Add. MS 32688, f. 526: William Hay to duke of Newcastle, Glynbourn, 19 Oct. [1733].

[24]BL, Add. MS 32688, f. 108: Thomas Hurdis to duke of Newcastle, Stompting, 15 Aug. 1733.

[25]BL, Add. MS 32688, f. 379: William Hay to duke of Newcastle, Glynbourn, 24 Sept. 1733. See also ff. 293, 325, and 337.

[26]BL, Add. MS 32688, f. 170: Sir William Gage to duke of Newcastle, 23 Aug. 1733. BL, Add. MS 32688, f. 224: John Crawford to Peter Forbes, Lyhoth, Aug. 1733. Since the second letter lacks a precise date, it is possible that both letters referred to the same event.

[27]BL, Add. MS 32688, f. 253: Robert Burnett to duke of Newcastle, Dallington, 4 Sept. 1733.

[28]BL, Add. MS 32689, f. 3: John Collier to duke of Newcastle, Hastings, 1 Nov. 1733.

[29]BL, Add. MS 32688, f. 567: Thomas Pelham to duke of Newcastle, Lewes, 23 Oct. 1733. For the opposition meeting, see f. 383.

[30]BL, Add. MS 33073, f. 84: duke of Newcastle to duchess of Newcastle, Bishopstone, 7 Dec. 1733.

The final push to get voters to the polls came just before the elections. Newcastle and the candidates toured the county in the days leading up to the poll, meeting as many potential voters as possible in receptions, dinners and breakfasts.[31] They also arranged transportation and lodging for voters who lived some distance from the polling place.[32] These events were apparently quite festive, although Newcastle assured his wife in a postscript to a letter recounting a dinner with over 600 people, 'I was yesterday quite sober'.[33] By this time, as the duke of Somerset's experience showed, it was far too late to persuade voters. These events were purely about getting them to the polls.

In Lewes, agents were able to put more direct pressure on voters. Starting in December 1733, both campaigns undertook legal proceedings to terminate leases, evict and otherwise 'turn out' uncooperative tenants.[34] Similar threats were made by both sides not to employ tradesmen who supported the opposition, along with promises to patronise loyal voters.[35] While in theory the same type of leverage could be used in the county, in practice the sheer number of eligible voters probably made it impossible. Even in Lewes, the ability to target individuals in this way was possible largely due to the documented efforts of local gentleman William Hay, efforts that Hay portrayed as unusual.[36]

Although the leverage landlords and patrons had was theoretically very strong, there were practical limits. Only tenants with a short-term or about-to-expire lease were seen to be susceptible. As Hay wrote in December, 'if a Tenant has a right to stay in till next Michaelmas [29 September 1734], nothing is to be done'.[37] As a result, he only listed 15 voters on both sides who were susceptible to removal. The number of vulnerable voters was also reduced because having been evicted by one side gave voters a strong claim to favour from the other. Hay told a Lewes pipe-maker named Harman, who was threatened with eviction by his Tory landlord, 'not to be frightened … for if he turned him out of his House, I could promise him another one in that neighbourhood'.[38] In addition, there was no guarantee that election-time threats would be acted upon. Writing in July 1734, for instance, Thomas Pelham explained how important it was to boycott tradesmen who supported the opposition in Lewes and that, 'I have therefore try'd to convince our friends how necessary it is'. While he professed confidence that 'the greatest part' would do so, it seemed to be far from a sure thing.[39] Undoubtedly it was easier to make the threat than to carry it out. Certainly, in a larger constituency, it would be impracticable to influence a significant number of voters this way.

---

[31] BL, Add. MS 32689, f. 228: Thomas Bak to duke of Newcastle, Chichester, 6 May 1734.

[32] BL, Add. MS 32689, f. 232: duke of Wilmington to Newcastle, East Bowen, 6 May 1734.

[33] BL, Add. MS 33073, f. 87: duke of Newcastle to duchess of Newcastle, Goodwood, 23 April 1734.

[34] BL, Add. MS 32689, f. 86: William Hay to duke of Newcastle, Lewes, 18 Dec. 1733. See also ff. 104, 128, and 130.

[35] For example, see BL, Add. MS 32688, f. 526: William Hay to duke of Newcastle, Glynbourn, 19 Oct. 1733.

[36] See for example BL, Add. MS 32689 f. 24: William Hay to duke of Newcastle, Glynbourn, 15 Nov. 1733. While Hay had obvious motives to embellish his efforts, there is nothing in the correspondence that approaches his level of specificity for the county or indeed for other boroughs in Sussex.

[37] BL, Add. MS 32689, f. 90: William Hay to duke of Newcastle, Lewes, 22 Dec. 1733.

[38] BL, Add. MS 32689, f. 13: William Hay to duke of Newcastle, Lewes, 8 Nov. 1733.

[39] BL, Add. MS 32689, f. 316: Thomas Pelham to duke of Newcastle, Lewes, 20 July 1734. For an example of the difficulty in following through on evictions, see BL, Add. MS 32689, f. 263: William Hay to duke of Newcastle, Glynbourn, 6 June 1734.

Conclusion

Most voters in the early 18th century were partisans. They knew which party they supported, even if they occasionally had to be reminded why. In the 1734 Sussex elections, for example, the opposition candidates reiterated the dangers of excise while Whig candidates brought up memories of Tory measures like the Schism Bill. To use 21st-century terminology, these were 'base elections' characterised by a relatively small number of swing voters.

Despite their partisanship, those who were eligible to vote were not reliable participants in elections. It is not possible to ascertain with certainty the reason why potential voters did not vote. Undoubtedly there were as many reasons as there were non-voters, and in most constituencies we cannot even establish how many potential voters there were. But it is possible, based on the evidence here, to suggest a conceptual framework for voter participation.[40] The act of voting presented challenges, the severity of which varied with the voter and the constituency. Whether or not the eligible voter participated depended on whether their investment in the process outweighed those challenges.

First, there were practical obstacles to voting. This was especially true in the counties, where there was generally only one polling place. Participating often required overnight travel, costing time and money (although as we saw for Sussex candidates, they usually tried to defray those costs by providing transportation for some voters). Borough elections required less travel, at least for resident voters, but participating in the poll still required a significant time commitment.

Second, voters faced the consequences of displeasing powerful people with their vote. Like the practical challenges of time and distance, the severity of these repercussions varied. An independent gentleman might risk a loss of friendship, while a tradesman or tenant risked a catastrophic loss of livelihood. These consequences were real but should not be overstated to the extent of claiming elites controlled voters. A sufficiently determined voter could overcome even the most extreme retaliation. As William Hay reassured the pipemaker Mr Harman, what better recommendation for favour could there be than to have been turned out by supporters of the rival campaign? Even in a very small constituency like Lewes, elites found it onerous to follow through on threats to turn out or boycott voters. In larger constituencies, not voting was probably a safe way to avoid following through if a voter had felt obliged to promise against their partisan inclinations. But would-be voters who were more cautious or less dedicated might decide that abstaining from the poll was a more elegant response to pressure from landlords and other elites.

In terms of explaining voter participation, however, this pressure could also provide encouragement. It is plausible that the discrepancy between the small proportion of promised Lewes voters and the larger percentage of promised Sussex voters who did not appear at the poll was due to the increased scrutiny the former faced from the likes of William Hay and other agents. They may have feared retaliation for not voting more than their peers in the county did, although I have been unable to find specific examples of promised voters being punished for not appearing at the poll. While a hypothesis at this point, it seems reasonable to suggest that the practical challenges of voting were more significant in numerically and

[40] Given that most of this evidence comes from the Newcastle correspondence, it might be more accurate to say this is a framework for how elites understood voter participation.

geographically larger constituencies while the danger of displeasing elites was more acute in smaller constituencies.[41]

To overcome the challenges posed by voting, potential voters needed to feel invested in the process. Perhaps most obviously, the potential voter might care about the outcome of the election. Given the high levels of partisanship described in Part I, it is reasonable to assume that most voters had at least a nominal investment in whether Tories or Whigs won, even if only to see their 'team' come out on top. The Sussex campaigners who reminded voters of the policy consequences of defeat, referencing the Excise or Schism bills for instance, were trying to make potential voters care enough about the outcome to participate.

The creation of a social obligation, described for Sussex in Part II, was another way potential voters could become invested in the process of voting. This could function independently of the voters' interest in the outcome of the election. That is, a desire to fulfil one's promise and to repay the favour granted through treating gave the potential voter a reason to participate separate from their concern about the outcome.

Finally, the various election-related events generated enthusiasm for the election and made participating in it seem more valuable. Festivities, food and drink offered on the day of the election made the potentially long journey to the polling place more attractive. In the months before, balls and breakfasts, appearances at fairs and cricket matches, treats and stag hunts all served to keep the upcoming election in prospective voters' minds, even after they had already promised their support. Even circular letters, which ostensibly explained why a potential voter should support a candidate, were intended 'to whet up their memory'.

Like other electioneers, Newcastle and his allies in Sussex understood that not voting was common. In providing transportation to and lodging at the polling place and offering succour to friendly voters who faced retaliation, they attempted to mitigate two of the main obstacles to voting. They also made sustained efforts to motivate voters by giving them reasons to participate in the poll. While they would undoubtedly have been happy to persuade opposition voters to switch their vote, driving participation by their own partisans was the key to victory. Just like a present-day 'base election', the outcome depended on turning out supporters rather than winning over opponents.

Appendix

Sources of Poll Book Data

Bedfordshire 1715: *A Copy of the Poll for Knights of the Shire for the County of Bedford. Taken at the Town of Bedford, February Sixteenth, 1714/5* (1715).

Bedfordshire 1722: *A Copy of the Poll for the Knights of the Shire for the County of Bedford. Taken at the Town of Bedford the 4th of April, Anno Dom. 1722* (1722).

Bedfordshire 1727: *How Bedfordshire Voted, 1685–1735: The Evidence of Local Poll Books*, ed. James Collett-White (2 vols, Bedfordshire Historical Record Society, lxxxv, 2006).

Bedfordshire 1734: *How Bedfordshire Voted*, ed. Collett-White.

---

[41] This contrast should be taken as tentative, since the surviving poll books that comprise this article's dataset are heavily biased towards larger constituencies.

Bristol 1722: *An Exact List of the Votes of the Freeholders and Freemen, of the City and Council of Bristol, Taken at the Election of Members of Parliament, before John Rich, Esq; and Noblet Ruddock, Esq; Sheriffs* (Bristol, 1722).

Bristol 1734: *A List of the Free-Holders and Free-Men, Who Voted at the Election for the City and County of Bristol, Begun Wednesday May 15* (Bristol, [1734]).

Derby 1727: *Poll of the Burgesses of the Borough of Derby* (Nottingham, 1727).

Derby 1734: *A List of the Poll for the Borough of Derby Taken the 27th Day of April 1734* ([1734]).

Essex 1710: *List of the Names of the Gentlemen and other Free-Holders That Voted for Knights of the Shire for the County of Essex: As the same was Taken the 24th of October, 1710* (1711).

Essex 1715: *An Exact List of the Names of the Gentlemen and other Freeholders That Voted for Knights of the Shire for the County of Essex, (In the Room of Thomas Middleton, Esq; Deceas'd) As the same was Taken the 31st of May, 1715* (1715).

Essex 1722: *A List of the Names of the Gentlemen, and other Freeholders, that Voted for Knights of the Shire, for the County of Essex. As the same was taken the 27th of March, 1722* (1724).

Essex 1734: *The Poll for Knights of the Shire to Represent the County of Essex; Taken at Chelmsford, on Tuesday the 7th Day of May, 1734* (1734).

Hampshire 1710: *The Poll at the Election of Knights of the Shire for the County of Southampton, Anno 1710* (1714).

Hampshire 1713: *A True Copy of the Poll for the Electing of Knights of the Shire for the County of Southampton; Taken at the Castle of Winchester, On Wednesday, August the 26th … 1713* (1714).

Hertfordshire 1722: *A Copy of the Poll for Knights of the Shire, Taken at the Town of Hertford, April 3, 1722* (1722).

Hertfordshire 1727: *A Copy of the Poll for Knights of the Shire, Taken at the Town of Hertford, Sept. 7, 1727* (n.p., n.d.).

Hertfordshire 1734: *Copy of the Poll for Knights of the Shire for the County of Hertford, Taken at the Town of Hertford, May 2 1734* (1734).

Lewes 1734: *An Exact State of the Poll, Taken by Tho. Friend, and James Reeve, Constables of the Borough of Lewes, On the 27th Day of April, 1734. For the Election of Members to serve in this present Parliament* (1734).

Newcastle 1722: *The Poll at the Election of Members to serve in Parliament, for the Town and County of Newcastle upon Tyne, taken before Stephen Coulson, esq; Sheriff, the 4th and 5th of April, 1722.* (n.p., n.d.).

Newcastle 1734: *The Poll at the Election of Members to serve in Parliament for the Town and County of Newcastle upon Tyne* (Newcastle, 1734).

Northumberland 1710: *Poll Books, &c. County of Northumberland* (Newcastle, 1898).

Northumberland 1716: *The Poll Book of the Contested Election for the County of Northumberland, Taken on the 2nd Day of February, 1715* (Newcastle, 1899).

Norwich 1734/35: *An Alphabetical Draught of the Polls of Sir Edward Ward, Bart. Miles Branthwayt, Esq; And of Horatio Walpole, Waller Bacon, Esqs; for Members of Parliament for the City of Norwich: Taken May the 15th, 1734. And of Miles Branthwayt, Esq; and Thomas Vere, Esq; Taken February the 19th, 1734* (Norwich, 1735).

Surrey 1710: *The Poll for Knights of the Shire for the County of Surrey. Taken at Guildford the 11th and 12th Days of October 1710. Published at the Request of the Gentlemen and Freeholders of the County: By the Order of The Hon'ble Heneage Finch, Esq.* (1710).

Surrey 1713: *The Poll for Knights of the Shire for the County of Surrey Taken at Guildford the 9th and 10th Days of September, 1713* (1713).

Surrey 1717: BL, Add. MS 11571, ff. 10–56.

Surrey 1719: *The Poll for a Knight of the Shire for the County of Surrey, Taken at Guildford the Fifteenth and Sixteenth Days of December, 1719* (1720).

Sussex 1734: *A Poll Taken by Henry Montague Esq; (Sheriff of the County of Sussex) At the City of Chichester, on Thursday and Friday the Ninth and Tenth Days of May 1734. For the Election of Two Knights to serve for the said County in this present Parliament* (1734).

Parliamentary History, Vol. 43, pt. 1 (2024), pp. 36–52

A Tale of Two Poll Books – Wareham 1702 and Dorchester 1705

KEVIN TUFFNELL

The politics of Queen Anne's reign are characterised as the rage of party; Whigs and Tories contended over religion, the constitution and the succession, and foreign policy. This struggle was taken to the electorate in five elections during Anne's reign, and these raise a question concerning electors' motivations, the answer to which remains elusive: were they acting according to principle, or reflecting the electoral interests to which they were subject? This article analyses the two surviving poll books for Dorset elections in the age of Anne, those at Wareham in 1702 and at Dorchester in 1705. It focuses principally on the voting behaviour of those engaged in the towns' governance structures: corporation members, councils of freemen and local parishes. However, it also considers the behaviour of other categories of voter: politicians, the clergy and non-conformists. The analysis shows how electoral interest was mediated through the towns' governing institutions and suggests that (at least in these two cases) negotiation between the parties had a greater role in the outcome than has sometimes been suggested. It also demonstrates the limits of the electoral influence of the boroughs' elites: significant numbers of voters were simply not prepared to be led.

Keywords: election; interest; poll book; Whig; Tory; deference; participatory; voter; borough; corporation; Wareham; Dorchester

Introduction

Why did early 18th-century electors cast their votes as they did? Did they vote on the issues of the day, or were they responding to the electoral interests to which they were subject? The voters are unable to help: as Bill Speck put it, one cannot conduct an opinion poll of the dead.[1] Nonetheless, the question remains pertinent and this article considers the conclusions which can be drawn from analysis of the two Dorset elections conducted during the reign of Queen Anne for which poll books survive: those for the boroughs of Wareham in 1702 and of Dorchester in 1705.[2]

British politics under Anne was defined by the conflict between Whigs and Tories: the rage of party. To quote Geoffrey Holmes: 'whatever the complexities of the body politic in the early years of the eighteenth century, its lifeblood was the existence and

---

[1] W.A. Speck, *Tory and Whig: The Struggle in the Constituencies, 1701–1715* (1970), 114.

[2] Dorset History Centre (hereafter DHC), D/BOH X3: Wareham poll book; DC/DOB 33/1: Dorchester poll book.

conflict of two major parties'.[3] Party divisions centred on three principal issues.[4] First, the protestant succession. The death of Anne's only surviving child, the duke of Gloucester, in 1700 had reopened the issue; although apparently resolved by the Act of Settlement of 1701, it continued to be a source of contention. While the Whigs adhered firmly to the revolution settlement of 1688/9, continuing Tory discomfort was heightened by some Tories' inclination to Jacobitism.

The second issue concerned foreign policy. England had embarked on the War of the Spanish Succession at the outset of Anne's reign to prevent Louis XIV accepting the throne of Spain for his grandson, Philip of Anjou. A subsidiary cause was Louis' recognition of the Pretender (James II's son) as James III in September 1701. Both played into longstanding English fears of French Catholic hegemony in continental Europe and of popery and arbitrary government at home. At issue initially was not the war itself, but its conduct. The Tories wished to focus on naval operations; the Whigs, supporting the ministry of Godolphin and Marlborough, promoted Marlborough's land campaigns. Later, differences over foreign policy centred on Tory enthusiasm for making peace, an objective ultimately secured with the making of the treaty of Utrecht in 1713.

Finally, Anglicanism's status as the established religion was contentious; indeed, religion has been seen as lying at the heart of the division between the parties.[5] Tory enthusiasm for the primacy of the Church of England and inclination to the 'high-church' elements within it came into conflict with the Whigs' support for toleration of religious (most obviously protestant) dissent and their 'low-church' sympathies. Religious issues were particularly prominent in the elections of 1705 and 1710, but the Tories rarely missed an opportunity to raise the cry of 'the Church in danger'.[6]

The inter-party battle was fought not only in parliament and in London's clubs and coffee houses. Holmes also traced the conflict through social relations, the press, the churches and the theatre, presenting a picture of a deeply divided society. These divisions permeated the provinces as thoroughly as they did London, as Paul Halliday's and John Miller's studies of politics in provincial towns have shown.[7] This partisan contention was fuelled by frequent elections, conducted among an electorate of a quarter of a million voters. There were no fewer than five elections in Anne's 12-year reign, conducted in each of the counties and in those towns with borough status. The focus in this article is on two of these elections. In 1702 the recent accession of Anne, a staunch supporter of the established Church, enabled the Tories to campaign on the issue of 'church and state', and secure a substantial victory. Two events led to a Tory setback in 1705: first, the support of some Tories for the 'tack', a contentious attempt to pass legislation against dissenters who occasionally conformed to the Church of England by attaching it to a tax bill; and secondly, Marlborough's victory at Blenheim, an apparent vindication of Whig enthusiasm for military engagement on the

[3] G.S. Holmes, *British Politics in the Age of Anne* (rev. edn, 1987), 6.

[4] For an introduction to the issues, see Holmes, *British Politics*, 51–81.

[5] Tim Harris, *Politics under the Later Stuarts: Party Conflict in a Divided Society, 1660–1715* (Harlow, 1993), 203; G.S. De Krey, *A Fractured Society: The Politics of London in the First Age of Party, 1688–1715* (Oxford, 1985), 18; P.D. Halliday, *Dismembering the Body Politic: Partisan Politics in England's Towns, 1650–1730* (Cambridge, 1998), 306.

[6] Harris, *Politics under the Later Stuarts*, 83–4; Holmes, *British Politics*, 69.

[7] Holmes, *British Politics*, 15–48; G.S. Holmes and W.A. Speck, *The Divided Society: Party and Politics in England, 1694–1716* (1967), 2; Halliday, *Body Politic*; John Miller, *Cities Divided: Politics and Religion in English Provincial Towns, 1660–1722* (Oxford, 2007).

continent. This pattern was broadly reflected in the outcome of those two elections across Dorset's nine constituencies, with the total number of Whig MPs returned increasing from seven to nine between 1702 and 1705.[8]

How did voters respond to this febrile political environment: did they vote according to their political principles, or did they bend to the various interests and pressures to which they were subject? Attempts to answer this question inevitably face the problem of an absence of sources providing direct evidence of voters' intentions. Rare indeed was the voter in the Weymouth and Melcombe Regis election of 1713 who explained his motives during parliamentary proceedings: he had been promised two guineas for his vote.[9] Some examples of personal appeals to individual electors for their votes have survived (though not in the case of the two polls that are the subject of this article).[10] But even where it might be shown that the voter acted as asked, there can be no certainty that he was motivated by the appeal made to him, rather than by some other reason. Seeking conclusions concerning voters' motivations must therefore involve drawing inferences from circumstantial evidence: the prosopography of the voters themselves; electoral literature; and the correspondence of those seeking to exercise their own electoral interest, or to do so on behalf of others. The more limited the sources on which to ground these inferences, the greater the element of speculation inevitably introduced into the exercise.

Nonetheless, the question of voter motivation remains an important one, and has attracted considerable attention. In his analysis of the elections of Anne's reign, Bill Speck emphasised the volatility of the electorate and the impact of voters whose party allegiance changed between elections.[11] The importance of these floating voters was also the theme of more detailed analyses of selected poll books which he undertook alongside others.[12] Recognising the impossibility of certainty on questions of voter motivation, Speck concluded that electors were voting on principle, reflecting the issues of the day and the impact of partisan propaganda.[13] Tim Harris has concurred.[14]

In opposition to this participatory model of voter behaviour stands the deference model, which posits that voters acted in response to the pressures and electoral interests to which they were subject, be they from their landlords, neighbouring landowners and other social superiors, or from those participating in local government.[15] A study of the behaviour of voters in the Cheshire county elections of the early 18th century by Stephen Baskerville, Peter Adman and Katharine Beedham concluded that landlords had considerable influence over how their tenants cast their votes.[16] While the authors accepted that the records

[8] *HPC, 1690–1715*, www.historyofparliamentonline.org/ (accessed 13 Mar. 2023), s.v. constituencies.

[9] *CJ*, 27 May 1714.

[10] E.g., TNA, PRO 30/24/22/1/93: Shaftesbury to Trenchard, 16 Jan. 1701, in which Shaftesbury requested Trenchard's vote in Poole for his brother-in-law, Edward Hooper.

[11] Speck, *Tory and Whig*, 114.

[12] W.A. Speck and W.A. Gray, 'Computer Analysis of Poll Books: An Interim Report', *BIHR*, xliii (1970), 105–12; W.A. Speck, W.A. Gray and R. Hopkinson, 'Computer Analysis of Poll Books: A Further Report', *BIHR*, xlviii (1975), 64–90.

[13] Speck, *Tory and Whig*, 78–9, 114.

[14] Harris, *Politics under the Later Stuarts*, 176–96.

[15] For a fuller explanation of these models, see Speck, Gray and Hopkinson, 'Further Report', 64–5.

[16] S.W. Baskerville, Peter Adman and K.F. Beedham, 'The Dynamics of Landlord Influence in English County Elections, 1701–1734: The Evidence from Cheshire', *Parliamentary History*, xii (1993), 126–42.

available to them made it difficult to extrapolate their results to the behaviour of borough voters, they cast doubt on the uncritical assumption of greater electoral freedom in the towns.[17] By contrast, writing of the Devon borough of Tavistock, Jon Rosebank found little evidence of landlords exercising influence over the voting behaviour of their tenants.[18]

Norma Landau considered another potential source of electoral influence: the local justices of the peace.[19] Her study of Kent's early 18th-century elections led her to conclude that a gentleman's appointment as a magistrate greatly increased his powers of electoral persuasion. Landau was not, however, an uncritical adherent of the deference model of voter behaviour. Rather, she suggested an alternative which combined deference and participation: 'most voters acted in a manner which both preserved their integrity, and showed due regard for the opinions of their superiors'.[20] Mark Knights has also cautioned against drawing too clear a distinction between a voter acting according to principle and according to influence, identifying the paradox that a voter might cherish the right to vote based on his own judgment yet recognise the ability of his betters to guide that judgment.[21] This would potentially explain why local landowners might, irrespective of whether they were landlords to a significant number of voters, and aside from their patronage of businesses based in a nearby borough, expect to be able to exercise significant influence over that borough's voters.[22]

Landau's study used appointment as a justice of the peace as an indicator of superior social position: these were members of the gentry.[23] But consideration of the role of justices points to other potential sources of influence within electoral boroughs: the borough corporation and other instruments of local administration. Paul Halliday saw the corporations as being at the heart of the struggle for political control, with greater influence than that of national political figures and regional magnates. John Miller, however, cautioned against placing too much stress on the role of the borough corporations: in his view their electoral influence, and the opportunities for voters to act independently, varied greatly.[24] And a borough's administration went beyond the corporation: in his study of seven west-country towns, Jon Rosebank painted a picture of complex governance structures and communities, concluding that this made them difficult for outsiders to control.[25]

While Halliday and Rosebank weighed the competing claims to influence of borough corporations on the one hand and national and regional political magnates on the other, an objective here is to seek evidence of how borough corporations and other elements of

---

[17] Baskerville, Adman and Beedham, 'Dynamics of Landlord Influence', 139.

[18] Jon Rosebank, *Partisan Politics: Looking for Consensus in Eighteenth-Century Towns* (Exeter, 2021), 163.

[19] Norma Landau, 'Independence, Deference, and Voter Participation: The Behaviour of the Electorate in Early-Eighteenth-Century Kent', *HJ*, xxii (1979), 561–83. More generally, see L.K.J. Glassey, *Politics and the Appointment of Justices of the Peace, 1675–1720* (Oxford, 1979).

[20] Landau, 'Independence', 562.

[21] Mark Knights, *Representation and Misrepresentation in Later Stuart Britain: Partisanship and Political Culture* (Oxford, 2005), 174–81.

[22] See M.A. Kishlansky, *Parliamentary Selection: Social and Political Choice in Early Modern England* (Cambridge, 1986), 149; cf. Speck, *Tory and Whig*, 45.

[23] Landau, 'Independence', 569.

[24] Halliday, *Body Politic*, 332; Miller, *Cities Divided*, 128–9.

[25] Rosebank, *Partisan Politics*, 76. See also Rosemary Sweet, *The English Town, 1680–1840: Government, Society and Culture* (Harlow, 1999), 27, 124–5.

local government mediated between voters and those seeking to exercise electoral interest. Was Speck right to cast doubt on the role of negotiation in the outcome of borough elections, or, as Miller suggested, were corporation members seeking accommodations between competing electoral interests?[26]

At first glance, the two Dorset boroughs being studied, Wareham and Dorchester, are promising subjects for analysis. Both adopted a relatively broad franchise: the town's freeholders and those residents paying poor rates ('scot and lot'). As was the case in almost all constituencies, each elector had two votes, with each borough returning two MPs.[27] The electorate (those entitled to vote) in each case was consequently relatively large, and this was reflected in the numbers who actually voted: 140 in Wareham's election in 1702; 244 in Dorchester's in 1705.[28] Nonetheless, some significant issues need to be acknowledged. First, these poll books are hardly a representative sample: across Dorset there were 45 constituency elections in Anne's reign, of which 12 were contested.[29] Secondly, the purpose for which the books were prepared is unclear: were they an official record taken at the poll, or compiled by party agents to support subsequent election campaigns?[30] Thirdly, there is the practical question of legibility: the authors of the two (identical) copies of Wareham's book had impeccable handwriting; the same cannot be said of the compiler of the Dorchester book, who seems to have spilt his beer on it. Fourthly, instead of the more usual four candidates, two on each party ticket, these contests featured only three. And finally, there is an important difference between the two boroughs: Wareham's seats were 'safe', while Dorchester was more volatile. Wareham was represented throughout almost the entirety of Anne's reign by one Tory and one Whig MP. Dorchester, by contrast, elected two Tories in 1702, returned one Tory and one Whig in 1705, and in 1708 (the reign's least successful election for the Tories) returned two Whigs.[31]

There are also other problems. Poll books for the same constituency for a run of consecutive elections would allow for the type of analysis of change over time, which enabled Bill Speck to identify a significant number of floating voters (those who had changed their party allegiance between polls), and led him to conclude that many electors were voting on the issues of the day.[32] Having poll books for the same general election in different constituencies subject to different types or degrees of electoral interest might indicate the

[26]Speck, *Tory and Whig*, 57; Miller, *Cities Divided*, 129. See also Rosebank, *Partisan Politics*, 137.

[27]The exceptions were the city of London and the combined Dorset boroughs of Weymouth and Melcombe Regis, both of which returned four MPs.

[28]*HPC, 1690–1715*, s.v. Dorchester and Wareham.

[29]Derived from *HPC, 1690–1715*, s.v. constituencies. Of these 45 elections, 12 were contested, increasing to 13 if one includes the rerun in Weymouth in 1711 after the 1710 election was voided.

[30]See the discussion in S.W. Baskerville, Peter Adman and K.F. Beedham, 'Manuscript Poll-books and English County Elections in the First Age of Party: A Reconsideration of their Provenance and Purpose', *Archives*, xix (1991), 384–403, which makes the point that from 1696 (under the Parliamentary Elections Act of 1695) it was a legal requirement that returning officers make copies of poll books available on demand. In the present case, some inference might be drawn from the fact that the Wareham poll book is to be found in the papers of Denis Bond, one of the candidates, while that for Dorchester is among the borough corporation's own records.

[31]*HPC, 1690–1715*, s.v. Dorchester, Wareham and John Churchill. The biography identifies Churchill (who was elected for Dorchester alongside Awnsham Churchill in 1708) as 'probably a Whig'. Speck estimated that in the period there were some 189 'safe' seats out of a total of 513: Speck, *Tory and Whig*, 64.

[32]Speck and Gray, 'Interim Report'; Speck, Gray and Hopkinson, 'Further Report'; W.A. Speck and W.A. Gray, 'London Poll-books, 1713', in *London Politics, 1713–1717*, ed. H.J. Creaton, (London Record Society, xvii (981), 62–129.

respective weights that voters attached to principle and to electoral interest in deciding how to vote.[33] These issues notwithstanding, close study of the Wareham and Dorchester poll books, alongside related primary sources, sheds significant light on the role of borough corporations and other elements of their governance structures in electoral politics. It also enables conclusions to be drawn as to the extent to which, despite the pressures to which they were subject, electors chose to follow their principles when casting their votes.

Local Understanding of 'Whig' and 'Tory'

Before considering the two poll books, and the votes garnered by Tory and Whig candidates, there is an initial question to be addressed: to what extent did Dorset's voters identify as Tory or Whig, or at least align themselves with the parties' respective positions in a way which allows it to be inferred that they voted for candidates whose principles matched their own? Halliday, while emphasising the prevalence of partisan division in England's towns, noted that the terms 'Whig' and 'Tory' originated in London: even under Queen Anne, they rarely appeared in cases before the queen's bench concerning local electoral disputes.[34] Rosebank made the point that the picture in the provinces could be considerably more complex than focusing on a straightforward Whig/Tory opposition might imply.[35] Nonetheless, contemporary sources relating to Dorset provide evidence of political affiliations following party lines.

Considering first the printed sources: Corfe Castle's loyal address on the queen's accession in 1702 demonstrated an awareness of the main issues of the day, referring to the protection of the Church, the succession (the queen should defend her crown and religion against the 'pretended Prince of Wales'), and the threat of the 'exorbitant power of France'.[36] During the contention over the trial of the 'high-church' cleric Dr Sacheverell in 1710, which broke along party lines, Dorchester's address followed the county's in taking a firm Tory stance. Attacking the 'daring insolence and base ingratitude of a sett of men' who propagated 'sedition and anti-monarchical notions' (an unambiguous reference to the Whigs), the address declared that the town's inhabitants would in future take care to be represented by men 'conspicuous for their zeal for our holy Church' (i.e., Tories).[37] Later Dorset addresses of the queen's reign demonstrated similar adherence to party-political positions.[38]

---

[33] Landau undertook a similar exercise using the Kent county poll books for 1713 and 1715, which identified the parish in which each voter held his qualifying freehold; using this information, she compared the behaviour of voters in parishes subject with different levels of government influence. Landau, 'Independence', 565–8.

[34] Halliday, *Body Politic*, 17–18.

[35] Rosebank, *Partisan Politics*, 164.

[36] *London Gazette*, 16 Apr. 1702. There remains the question of the extent to which addresses can be seen as a true reflection of local feeling, as opposed to having been orchestrated centrally. However, Edward Vallance (among others) has concluded that they represented an important opportunity for those subscribing to them to participate in political discourse: Edward Vallance, *Loyalty, Memory and Public Opinion in England, 1658–1727* (Manchester, 2019), 93–119.

[37] John Oldmixon, *The History of Addresses. With Remarks Serious and Comical. In which a Particular Regard is had to All Such as Have Been Presented since the Impeachment of Dr. Sacheverell. Part II* (1711), 227–8: Dorchester's address of 1 Aug. 1710.

[38] *London Gazette*, 26 Aug. 1712: Dorset's address; *London Gazette*, 23 Sept. 1712: Shaftesbury's address.

Pamphlets targeted at Dorset or West Country voters, albeit also from the later years of the queen's reign, are similarly suggestive. The *Letter to the Gentlemen and Freeholders of the County of Dorset*, which was published in advance of the 1713 election, advocated the Hanoverian succession and toleration of Protestant dissent, and encouraged voters to return 'lovers of our constitution'. It expressly used the terms 'Whigs' (in support of whom it was written) and 'Tories'.[39] In the same year, the *Letter to a West-Country Clothier* (many of whom would have been Dorset men) contained both a list of local MPs voting for and against the French commerce treaty which the Tory ministry had negotiated alongside the treaty of Utrecht, and a narrative making the case against it. Directed at a local audience, its purpose was clear: to denigrate the county's Tory MPs, and generate support for Whig opposition to the treaty.[40]

If the printed sources allow some inferences to be drawn about the political terms in which Dorset's electors were thinking, or were perceived to be thinking, the motivation of some of those seeking their votes is easier to determine. The earl of Shaftesbury, a principled Whig who played a leading role in Dorset politics in Anne's reign, clearly conceived his electoral activities in terms of party and policy advantage. From as early as 1700, he worried that a Tory-dominated Commons would jeopardise the succession, 'and bring us back to where we were before the revolution'.[41] The Whig Awnsham Churchill struck the right note when writing to Shaftesbury in 1705 seeking his support in the forthcoming Dorchester election: 'I cannot but tremble at the prospect of a Tory house'.[42] Five years later, the election to be held in the aftermath of the Sacheverell affair threatened a Tory-dominated house of commons which would support the new Tory ministry in seeking peace with France; Shaftesbury told General Erle (Whig MP for Wareham) that he hoped that success in that election would prevent a 'perfidious and corrupt party at home' (evidently the Tories) making an ignoble peace.[43]

More intriguing is the evidence of a canvass return for an election in the Dorset borough of Shaftesbury, probably 1701. The canvasser marked a list of the town's worthies with the annotations 'WW', 'TT' and 'TW', presumably to indicate their voting intentions: both votes for the Whig candidates, both for the Tories, or a split of one vote for each. Confident of his persuasive powers, he noted that one voter 'seem'd to come off from Toryism and assented heartily to my discourse'.[44] Wareham and Dorchester's electorates can therefore be inferred to have possessed a degree of political sophistication; but was this manifested in their voting behaviour, or did it reflect the electoral interests to which they were subject, and the influence of the urban elites which governed their towns?

[39] *Letter to the Gentlemen and Freeholders of the County of Dorset* (1713).

[40] *Letter to a West-country Clothier* (1713).

[41] *Original Letters of John Locke, Algernon Sidney and Lord Shaftesbury: With an Analytical Sketch of the Writings and Opinions of Locke and other Metaphysicians*, ed. Thomas Forster (1847), 76.

[42] TNA, PRO 30/24/20/214: Churchill to Shaftesbury, 1 Feb. 1705.

[43] Churchill College, Cambridge, Churchill Archives Centre (hereafter CAC), GBR/0014/3/16: Shaftesbury to Erle, undated.

[44] TNA, PRO 30/24/21/335 and 337: Shaftesbury canvass returns.

Wareham 1702

Lying upriver from Poole harbour, Wareham comprised just two streets and some 200 houses at the beginning of the 18th century; contemporary commentators gave the impression of a town that had seen better days.[45] Its government was closely controlled by the principal townsmen, although before the queen granted the town a charter in 1703, its administration seems to have been a matter of custom and practice.[46] In petitioning for the charter, the mayor and townsmen referred to the problems of governance that they were facing, due not least to there being no justices of the peace to keep order, and the charter itself recited the desire for 'one certain and undoubted modus in the said town, for the preservation of the peace, and for [its] good rule and governance'.[47] The resulting charter is the best indication available of how the town was governed in the preceding years. It provided for a corporation of seven burgesses and 12 assistants, each appointed for life; together they comprised the common council, which each year appointed one of the burgesses to act as mayor. The mayor, the recorder (also a life appointment) and the immediately past mayor were to act as justices. On the death of a burgess, a replacement was to be elected from among the assistants; new assistants were to be elected from among the town's freemen.[48] These elections were in the hands of the corporation's existing members, who could therefore influence its political complexion for a significant period into the future: the corporation was, in Rosemary Sweet's terms, a self-selecting oligarchy.[49]

The official candidates at Wareham's 1702 election were the Whig General Erle, an associate of Marlborough's, and the Tory George Pitt, both of whom had been returned in the two elections of 1701, together with Denis Bond, a second Whig. How the candidates came to be selected is frustratingly unclear, as Bond's candidacy was probably unwelcome to both of the other candidates and to the corporation; moreover, a number of electors took the unusual step of voting for individuals not formally on the ballot.[50]

Erle's electoral interest seems to have derived from a combination of the influence arising from ownership of his estate at nearby Charborough Park, and his charitable support: in the 1690s, he had donated the local manor to the corporation, providing a valuable source of rental income to be applied in securing apprenticeships for poor children of the town.[51] He was also in a position to procure offices and employment: in 1698, for instance, he had given a reference for Thomas Shittler, a carpenter in Portsmouth's naval dockyard.[52] Although, if

---

[45] Browne Willis, *Notitia Parliamentaria: Or, an History of the Counties, Cities, and Boroughs in England and Wales. Shewing what Boroughs were Anciently Parliamentary, but now Disus'd* (2 vols, 1715–16), ii, 485; Daniel Defoe, *A Tour Through the Whole Island of Great Britain* (3 vols, 1724), i, letter iii, 61. While the *Tour* was published in 1724, it has been suggested that much of the material was gathered during Defoe's electoral perambulations in the early 1700s.

[46] Willis, *Notitia Parliamentaria*, ii, 488.

[47] John Hutchins, *History and Antiquities of the County of Dorset* (2 vols, 1861–74; repr. 1973), i, 127; TNA, SP 44/239, f. 113.

[48] Hutchins, *History*, i, 127–34.

[49] Sweet, *English Town*, 36. Although Rosebank cautioned against thinking of urban governance in terms of oligarchy, stressing instead the degree of interdependence between those at the top of local government structures and the wider population of the town: Rosebank, *Partisan Politics*, 15, 123.

[50] On the opacity of candidate selection, see Kishlansky, *Parliamentary Selection*, 183.

[51] Willis, *Notitia Parliamentaria*, ii, 488.

[52] CAC, GBR/0014/3/24: certificate, 19 Aug. 1698.

this was the same Thomas Shittler who voted in Wareham in 1702, Erle's patronage was wasted: Shittler did not vote for him. In 1705, Wareham's burgesses themselves sought Erle's patronage, asking him to obtain a customs office for a local resident.[53]

The sources of Pitt's electoral interest were various. As well as owning the priory in the heart of the town, he seems to have held the freehold of a significant number of tenanted houses.[54] By 1702, he was patron of two of Wareham's three parishes and presumably therefore had the benefices within his gift.[55] Pitt's family had also made significant charitable gifts to the town: in his will, his father had left the revenues of two churches, together with liberty to cut peat on a nearby common, to fund the salary of a schoolmaster.[56] Where Pitt stood politically within the Tory party is unclear. While he was subsequently alleged to have had Jacobite sympathies, an analysis of MPs printed after the 1705 election identified him (alongside Erle) as 'low-church', and it seems that he did not support the 'tack'.[57]

It is clear that Erle and Pitt had an electoral pact to split the representation of the borough between them; in advance of the 1708 election, Pitt would assure Erle, who was absent on campaign, that he would look after Erle's interests, the town being 'much troubled to be deprived of the pleasure of seeing you here'.[58] The arrangement seems to have reflected their balanced electoral interests: in advance of the 1705 poll, Pitt informed Erle of his intention to visit Wareham, 'where your interest Sir is undoubted, but were it not should be considered equally with mine own'.[59] That the members of the corporation were supportive of the arrangement is clear from a letter to Erle, again sent shortly before the 1705 poll. Signed by all but one of the burgesses, it assured him that they were very sensible of his and Pitt's repeated good services to the town, and would seek to ensure that no other candidate would stand.[60]

But three years earlier, in 1702, that is exactly what had happened: Denis Bond had attempted to break into the arrangement for Wareham's representation. Bond would become an accomplished political operator, later sitting as a Whig MP for Dorchester, Corfe Castle and Poole. The source of any electoral interest he had in Wareham is uncertain; it may have arisen from his father's ownership of Creech Grange, an estate five miles from the town. What is clear is that his candidacy in 1702 was unwelcome, at least to Pitt. Erle's son-in-law, Edward Ernle, warned Erle before the poll that Pitt was highly dissatisfied; if Erle did not immediately write to the corporation to confirm that he would be standing alongside Pitt,

[53] CAC, GBR/0014/2/36: Kaines and others to Erle, 28 Apr. 1705. See also CAC, GBR/0014/2/36: Kaines to Erle, 2 May 1705.

[54] Unfortunately, while there is an extant list of the town's freeholders and tenants, it probably dates from the early 1690s, and so cannot reliably be used to assess Pitt's ability to influence his tenants' votes a decade later: DHC, D/BOH X2.

[55] Hutchins, *History*, i, 102–3.

[56] TNA, PROB 11/422/161: will of George Pitt.

[57] W.D. Montagu, 7th duke of Manchester, *Court and Society from Elizabeth to Anne* (2 vols, 1864), ii, 116–19; *A Numerical Calculation of the Honourable Mem—rs as Were Elected for the Ensuing Parl—nt* (1705); Stephen Whatley, *A Collection of White and Black Lists; Or, A View of those Gentlemen who Have Given their votes in Parliament for and against the Protestant Religion* (3rd edn, 1715), 37.

[58] CAC, GBR/0014/3/14: Pitt to Erle, 9 May 1708.

[59] CAC, GBR/0014/3/14: Pitt to Erle, 27 Feb. 1705.

[60] CAC, GBR/0014/2/36: Kaines and others to Erle, 28 Apr. 1705.

Table 1: *Wareham – analysis of voting combinations.*

Candidates ('W' indicates Whig; 'T' indicates Tory)	Number of voters	Percentage of voters
Erle (W) and Pitt (T)	54	38.6
Erle (W) and Bond (W)	52	37.1
Bond (W) and Pitt (T)	14	10.0
Bond (W) only	16	11.4
Pitt (T) only	4	2.9
Erle (W) only	Nil	Nil

Note: this table takes no account of votes cast for those not formally standing as candidates.

and no one else, Pitt was threatening to 'bring down a merchant that will spend £1,000 [to] turn you out'.[61]

If these were the dynamics of electoral interest in Wareham, how did they play out in the polling? Votes were cast by 140 electors in 1702. Erle led with 106 votes, Bond polled 82 and Pitt 72. In addition, 17 voters cast one of their two votes for individuals not formally standing as candidates, including the mayor and two other townsmen.[62] Despite Bond receiving ten more votes than Pitt, the mayor returned Pitt alongside Erle. The election was not disputed, and the reasons are unknown; however, one plausible explanation is that the mayor was using his position to ensure that the corporation's preferred candidates were returned.

More instructive than these bare numbers are the combinations in which electors voted: (Table 1).

The correspondence previously referred to suggests that the cross-party combination of Erle and Pitt might be considered the 'establishment ticket', favoured by the borough corporation, and that can first be tested by considering how the corporation members voted. There is no extant list of the corporation's membership for 1702, but it is reasonable to assume that its composition was close to that provided for in the 1703 charter.[63] Of the seven 1703 burgesses (the senior members), all voted for Erle and Pitt; of the ten assistants who voted, eight voted for Erle and Pitt, and two for other combinations of candidates. Thus over 88 per cent voted for the Erle/Pitt combination.

Although Rosemary Sweet stressed the importance of looking beyond the corporation when seeking sources of authority in an English town, in Wareham this is problematic: it seems from the petition for the 1703 charter that in 1702 the town had no justices in office and, while that charter refers to freemen of the town, no records survive of who they were (beyond the members of the corporation themselves). Parishes also played a significant role in town governance, and surviving records for one of Wareham's three parishes reveal some of those who acted as churchwardens or attended vestry meetings in the years either side of the Wareham poll; however, the voting pattern of those individuals is much closer to

---

[61] CAC, GBR/0014/2/20: Ernle to Erle, 1 June 1702.

[62] These votes were recorded in the margins of the poll book. The entry opposite the name of the first voter who attempted to cast a vote in this way included an additional note to the effect that the mayor did not allow the vote: DHC, D/BOH X3.

[63] Hutchins, *History*, i, 127–34.

that of the voters as a whole than it is to that of the corporation members.[64] The impression of an establishment ticket is nevertheless reinforced by the voting of those who might be regarded as active members of the political class: those who themselves had been, or who would in due course become, members of parliament. Of the five who voted in Wareham in 1702, three voted for Erle and Pitt, with another, the county MP and 'high-church' Tory Colonel Strangways, voting for Pitt alone. Strangways' father had fought in the West Country on the royalist side during the Civil Wars, and he presumably could not bring himself to vote for Erle, whose grandfather had led the opposing parliamentary forces there.[65]

Across the entirety of the poll, the vote for the corporation's favoured ticket of Erle and Pitt is substantial, but hardly overwhelming: 54 voters selected this combination, amounting to just under 39 per cent of the total. Indeed, the straight 'Whig vote', for Erle and Bond, is only slightly less, and on the face of the poll book it appears that these two candidates won the poll. These 52 solidly Whig votes can be contrasted with a purely Tory vote of only four (those voters plumping for Pitt alone). Given the Tories' strong national performance in 1702, this suggests a town with significant Whig sympathies, the most likely explanation for which lies in the fact that during Anne's reign most of the inhabitants of the town were dissenters.[66] They are not, however, easy to find among the voters: only seven can be identified with confidence, but all of them voted for the Erle and Bond combination; this is as one would expect, given Whig toleration of religious non-conformism.[67] By contrast, the local clergy would have been expected to be Tory sympathisers.[68] Here, the Wareham sample is even smaller: only one of the local Anglican ministers, Edward Sutton of St Peter's, participated in the election, voting for Erle and Pitt, which is hardly surprising given that George Pitt held the patronage of his parish.[69]

The actions of those who voted for a combination of Pitt and Bond (one Tory, the other Whig) appear eccentric: if a voter wished to split his vote between parties, then the establishment ticket of Erle and Pitt seems a natural choice. However, there are several possible explanations for the polling of the 14 voters who did so, aside from a simple reluctance to waste their second vote having cast the first in line with interest or principle.[70] First, they could have been responding to Bond's electoral interest, casting their second vote for Pitt either because of his own interest or to reflect their Tory principles. Alternatively, Whig sympathisers subject to Pitt's influence as to one of their votes may have been voting tactically with the second: if Erle was clearly going to have the greatest number of votes, casting

[64]DHC, PE-WA/CW/1/1: Wareham, Holy Trinity, churchwardens' accounts; Rosebank, *Partisan Politics*, 11. However, Sweet suggested that vestry influence was greater in the unincorporated towns: Sweet, *English Town*, 32.

[65]ODNB, www.oxforddnb.com (accessed 13 Mar. 2023), s.v. 'Sir Walter Earle', Giles Strangways.

[66]William Densham and Joseph Ogle, *The Story of the Congregational Churches of Dorset, from their Foundation to the Present Time* (Bournemouth, 1899), 340.

[67]Wareham's and Dorchester's dissenters have been identified from several sources, including the Dorset county quaker minute book (DHC, NQ-1/A/1) and Densham and Ogle, *Congregational Churches of Dorset*.

[68]Speck and Gray, 'Interim Report', 110, 112; Speck, Gray and Hopkinson, 'Further Report', 68–9.

[69]Hutchins, *History*, i, 102–3.

[70]Citing the Rutland poll of 1713 as an example, Speck, Gray and Hopkinson concluded that in circumstances where there were only three candidates, some voters might be motivated by a desire not to 'waste' their second vote. They went on to note, however, that such contests could sharpen party conflict by encouraging 'plumping': casting one vote only, for the candidate standing alone on his party ticket. Speck, Gray and Hopkinson, 'Further Report', 84–7. See also James Harris, 'Partisanship and Popular Politics in a Cornish "Pocket" Borough, 1660–1714', *Parliamentary History*, xxxvii (2018), 367.

the second vote for Bond rather than Erle could lead to a double Whig victory (the actual result on the face of the poll book). But the first explanation is more likely: most of these Pitt/Bond voters voted early – before the scale of Erle's victory had become clear – and although Bond gained votes faster than Pitt in the second half of the poll, this was mainly due to 'Whig' voters – those voting for both Erle and Bond. In any event, such tactical voting would hardly have been welcomed by Pitt himself.

Finally, there are the 16 voters who cast one vote for Bond, and voted for neither of the other official candidates; 15 of these voters cast their second vote for an 'unofficial' candidate. It is hard to see this as anything other than a protest vote against the establishment ticket. If a voter voted for Bond due to electoral interest, he could, had he wished, have deployed his second vote in accordance with his principles: voting for Erle if he favoured the Whigs or for Pitt if he favoured the Tories. And if he voted for Bond to reflect his Whig principles, then a second vote for Erle seems a natural option. Yet over 10 per cent of those polling chose not to cast their second votes for either Erle or Pitt. Taken with the fact that fewer than 40 per cent of voters supported the corporation's favoured Erle/Pitt combination, this protest vote for Bond strongly suggests that a significant element of the electorate was unwilling to be led.

Dorchester 1705

Daniel Defoe was in two minds about Dorchester, writing in 1705 that it was a 'good for nothing town', while in his *Tour*, published two decades later, he described it as a 'pleasant agreeable place to live'.[71] He was consistent, however, in ascribing moderation to its townspeople: while differing as to religion and politics, they did not 'separate into parties and factions' as happened elsewhere.[72] The Anglican clergy and dissenting ministers drank tea together, 'conversing with civility and good neighbourhood'.[73]

Dorchester's 1629 charter provided for 15 capital burgesses, comprising the mayor (appointed annually), six further aldermen, six burgesses and two bailiffs. The capital burgesses and the recorder held office for life, and appointed their own successors; as in Wareham, the corporation was in the hands of a tight and self-perpetuating group. The charter also provided for a common council of 24 freemen, led by a governor. Only those admitted as freemen by the common council could trade in the town.[74]

Three candidates stood in 1705: Captain Nathaniel Napier, an army officer; Awnsham Churchill, a London bookseller; and Sir John Darnell, a prominent lawyer. Defoe ascribed the election of Captain Napier, a Tory, to the interest of Colonel Strangways, but the Napiers, another landed Dorset family, had cultivated their own interest.[75] The family had founded almshouses in the town and the captain's father (another alleged Jacobite) had promoted the rebuilding of the local grammar school and donated a further £20 annually for

[71] Defoe, *Tour*, i, letter iii, 63–4; *The Letters of Daniel Defoe*, ed. G.H. Healey (Oxford, 1955), 108–13.
[72] Defoe, *Tour*, i, letter iii, 63–4.
[73] Defoe, *Tour*, i, letter iii, 63–4.
[74] C.H. Mayo, *Municipal Records of Dorchester* (Exeter, 1908), 56–9; Willis, *Notitia Parliamentaria*, ii, 414.
[75] *Letters of Daniel Defoe*, ed. Healey, 108–13; HPC, *1690–1715*, s.v. Dorchester.

its funding.[76] In April 1702, Captain Napier, already an MP, had sponsored legislation to construct the workhouse for which the borough had petitioned parliament and, following the 1702 election, he and his father held the town's two seats for the Tories.[77] Captain Napier's position on the 'tack', a significant political issue at the 1705 election, is unclear: while he did not vote in favour, there is disagreement as to whether he was among the 'sneakers', those who sneaked out of the Commons' chamber in order to avoid voting on the issue at all.[78]

Churchill, a Whig, seems to have relied on the electoral interest of two Whig aristocrats: the earl of Shaftesbury and the duke of Newcastle, who was Dorchester's high steward and owned significant property there.[79] Newcastle financed almshouses in the town and gave a total of £53 between 1702 and 1704 to support the poor, generosity which the corporation acknowledged in a fulsome letter of thanks.[80] He had been appointed to the cabinet as lord keeper of the seal two months before the 1705 election, with a view to his exercising his electoral interest across the country in support of the Godolphin ministry and its desire for a balanced outcome to that election.[81] The corporation marked the appointment with a public celebration where large crowds were entertained with church bells, music and fireworks, an event which can only have enhanced Newcastle's standing in the town.[82]

Churchill appears to have had little interest of his own; although born in the town, there is no evidence that he owned property there, and the Dorset manor he bought in 1704 lay some 20 miles away. One modest attempt to construct an interest may lie in the subscription of ten guineas he paid on election as a freeman just a week before the 1705 poll; the usual sum was between one and ten shillings. By contrast, Napier's father had paid £5 in 1700, while Darnell is not recorded as paying anything at all.[83]

There is also no evidence of Darnell's electoral interest in the town. His appointment as the town's recorder in 1701 indicates political ambition, but he was never elected as an MP in Dorchester or elsewhere. Discerning Darnell's political affiliation is difficult, and the evidence that can be gleaned from the legal cases he took on is ambiguous. An inclination to toryism is suggested by the fact that in 1704 he was engaged for the ministry in prosecuting the author of the whiggish *Observator* for seditious libel.[84] Yet five years earlier

---

[76] *Notes and Queries for Somerset and Dorset*, v (1897), 172, and xxvii (1961), 51–2; Montagu, *Court and Society*, ii, 116–19.

[77] *HPC, 1690–1715*, s.v. Dorchester; *CJ*, 8 Apr. 1702.

[78] Napier is described as having been identified as a 'sneaker' in his biography in *HPC, 1690–1715*. This description probably refers to *A Numerical Calculation of the Honourable Mem—rs*, which includes Napier as a 'sneaker'. However, a list republished in 1715 includes him as one of those 'not number'd among the tackers nor sneakers': Whatley, *A Collection of White and Black Lists*, 35.

[79] *HPC, 1690–1715*, s.v. Dorchester; TNA, PRO 30/24/20/214: Churchill to Shaftesbury, 1 Feb. 1705.

[80] BL, Add. MS 70504, unfoliated: note to William Damer at Dorchester; DHC, DO[HT]/CW/1/1 and /2: Trinity, Dorchester, churchwardens' accounts; Mayo, *Municipal Records*, 443; Inspire Nottinghamshire Archives, DD/P/6/1/24/9: Dorchester corporation to duke of Newcastle, 8 Nov. 1703.

[81] HMC, *The Manuscripts of His Grace the Duke of Portland, preserved at Welbeck Abbey* (11 vols, 1892–1931), ii, 186; Speck, *Tory and Whig*, 84. Holmes, *British Politics*, 225n. identifies ten MPs in the 1705–8 parliament (including Awnsham Churchill) who owed their election wholly or mainly to Newcastle's influence.

[82] *Post Man*, 5 Apr. 1705.

[83] Mayo, *Municipal Records*, 428–9.

[84] *Dictionary of National Biography*, https://en.wikisource.org/wiki/Dictionary_of_National_Biography,_1885-1900/Darnall,_John_(1672-1735) (accessed 13 Mar. 2023).

Table 2: *Dorchester – analysis of voting combinations.*

Candidates	Number of voters	Percentage of voters
Churchill (W) and Napier (T)	159	65.2
Churchill (W) and Darnell	54	22.1
Napier (T) and Darnell	29	11.9
Napier (T) only	1	0.4
Darnell only	1	0.4
Churchill (W) only	Nil	Nil

he had represented a dissenting schoolmaster who was defending his licence to run his school against a clergyman seeking to revoke it because of his religious non-conformity.[85] Looking beyond his legal career, Whig sympathies might be inferred from the fact that in 1694 Darnell petitioned Baron Somers (a member of the junto of leading Whigs) for his appointment as king's serjeant, a position to which he was appointed in 1698 after Somers had become lord chancellor.[86] This impression is reinforced by the fact that Newcastle had approved, perhaps actively promoted, Darnell's appointment to the politically influential position of recorder.[87]

In Dorchester's 1705 poll, 244 voters cast a total of 486 votes. Churchill led with 213 votes, followed by Napier (also elected) on 189, with Darnell on 84. The electors cast their votes in the combinations represented above in Table 2.

In contrast to Wareham, no correspondence survives which gives any indication of the role of the corporation in the elections of Anne's reign, although it is possible to draw inferences from the voting behaviour of its 1705 members, 14 of whom can be identified.[88] Three of those 14 abstained (including the mayor). Of the 11 who voted, eight opted for the Churchill/Napier combination (73 per cent, slightly ahead of the percentage of all voters who did so). The town's government structures were not, however, limited to the corporation and its members.[89] While all the justices of the peace at the time of the election, except Darnell, were aldermen or burgesses, the company of freemen was more broadly constituted.[90] Of the governor, wardens and common councilmen 16 voted, with 11 (69 per cent) choosing the Churchill/Napier combination, marginally higher than the proportion of voters as a whole. That Whig/Tory ticket therefore had the substantial backing of both the corporation and the council of freemen. The votes of Richard Hutchins, vicar of All Saints, for Churchill and Napier provide modest corroboration for the idea of that being the establishment ticket; his living was under the patronage of the mayor and corporation. Not

[85] *Flying Post*, 23 Nov. 1699.

[86] Surrey History Centre, 371/14/L/1: Darnall [sic] to Somers, 26 Feb. 1694.

[87] Inspire Nottinghamshire Archives, DD/P/6/1/24/9: Dorchester corporation to duke of Newcastle, 8 Nov. 1703.

[88] DHC, DC-DOB/16/6: Dorchester corporation minute book, minutes for 2 Oct. 1704 and 1 Oct. 1705.

[89] Sweet, *English Town*, 27, 124–5.

[90] DHC, DC-DOB/1/1: Dorchester quarter sessions minute book, minutes for Sept. 1704; DHC, DC-DOB/13/2: Dorchester company of freemen minute book, minutes for 27 Sept. 1705.

so the voting of those who acted as churchwardens or overseers of the poor, or attended vestry meetings, for those of Dorchester's parishes for which records survive: just 58 per cent voted for Churchill and Napier (with 32 per cent opting for Churchill and Darnell and 10 per cent for Napier and Darnell).[91]

It follows that the idea of an establishment ticket is less compelling here than in the case of Wareham, but the Churchill/Napier combination comes close, and across the whole poll the strength of the vote for this pairing is an impressive 65 per cent (compared to 39 per cent for Erle and Pitt in Wareham in 1702). This could suggest an electorate more willing to follow their corporation's lead, but equally it could reflect balanced electoral interests, with the Whig influence of Newcastle and Shaftesbury offsetting the Tory interest of the Napiers and Colonel Strangways. And that balance of interests also points to the possibility of an electoral pact. While (unlike in the case of Wareham) no contemporary correspondence provides evidence of such an arrangement, the behaviour of those voters who might be described as politicians (those who were, or would become, MPs) is suggestive: the Tory Colonel Strangways and two Whigs (including Shaftesbury's brother Maurice) all supported the cross-party Churchill/Napier combination. These were sophisticated voters; they would not have cast a second vote for a candidate of the opposing party simply in order not to waste it.

If the evidence concerning the motivation for those voting for the Churchill/Napier combination is ambiguous, what of those voting for the other combinations, particularly for Churchill and Darnell? Uncertainty regarding Darnell's political affiliation makes drawing conclusions difficult, but some insight can be gained by considering the voters who were religious dissenters. While, by the reign of Anne, Dorchester was no longer the centre of religious dissent described in David Underdown's account of the town in the 17th century, it maintained a strong non-conformist presence.[92] As in Wareham, the sample size is small: it has been possible to identify with confidence only five dissenters among the voters. Four of these voted for Churchill and Darnell, rejecting Napier as a candidate in the 'high-church' Tory mould and (perhaps) as a man who reputedly could not be relied upon to vote against the 'tack'. If this pattern was repeated among the remainder of the town's dissenting voters, it would explain the significant Churchill/Darnell vote (at 22.1 per cent) and reinforce the impression that Darnell was, more likely than not, a Whig. Even were that not the case, it seems that those voters were rejecting Captain Napier as a matter of principle.

Among those voting for Churchill and Darnell were Robert Weare, a corporation member and former justice who had managed Newcastle's local affairs in 1703 and 1704, and the Anglican minister Samuel Conant, whose living of St Peter's was under the duke's patronage.[93] These votes imply that Newcastle preferred Darnell to Napier, a preference which would again be consistent with Darnell sharing Newcastle's whiggism. Whatever Darnell's politics, for Newcastle to have favoured him over Napier implies a rift between the duke and the greater part of the town's corporation. The presentation under which Conant's appointment was confirmed shortly before the poll provides further evidence of this, and of differences of opinion within the corporation itself. Four corporation members

[91] DHC, DO[AS]/CW/1/1: Trinity, Dorchester, churchwardens' accounts; DHC, PE-DO[AS]/OV/1/3: All Saints, Dorchester, churchwardens' and overseers' accounts.

[92] David Underdown, *Fire from Heaven: The Life of an English Town in the Seventeenth Century* (1992), 262.

[93] Inspire Nottinghamshire Archives, DD/4P/54/111-125: estate accounts 1703-4.

(presumably all members of the vestry) joined the duke in signing the document, but another four failed to do so. Three of those who refused voted, and all did so for Churchill and Napier (the combination favoured by a substantial majority of the corporation). Those who signed voted for various combinations, but three out of the four cast one vote for Darnell (compared with only one-third of all voters who did so).[94]

Of those four corporation members who joined the duke in signing Conant's presentation, two voted for a combination of Napier and Darnell. Unfortunately, however, there appear to be no other common factors between them and the remaining 27 voters who selected that combination; discerning their motivation is impossible. If Darnell was standing as a Tory, or independently, then a vote for the Napier/Darnell combination would make sense as a safe haven for those who inclined to the Tories and wanted neither to cast their second vote for the Whig Churchill, nor to waste it. But this tends to contradict the inferences as to Darnell's whiggism drawn from the votes of the dissenters and other evidence.

The picture in Dorchester is therefore mixed: at first glance, a balance of electoral interests, perhaps leading to an agreement to promote Churchill and Napier that was supported by a substantial majority of the corporation, appears to have driven the result. But issues of principle also played a part, with the result reflecting the nationwide trend towards the Whigs in 1705. The borough had been held unopposed by the Napiers for the Tories in 1702, following split Whig/Tory representation in both 1701 elections, suggesting that interest alone was not sufficient to secure victory, and that issues mattered. This conclusion is consistent with the fact that over 87 per cent of electors voted for Churchill, with the votes of the dissenters, and with the 1705 result nationwide.[95]

Conclusion

John Miller has suggested that corporations' electoral influence and the opportunities for voters to act independently varied greatly; the experience of Wareham and Dorchester bears this out. In Wareham in 1702 what might be called the borough establishment swung strongly behind the cross-party Erle/Pitt combination. Yet despite the relatively modest size of the electorate, voters were reluctant to follow their lead; indeed, there was a substantial protest vote by those who voted for Bond, and for neither of the other official candidates. In Dorchester the establishment showed somewhat less commitment to the Churchill/Napier ticket, yet that combination secured significantly more support than had Erle and Pitt in Wareham three years earlier.

These corporations were not operating in a vacuum; they were acutely conscious of the competing electoral interests in their towns, and indeed acted as intermediaries between them. In Wareham, the corporation members were party to a pact between Erle and Pitt that reflected the balance of their interests, and the behaviour of some of Dorchester's voters in 1705 implies a similar arrangement. If Speck was correct that such pacts were rare in borough elections, then Dorset may have been an exception.[96]

---

[94] Mayo, *Municipal Records*, 610.

[95] See Speck's analysis of the 1705 election: Speck, *Tory and Whig*, 98–109.

[96] Speck, *Tory and Whig*, 36, 57.

There remains, however, the question of the extent to which voters were acting on principle. These two poll books hardly seem a promising starting point, but conclusions can be drawn. In Wareham, the strength of the Whig vote for Erle and Bond in the face of both establishment pressure to split the borough's representation and a strong national result for the Tories in 1702, is highly suggestive. In Dorchester's case, the strength of the vote for Churchill, and the inferences which can be drawn as to the voting of the town's religious non-conformists, also suggests that many voters were motivated by the issues. And the fact that in this volatile constituency the two parties may have agreed to exercise their influence to split the representation in 1705 implies that electoral interest bowed to principle, the Tories recognising that in the climate of the time they could not expect to retain both seats.

Parliamentary History, Vol. 43, pt. 1 (2024), pp. 53–71

Controverted Elections, Electoral Controversy and the Scottish Privy Council, 1689–1708★

ROBERT D. TREE

Both the privy council and elections in early modern Scotland are understudied. The council itself has largely been described as a tool for crown management of elections. But it was fundamentally a court and standing committee charged with government administration, which was often supplicated to deal with cases of electoral impropriety and controversy. As elections became increasingly contested throughout the later 17th century, so the council's role developed into a form of elections committee which adjudicated over controverted elections. This, in some ways, reflected the business conducted by parliament's own elections committee, although the council was largely concerned with elections in the royal burghs while it also dealt with other electoral issues. This article explores the privy council's engagement in a complex range of electoral business between the Revolution of 1689 and its abolition in 1708.

Keywords: privy council; elections; burghs; parliament; committees; government administration; procedure

The Scottish privy council was an omnicompetent institution of the law and government that emerged in the 16th century and which after 1689 was made up of officers of state, noblemen, parliamentarians, lawyers, civic officials and military officers. The council's remit was that of an executive, which supposedly 'inferior' institutions such as burghs looked to for advice and authority, and utilised its judicial functions as an appellate court. It acted as the chief organ of central government in Edinburgh and it was made up of individuals of different political and religious persuasions, appointed by the monarch, who dealt with what Laura Rayner calls 'everyday government' in the 1690s.[1] During and after the Williamite Revolution, the Scottish parliament and privy council were further empowered, and the Scottish electoral landscape was fundamentally altered.[2] In the decades following the Revolution, we see the emergence of distinct and well-organised opposition parties in Scotland, which would exert considerable political influence, especially the 'country party' after 1698 and the *squadrone volante* after 1703.[3] This development brought with it increased

★ I wish to express my gratitude to Dr Alastair Mann, Dr Laura Doak, and the editors of this special issue for comments on an earlier draft of this article.

[1]Laura Rayner, 'The Tribulations of Everyday Government in Williamite Scotland', in *Scotland in the Age of Two Revolutions*, ed. Sharon Adams and Julian Goodare (Woodbridge, 2014), 193–210.

[2]D.J. Patrick, 'People and Parliament in Scotland, 1689–1702', University of St Andrews PhD, 2002.

[3]J.R. Young, 'The Scottish Parliament and the Politics of Empire: Parliament and the Darien Project, 1695–1707', *Parliaments, Estates and Representation*, xxvii (2007), 175–190; Graham Townend, '"Rendering the Union

electoral competition and concomitant attempts at electoral manipulation, with which the privy council was often forced to deal.

There remains debate over whether there was a separate revolution in Scotland in 1689, but it is generally agreed now that the Scottish settlement was more radical than its English counterpart.[4] This largely rests on the constitutional settlement instituted by the convention of estates (a convention parliament without royal summons and with fewer powers than normal) in 1689, which produced the Claim of Right and declared that King James had 'forefaulted' the crown.[5] The religious dimension of the Revolution, which reintroduced a Presbyterian form of church government and overturned episcopacy in 1690, was also radical.[6] Despite its members largely supporting the Revolution, an empowered autonomous Scottish parliament after 1689 posed serious problems for crown management, one of which was an increasing trend towards electoral competition.

Although there were no general elections between 1689 and 1702, elections to burgh councils and of some parliamentary commissioners were still held throughout the 1690s.[7] The early modern Scottish parliament was often referred to as 'the estates', since it was unicameral but made up of three or four estates: the clergy and nobility, the burghs, and the shires, in addition to officers of state, who did not make up a separate estate. Officers of state and the nobility (and clergy, prior to their removal from parliament after the Revolution) sat in the estates because of their office or title. Therefore, it was only the burgh and shire commissioners (the label for elected members of the Scottish parliament) who were subject to election. Annual elections – usually around Michaelmas – to both were constitutionally established in acts of the 15th and 16th centuries. The 66 or 67 royal burghs – those with crown charters and special trading privileges – were represented in parliament, but also had their own similar body, the convention of royal burghs, which was less well attended than parliament in the 1690s. Lesser burghs, of regality and barony, were not represented in parliament. The burgh electorate was stipulated by an act of parliament in 1469.[8] Parliamentary elections in the burghs had previously included the entire burgess community but thereafter consisted of the elected burgh council and magistrates.[9] Elections for burgh councils generally included the old burgh council, but practices varied slightly, with some burghs involving deacon convenors (heads of trades) and larger numbers of burgesses, for example. Illustrative of the general process, though, was Peebles, where the town clerk recorded in 1682 that the old council chose the new one and then the newly elected council chose the magistrates (two bailies and a provost), with the burgh council itself always consisting of 17 members.[10] This burgh council and its magistrates then made up the electorate in the

---

more Complete": The *Squadrone Volante* and the Abolition of the Scottish Privy Council', *Parliamentary History*, xxviii (2009), 88–99.

[4] Tim Harris, *Revolution: The Great Crisis of the British Monarchy, 1685–1720* (2006), 395–403.

[5] 'The Records of the Parliaments of Scotland to 1707', ed. K.M. Brown (St Andrews, 2007–2023), https://www.rps.ac.uk/ (hereafter RPS), 1689/3/108. All RPS sources were accessed during June 2023.

[6] RPS, 1690/4/43.

[7] For burgh council elections during the Revolution, see: Alasdair Raffe, Scotland in Revolution, 1685–1690 (Edinburgh, 2018), chs 5–6.

[8] RPS, 1469/19.

[9] A.R. MacDonald, *The Burghs and Parliament in Scotland, c.1551–1651* (2007), ch. 2.

[10] National Records of Scotland (hereafter NRS), B58/19/6/27, memorials, minutes, tacks, petitions, writs and other papers of Peebles town council, 28 Feb. 1682.

polls for parliamentary commissioners representing the burgh. Hence the desire to control or influence burgh council elections in order to manage parliamentary elections in the burghs.

In shire elections, voting eligibility was based upon land-holding. The electorate, following changes to the property qualifications in 1661 and 1681 (which were retained until 1832), consisted of 40-shilling freeholders and those who held lands directly from the crown.[11] The size of the shire electorate is difficult to determine accurately as it varied heavily, with the entire Scottish parliamentary electorate probably numbering between 2,000 and 4,000.[12] There were 33 parliamentary shires and each shire was eligible to send two commissioners to parliament, who were elected each year at Michaelmas head courts. In 1690, the shires gained a further 26 representatives in parliament (with some larger burghs gaining more commissioners), which increased their voting strength as an estate to a maximum of 92.[13] Combined with the increasing involvement of the burghal estate from 1689, this stresses the augmented power of the 'commons' in the Scottish parliament in its final years.[14] This perhaps also hints at some nobles' concerns, which might explain anxious attempts to retain their privilege by managing elections via the privy council.

The 1689 electoral summons represented a clear innovation. The parliamentary elections in the burghs that year reverted to pre-1469 practice and engaged almost the entire burgess community. The Test – an assurance of loyalty imposed in 1681 – was removed as a qualification for electors in addition to a move to allow all Protestant burgesses a vote. Derek Patrick notes 'popular politics on a substantial scale' in these elections; for instance, at Selkirk on 27 February 1689, the electorate comprised 183 out of a possible 228 burgesses, meaning that there was a turnout of over 80 per cent.[15] At the Edinburgh election, also in February 1689, Sir John Hall of Dunglass was elected. In this hotly contested election, the results were as follows: 610 voted for Magnus Prince, 632 and 745 polled for John Baillie and George Stirling respectively, and an unassailable 789 voted for Hall.[16] Additionally, the record of the Perth election for its burgh commissioner to the convention in 1689 included the occupations of the voters in a contested election which included hundreds of burgesses. Here, the weavers, tailors, fleshers (butchers), bakers, shoemakers, and other craftsmen voted, and two candidates contested the election. The sitting (Jacobite) provost opposed a former bailie, and the election was decided in favour of the latter by parliament after the contest.[17]

---

[11]K.M. Brown and A.J. Mann, 'Introduction', in *The History of the Scottish Parliament, Volume II: Parliament and Politics in Scotland 1567–1707*, ed. K.M. Brown and A.J. Mann (Edinburgh, 2005), 49–50; A.R. MacDonald, 'Scottish Shire Elections: Preliminary Findings in Sheriff Court Books', *Parliamentary History*, xxxiv (2015), 284, 292.

[12]C.A. Whatley, *The Scots and the Union: Then and Now* (Edinburgh, 2014), 64–5.

[13]Brown and Mann, 'Introduction', 36–7.

[14]John Young has introduced the idea of the emergence of a Scottish 'commons' (of the burgh and shire estates) in the covenanter parliaments of the 1640s. But it should be noted that shire commissioners were largely lairds, from the minor nobility. J.R. Young, 'The Scottish Parliament and the Covenanting Revolution: The Emergence of a Scottish Commons', in *Celtic Dimensions of the British Civil Wars*, ed. J.R. Young (Edinburgh, 1997), 164–84.

[15]D.J. Patrick, 'Unconventional Procedure: Scottish Electoral Politics after the Revolution', in *History of the Scottish Parliament. Volume II*, ed. Brown and Mann, 214, 218.

[16]Patrick, 'Unconventional Procedure', 218.

[17]Perth and Kinross Council Archives, B59/34/7, Perth Burgh records, 28 Feb.–4 Mar. 1689; Patrick, 'Unconventional Procedure', 223.

© *2024 The Authors*. Parliamentary History *published by John Wiley & Sons Ltd on behalf of Parliamentary History Yearbook Trust*.

The electorate was reversed to the statutory *status quo ante* in all parliamentary elections thereafter, the 1689 electoral summons being a temporary fudge. For instance, the election for the burgh of Jedburgh's parliamentary commissioner in 1700 (which is discussed below) consisted of just 38 electors, though the town's records noted that the quorum for such an election was 21.[18] The electorate was therefore far smaller than it had been in 1689 and thus provided a more manageable number for manipulation, or so it might have first appeared. Complications to management nevertheless transpired throughout the decade as attempts at management caused backlashes from a highly politicised burgess community across Scotland and the council's hand was forced into concessions following, on some occasions, its own electoral duplicity.

This article begins by discussing the limited historiography of Scottish elections, before focusing in on the electoral context of the 1690s through an exploration of the parliamentary committee for controverted elections in that period. It will then move on to illustrate the privy council's role in three aspects of elections, between the Revolution of 1689 and the council's abolition in 1708. These were, firstly, the orchestration or organisation of elections and, secondly, the council's involvement within the electoral process, or electoral management. These two facets largely conform to current historiography that describes the council as a conduit for crown interference and control of elections, although existing histories downplay the council's influence in this respect.[19] However, the final aspect of the council's involvement was electoral adjudication, in which legal challenges to electoral controversy, corruption or illegality were brought before the board. Often, these were direct reactions to the privy council's earlier attempts at managing elections, particularly in cases where the executive was concerned with what we might call court-conciliar privilege. Therefore, the article aims to argue that the council's complex role in electoral politics has been undervalued in existing scholarship.

1690s Scottish elections in context

David Hayton lamented in 1996 the 'depressed area of historiography' that was 18th-century Scottish political history, within which the study of elections was the most striking 'black spot'.[20] Recent scholarship has gone some way into addressing Hayton's concerns, at least as far as 1707.[21] Historiographical orthodoxy also now challenges the dreariness with which the Scottish parliament was understood by some of its earliest historians, most notably expressed in Robert Rait's classic study, *The Parliaments of Scotland* (1924).[22] For instance, parliament's widespread taxation and judicial powers have been illustrated, along with its

---

[18] NRS, PC2/28, f. 14r, privy council register of decreta, 24 Oct. 1700.

[19] R.S. Rait, *The Parliaments of Scotland* (Glasgow, 1924), 302–4, 309–10; Whatley, *Scots and the Union*, 328.

[20] D.W. Hayton, 'Traces of Party Politics in Early Eighteenth-Century Scottish Elections', *Parliamentary History*, xv (1996), 74.

[21] See, for example, *History of the Scottish Parliament. Volume II*, ed. Brown and Mann; *The History of the Scottish Parliament. Volume III: Parliament in Context*, ed. K.M. Brown and A.R. MacDonald (Edinburgh, 2010); G.H. McIntosh, *The Scottish Parliament under Charles II, 1660–1685* (Edinburgh, 2007); MacDonald, *Burghs and Parliament*; Patrick, 'People and Parliament'.

[22] Rait, *Parliaments of Scotland*. Also relevant are two other early works: C.S. Terry, *The Scottish Parliament: Its Constitution and Procedure, 1603–1707* (Glasgow, 1905); E.E.R. Thomson, *The Parliament of Scotland, 1690–1702* (Oxford, 1929).

concern with social issues, with the estates' extensive role reaching far beyond legislation.[23] Elections, though, remain an understudied grey spot, while the Revolution and Union are bookends within which the 1690s and early 1700s often escape close analysis. Indeed, in terms of politics and government, post-Revolution Scotland has suffered what has recently been described as a 'strange neglect', tending to be scrutinised by historians to explain, often teleologically, the 1707 Anglo–Scottish parliamentary union.[24] Hence, the Revolution of 1689 until the Scottish privy council's abolition in 1708 provide the chronological basis for this article.

Notwithstanding the above, the landmark Scottish Parliament Project's published research consists of two compelling accounts of elections in the post-Revolution period. These demonstrate, first, thanks to Derek Patrick, the concerted electioneering campaign pursued by the nascent Williamite regime in 1689, which managed to secure many pro-Revolution (burgh) seats in the convention of estates.[25] The backbone of these efforts was the unprecedented expansion of the burgh electorate in the electoral summons, which stands as one of the few examples in Scotland, after 1469 of popular electoral activity. The convention became a full parliament on 5 June 1689 and thereafter there were no general elections held until 1702. Secondly, Keith Brown's study of the 1702–3 general elections illustrates an overhaul in parliamentary representation. Advances were made by around 70 (mainly Jacobite or Episcopalian) cavaliers, some 60 'country party' members, and 25 from the new *squadrone volante*, all of whom challenged the dominant Court Party.[26] Additionally, Brown has elsewhere accounted for the vibrant electoral culture in early modern Scotland, which had widespread elections, including for church matters.[27] Here, Brown also illustrates that there was a plethora of means through which people could engage with and influence elections, from petitioning to office holding, for instance.

Elections became increasingly contested throughout the later 17th century and particularly in two key periods. The first was after the Restoration of 1660, as party increasingly informed electoral politics. Such was the concern for the Scottish government that in 1669 a parliamentary committee for controverted elections was established, although it did not meet regularly until 1678.[28] Again, during the Revolution of 1688–91, the committee was an important cog with which the government machine attempted to manage elections, among other business. Its workload greatly increased thereafter. Edith Thomson notes, for instance, that of the 60 to 70 controverted elections dealt with by the committee in its entire lifespan, most came from the period after 1689.[29] Also, after 1689, the committee was appointed along with two other standing committees at the start of each parliament.

---

[23] A.J. Mann, 'The Law of the Person: Parliament and Social Control', in *History of the Scottish Parliament. Volume III*, ed. Brown and MacDonald, 186–215; A.M. Godfrey, 'Parliament and the Law', in *History of the Scottish Parliament. Volume III*, ed. Brown and MacDonald, 157–186.

[24] Amy Blakeway and L.A.M. Stewart, 'Writing Scottish Parliamentary History, c.1500–1700', *Parliamentary History*, xl (2021), 110.

[25] Patrick, 'Unconventional Procedure', 240–1.

[26] K.M. Brown, 'Party Politics and Parliament: Scotland's Last Election and Its Aftermath, 1702–3', in *History of the Scottish Parliament. Volume II*, ed. Brown and Mann, 273.

[27] K.M. Brown, 'Towards Political Participation and Capacity: Elections, Voting, and Representation in Early Modern Scotland', *Journal of Modern History*, lxxxviii (2016), 1–33.

[28] RPS, 1669/10/7.

[29] Thomson, *Parliament of Scotland*, 62.

These committees were introduced to oversee much of the business that had hitherto been conducted by *ad hoc* committees and the lords of the articles – a parliamentary steering committee and symbol of crown management that was abolished in May 1690.[30] The elections committee was reconstituted nine times from March 1689 until June 1702, although in its 1693 incarnation the parliamentary register did not record the names of its members.[31] From the eight that were recorded, it can be determined that there were 120 appointments to the committee (with five from each estate) and that 80 individuals sat on it. Interestingly, of this number 25 (31 per cent) also served as privy councillors at some point from the Revolution until 1708. Therefore, although not a critical mass, councillors (particularly noblemen) made up a sizeable minority on this committee.

Parliament's committee for elections often dealt with matters outside of its nominal remit. For instance, in the late 1690s and early 1700s there were a series of protests concerning the export of wool. The privy council dealt with some of these, including the case of a 'rabble' (crowd disturbance) of women headed by one Sarah Grier near Edinburgh in 1699, which prevented a consignment of wool being exported.[32] In 1701, the investigations of complaints concerning the export of wool were remitted to the committee for controverted elections.[33] Furthermore, in 1696, the committee introduced an act 'ordering a constant habit of clothes for men, and … for women, read the first time and ordered to lie on the table'.[34] This method – of committing to the first reading before letting a bill be sidelined for a while to be deliberated before second reading and voting – was normalised after legislation from 1695 and 1696, and prevented rushed bills making it onto the statute books.[35]

The privy council at times continued the unfinished business of parliament's committee for elections. This was in line with the council's overarching role as a standing committee charged with government administration (alongside its legal jurisdiction and other wide-ranging powers), which sat throughout the year and outwith parliamentary sessions. In 1701, for example, the council heard the petition of William Patton of Panholls, a lawyer and landowner in Perthshire.[36] Patton had held the village of Blackford (Perthshire) for the government in defence of the Jacobite army at the orders of Lord Cardross – himself a privy councillor and military commander – in 1689. He had incurred severe losses in doing so and had been the victim of depredations at the hands of Jacobite forces.[37] Patton had gone directly to the king in 1695 to seek redress and compensation, with his petition being henceforth handed around the administrative web. First, William had recommended his petition to parliament, where it had been read in 1696. The matter had then been remitted

---

[30] A.J. Mann, 'Inglorious Revolution: Administrative Muddle and Constitutional Change in the Scottish Parliament of William and Mary', *Parliamentary History*, xxii (2003), 121–2.

[31] RPS, 1689/3/6; RPS, 1690/4/24; RPS, 1693/4/18; RPS, 1695/5/12; RPS, 1696/9/13; RPS, 1698/7/21; RPS, 1700/5/34; RPS, 1700/10/25; RPS, 1702/6/22.

[32] NRS, PC1/51, p. 574, privy council register of acta, 8 June 1699.

[33] RPS, 1700/10/147.

[34] RPS, 1696/9/97.

[35] Bills were 'read' only twice in the Scottish parliament, but the 'voting' on a bill after the second reading in some ways resembled a third reading. For a bill to gain royal approval it then had to be touched by the sceptre. This four-step process was formalised by these acts: A.J. Mann, 'House Rules: Parliamentary Procedure', in *History of the Scottish Parliament. Volume III*, ed. Brown and MacDonald, 146.

[36] NRS, PC1/52, pp. 235–6.

[37] RPS, 1696/9/67.

by parliament to the Perthshire commissioners of supply – officials introduced in the Restoration, principally in charge of collecting tax in the regions but increasingly tasked with widespread aspects of local government – for concluding the matter and repaying his losses.[38] It is unclear whether this had been resolved by the commissioners of supply, but a clue may lie in the fact that Patton had returned to parliament with the petition again in late 1700 where he had presented the same requests. Parliament had read the petition once more and remitted the case onto its elections committee on 23 November.[39] On 18 January 1701, it had decided that the petition was to be dealt with on 'the next day that parliament proceeds to privat affairs'.[40] In the event this never materialised, because parliament was dissolved after 1 February 1701. Hence, the unresolved issue then came before the privy council, although not until 26 June. The board heard Patton's grievances and ordered the treasury to find money from vacant church stipends to pay him for his numerous and protracted tribulations.[41] This case exemplifies the interconnected government adminis- tration of early modern Scotland and the specific, yet at times overlapping, functions of the executive, the legislature and the multitudinous 'inferior' institutions, courts and officials which governed the nation. It also suggests that the privy council was the main institution which was supplicated to deal with matters – often in conjunction with the treasury – in a swift manner where they had previously been shelved or left unresolved by others.[42]

It is worth noting here that parliament's committee for controverted elections was pri- marily concerned with the elections of parliamentary commissioners. Whereas the privy council also oversaw elections for burgh and shire commissioners to parliament, it was largely involved in elections for burgh councils and burgh magistrates. These latter elec- tions nonetheless influenced parliamentary ones, since the elected burgh council and mag- istrates comprised the electorate for parliamentary commissioners representing the burghs. In many ways, the council acted, as part of its overarching executive function, as an elec- toral committee analogous to parliament's. Fundamentally, however, the privy council was a court, dealing with extensive judicial business and with appellate jurisdiction over 'inferior' magistrates, courts, civil officers and church institutions. As such, politics and politicking were not its primary function; instead, it was government and legal administration.

The privy council's role in elections has been all-but ignored, save for a few passing ref- erences in the 20th century, such as in Edith Thomson's and Charles Terry's early studies on parliament. For example, both note that electoral issues often came to the privy council prior to the establishment of parliament's elections committee, especially before 1641 and the curtailment of the council's business in the covenanting period in favour of a committee of estates.[43] This article aims to build upon this and recent scholarship discussed above in or- der to place the privy council within the framework where parliament has heretofore been the primary concern. It will demonstrate the complex centrality of the Scottish privy coun- cil to electoral politics from the Revolution to its abolition, although this was of declining

---

[38] RPS, 1696/9/67.

[39] RPS, 1700/10/71.

[40] RPS, 1700/10/193.

[41] NRS, PC1/52, p. 236.

[42] For the treasury and privy council in the 1690s, see Rayner, 'Tribulations of Everyday Government', 193– 210.

[43] Terry, *Scottish Parliament*, 41–2, 125; Thomson, *Parliament of Scotland*, 55.

importance after 1703. Parliament preferred to deal with disputed elections in full session rather than delegate to committees after Anne's accession, and there were generally fewer elections.[44] Also, the privy council appears to have seldom dealt with electoral issues after 1703, with its general business fizzling out after around 1705 and just one election annulled from then until its demise in May 1708. This was the 1704 Arbroath (Angus) burgh council election, which the privy council annulled in November 1705, following complaints about the dubiety of the sitting provost's successful election from his predecessor.[45] The council then called for a new election to take place and ordered the earl of Northesk (one of their number) to attend the election to monitor proceedings and ensure proper conduct.

Electoral Organisation

The privy council often arranged and announced elections, made historical enquiry into local practices, and gave the authority back to local communities to put into practice its orders. Burgh inhabitants and town councils that governed them sought guidance on legitimate electoral practices and also petitioned the privy council to solve issues surrounding elections. For example, the inhabitants of Brechin (Angus) petitioned the privy council in autumn 1689, noting that their (burgh council) election time was drawing near and they therefore had to apply to the executive so that it might be prorogued and 'cloathed with the saids lords authoritie', since the privy council was the only 'proper judicatory' which could do so.[46] In September 1692, moreover, the privy council was involved in determining the manner of election for St Andrews' burgh council. Their majesties' solicitor investigated the burgh's electoral precedents and found that, during episcopacy, the magistrates had been nominated by the town's archbishop.[47] It was decided, after investigation, that the power to nominate which had previously been in the hands of the archbishop would now be transferred to the town's sitting magistrates. Also, following the increase in shire representation in 1690 mentioned above, it was the privy council that determined the proper electorate, arranged the elections for new shire commissioners, sent out summons and ensured they were carried out.[48] Furthermore, in 1707, the privy council was charged with putting into execution the writs for 'Summoning, Electing and returning the Peers and Comones for Shires and Burghs in the Parliament of Great Brittain for and on the part of Scotland'.[49]

The privy council also ensured the correct electorate was being utilised for burgh council elections where there had previously been intrusive crown policies enforced. For instance, in Paisley (Renfrewshire) in 1689 the privy council heard that there had been no 'free electiones' during the Restoration, since the council and magistrates had been chosen by way of letters from the chancellor. This had consequently, the petitioners claimed, 'impowerished' the burgh, in addition to discouraging godly ministers and disrupting the proper running

---

[44] Rait, *Parliaments of Scotland*, 313; Brown, 'Party Politics and Parliament', 275.

[45] NRS, GD124/10/449/4, papers of the Erskine family, earls of Mar and Kellie: journals of privy council, 1705–8, 29 Nov. 1705.

[46] *Register of the Privy Council of Scotland* (hereafter *RPCS*), ed. J.H. Burton *et al.* (37 vols, Edinburgh, 1877–1970), 3rd ser., xiv, 332.

[47] NRS, PC2/24, f. 117r.

[48] *RPCS*, 3rd ser., xv, 353–4.

[49] TNA, warrant for a new commission to the privy council in Scotland, PC1/2/62/1, 20 Mar. 1707.

© 2024 The Authors. Parliamentary History *published by* John Wiley & Sons Ltd *on behalf of* Parlimentary History Yearbook Trust.

of local schools and, more generally, local government.[50] The privy council's authority was sought to carry out a free election, which was duly organised and a council committee was appointed to see the matter to completion. Similarly, in Burntisland (Fife), the privy council annulled the 1689 election as the electors were not resident tradesmen and had not sworn the oath of allegiance. Thereafter the privy council authorised a new free election in the burgh and explicitly excluded unqualified voters so as to ensure a legal election process.[51]

The privy council had an important role in ceremonial aspects of parliamentary procedure as well.[52] The 'riding of parliament' was a public ceremony, where parliamentarians processed on horseback to the legislature at the start ('downsitting') and end ('rising') of parliament, but not each session.[53] This was closely choreographed by the privy council. It also ensured there was no outside interference from Edinburgh crowds, since the parliamentarians publicly processed from Holyrood up the Royal Mile to Parliament House.[54] The last of these occurred in Queen Anne's first parliament of 1703. The council ordered that controverted members and those with double elections were either not to ride in the procession or were afforded a specific place away from other members, thus symbolically reinforcing their disputed election.[55] This implied superiority of membership according to the commissioners' electoral status. The privy council's symbolic power over the candidates in controverted elections was thereby openly reflected in the procession.

Electoral Management

Following the Revolution, the council was often proactive in its interference in local issues, engaging in conciliar management. For example, a petition from 'several hundred' burgesses and inhabitants of Glasgow in June 1689 asked for the executive to organise a new burgh council election.[56] Inspired by policy implemented elsewhere, the privy council called for a list of three potential provosts, which was to be passed on to his majesty for perusal and approval and then sent back to the burgh for selection.[57] Thus, the choice of magistrates was closely monitored by the government and the electorate was ripe for a degree of manipulation.

The privy council dealt with the overturning of previously Jacobite-dominated magistracies immediately after the Revolution. For instance, parliament enacted on 18 April 1689 that fresh elections of burgh councils should occur and it was thereafter the privy council which oversaw these.[58] In Stirling, several Presbyterian inhabitants petitioned the council and cited that the burgh had been openly and illegally manipulated under James VII

---

[50] *RPCS*, 3rd ser., xiv, 320.

[51] *RPCS*, 3rd ser., xiv, 413, 415, 455.

[52] A.J. Mann, 'Continuity and Change: The Culture of Ritual and Procession in the Parliaments of Scotland', *Parliaments, Estates and Representation*, xxix (2009), 143–58.

[53] 'The Method and Manner of Ryding the Scottish Parliament', in *Miscellany of the Maitland Club*, iii, pt 1 (Edinburgh, 1842), 101–37.

[54] Mann, 'Continuity and Change', 154.

[55] NRS, PC1/52, pp. 558–62.

[56] *RPCS*, 3rd ser., xiv, 452.

[57] *RPCS*, 3rd ser., xiv, 459–60.

[58] RPS, 1689/3/134.

© 2024 The Authors. Parliamentary History published by John Wiley & Sons Ltd on behalf of Parliamentary History Yearbook Trust.

and that it was awash with Episcopalians.[59] They asked for a new burgh council election, which was granted, and the privy council compiled a list of potential burgh councillors, magistrates and deacon convenors, confirming that all the Presbyterian petitioners were eligible to vote. This policy had been effectively deployed in 1689 in Edinburgh, Glasgow, and Dundee, where the council had actively interfered, approved lists of candidates, and claimed to overturn the illegality of the quondam reign.[60] This was particularly ironic since supporters of the Revolution claimed to oppose James VII's interference in burgh affairs while openly committing to a similar policy.

If the intrusive arm of the state was not enough to cajole magistrates into supporting the government, then there were other tests of loyalty. New formal declarations of loyalty were introduced after 1689 in the oath of allegiance, the assurance (1694) and the association (1696). The former was a simple one-line statement of loyalty to the new joint monarchy, whereas the assurance enforced a recognition of William and Mary as *de jure* and *de facto* monarchs, and the latter bound swearers to defend his majesty and Protestantism.[61] Besides these, newly elected magistrates often came before the council to report on the new magistracy or to confirm their allegiance personally.[62] For instance, in 1694, a Stirling bailie and the town's deacon convenor were sent to Edinburgh, 'to give accompt of the last election to my lord chancellor, the advocat, and other lords of privy council'.[63] They reaffirmed their gratitude for the councillors' endeavours in traditional forms of loyal addressing and confirmed they would 'be ready on all occasiones to give testimonie therof and imploy their outmost endeavours for being serviceable to the government'.[64]

In 1689, the inhabitants of Kirkcaldy (Fife) petitioned the privy council in Edinburgh following the election for their burgh council. The election had been carried out only by a limited number of burgesses and two of the qualified residents petitioned the council for a new election, to no avail.[65] A Williamite party was installed as the new magistracy, led by privy councillor David Melville, third earl of Leven (1660–1728), whose father (the earl of Melville) and brother (master of Melville) also sat on the privy council. The family were solid Presbyterians who were part of the large Scottish expatriate community in the Netherlands which had attached itself to the Orange court during the Restoration.[66] Among the inhabitants' complaints were extensive quarterings, the large amount of cess (land tax) charged against them since the early 1680s, and declining trade. Additionally, they noted that the burgh council was voted in by a 'cabal' without the proper recourse to electoral precedent. The privy council refused to stop the quarterings on the town and declined to call a new election. The burgh's parliamentary commissioner following the

---

[59] *RPCS*, 3rd ser., xiv, 334.

[60] *RPCS*, 3rd ser., xiv, 459–60.

[61] Alasdair Raffe, 'Scottish State Oaths and the Revolution of 1688–1690', in *Scotland in the Age of Two Revolutions*, ed. Adams and Goodare, 185.

[62] A privy council committee for elections is mentioned in June 1701: NRS, PC1/52, p. 235.

[63] *Extracts from the Records of the Royal Burgh of Stirling*, ed. Robert Renwick (2 vols, Glasgow, 1889), ii, 72.

[64] *Extracts from the Records of Stirling*, ed. Renwick, ii, 72.

[65] *RPCS*, 3rd ser., xiv, 487.

[66] Ginny Gardiner, *The Scottish Exile Community in the Netherlands, 1660–1690* (East Linton, 2004).

Revolution was John Boswell, who was also part of the Williamite court interest up until around 1701.[67]

Kirkcaldy ignited into open revolt against the dominant court interest in 1702. Interestingly, there were clear links between the parliamentary opposition to the Court Party and the local opposition which had been articulated in the early stages of the Revolution. James Hamilton, fourth duke of Hamilton (1658–1712), was the most prominent of the parliamentary 'country party' opposition, which had emerged in the late 1690s and had become increasingly aligned to the Company of Scotland with the failure of the Darien scheme to set up a trading entrepôt in Panama.[68] On 9 June 1702, Hamilton led a walkout of parliament.[69] He was followed by scores of his colleagues, ostensibly to oppose the failure to adhere to the 1696 (Scottish) Act of Security, which had legislated that a parliament should be called within 20 days of the king's death.[70] Of course, this walkout was a gesture which was as much to do with opposition to Queen Anne's fledgling administration as it was about constitutional commitment.

In a similar fashion to this 'country party' walkout, the earl of Leven, who was the provost of Kirkcaldy from 1690 to 1702, explained to the privy council in September 1702 that at the election of the burgh's parliamentary commissioner, a great many abstained and left in protest. The election was contested and the protest was led by James Oswald, who had been chosen by many craftsmen.[71] The protest was in opposition to Leven's noble status, the fact that he already sat in parliament, and because his presence deterred free voting. This meant that there were insufficient numbers to conduct the election, so it was abandoned.[72] The privy council empowered Leven either to compel the abstainers to return, or if they absented themselves again to 'supply and fill up the vaccant places of those who shall not attend or doe remove with such able and sufficient burgesses as they shall think fitt to nominat'.[73] In stark contrast to the council's concern for electoral integrity elsewhere (as is explored below), the policy here was to pack the burgh electorate in order to return a favourable commissioner. As a result, Leven remained in office for another year despite the opposition. For the privy council there was no standardised response to these electoral issues, but a case-by-case basis was followed with at times – perhaps out of convenience – only a cursory commitment to upholding the rightful electoral process. In 1703, the Kirkcaldy election was contested again, this time between Boswell and James Oswald, with Oswald's election being disputed but upheld.[74]

---

[67] Patrick, 'People and Parliament', 427.

[68] Young, 'Scottish Parliament and the Politics of Empire', 175–190; Douglas Watt, 'The Company of Scotland and Scottish Politics, 1696–1701', in *Scotland in the Age of Two Revolutions*, ed. Adams and Goodare, 211–30; Patrick, 'People and Parliament', ch. 5.

[69] RPS, M1702/6/1.

[70] Bowie reports that between 60 and 80 members accompanied Hamilton and compiled an oppositional address which was signed by over 70 parliamentary commissioners plus many outside individuals: Karin Bowie, *Public Opinion in Early Modern Scotland, c. 1560–1707* (Cambridge, 2020), 35, 39, 229.

[71] NRS, PC1/52, pp. 453–4.

[72] Brown, 'Party Politics and Parliament', 267.

[73] NRS, PC1/52, p. 454.

[74] *The Parliaments of Scotland: Burgh and Shire Commissioners*, gen. ed. M.D. Young (2 vols, Edinburgh, 1993), ii, 557.

The Scottish executive's abolition in 1708 (proposed the previous December) serves as a reminder of the council's potential influence on elections. The year 1708 was an election year, which brought fears of an explosion in support for the opposition, especially due to the deeply unpopular parliamentary union of 1707. The English ministry was largely in favour of the council's abolition, but Sidney Godolphin, earl of Godolphin (1645–1712) and several in the administration were in favour of the council's continuation, while the *squadrone* pressed for abolition.[75] At this time, much of the council was personally opposed to the court's leader, James Douglas, duke of Queensberry (1662–1711), and several of its number outwith the opposition wanted abolition of Scottish executive powers in Edinburgh. On the contrary, proponents of the council's maintenance stated their support for its remaining for an indeterminate period – until the clamour against the Union had calmed down – in order to smooth the transition of government administration, in line with the 19th article of union.[76] Abolition has often been presented as an invigorated attempt to slight Queensberry, which is partly borne out in the evidence; however, as Riley points out, the court proposal that the abolition be delayed until October 1708 was defeated, since this would have been during the elections and opponents feared the council could influence the result.[77] The *squadrone* gained support from Whigs and the Junto in its bid to have the Scottish privy council abolished in May, which came to fruition after the bill passed in both the Commons and the Lords.[78]

Electoral Adjudication

In spite of the invasion of the Dutch fleet on 5 November 1688, Aberdeen burgh council remained under the control of a Jacobite faction under Alexander Gordon (1626–92). In late November 1688, Anne Drummond, countess of Erroll (1656–1719), was informed of the new burgh council's election, administered by way of a list sent from Edinburgh by the Jacobite-supporting 'dictator', David Eadie, one of the town's bailies.[79] Eadie had been a close confidant of the court interest in Edinburgh during the 1680s.[80] The perpetuation of Jacobites in the magistracy is not in itself significant as many burghs and regions remained loyal to the exiled Stewarts, but the Revolution was far from secure. Indeed, Aberdeen presented a key strategic challenge to the nascent Revolution regime.

Although he was blacklisted by the privy council, John Sandilands of Countesswells was elected as Aberdeen's provost in 1690. Sandilands was evidently disaffected towards the Williamite government and hostile towards the reintroduction of Presbytery. In June 1691 the lord advocate and the Kirk's lawyer reported to the privy council that Sandilands had been deliberately unreasonable with the visiting commissioners of the revived general assembly of the Church in March of that year.[81] He denied them access to a meeting house

---

[75] Townend, "'Rendering the Union more Complete'", 95, 97.

[76] RPS, 1706/10/257.

[77] P.W.J. Riley, *The English Ministers and Scotland, 1707–1727* (London, 1964), 95.

[78] *CJ*, xv, 511–12; *LJ*, xviii, 438–51.

[79] A.M. Munro, *Memorials of the Aldermen, Provosts, and Lord Provosts of Aberdeen, 1272–1895* (Aberdeen, 1897), 186.

[80] Raffe, *Scotland in Revolution*, 89.

[81] *RPCS*, 3rd ser., xvi, 347–9.

© 2024 The Authors. Parliamentary History *published by John Wiley & Sons Ltd on behalf of Parliamentary History Yearbook Trust.*

and instead instructed them to meet in the town's tolbooth and council chamber, where they were surrounded by an armed mob. Sandilands had turned a blind eye to this 'tumult', and consequently he was duly imprisoned by the privy council and removed from office.[82] As he had also failed to swear the oath of allegiance to William and Mary, he was thus viewed as both politically and religiously opposed to the Revolution. The privy council thereafter ordered a new burgh council election to be carried out and Walter Cochrane of Drumbreck was elected as provost in July 1691.[83] It is unclear where his allegiances lay, but it is likely he was at least acquiescent to the Revolution regime.

Controversy continued in the Aberdeen magistracy throughout the 1690s. In 1693, former bailie Robert Cruickshank of Banchory (1623–1717) was elected as provost, a position he was to serve in for the next four years. It was under his leadership that the burgh council finally took measures to impose the Presbyterian church settlement on an inert town, not without obstruction, however. The Episcopalian session continued to practise clandestinely, disruptive Quakers permeated the region, and there were large numbers of Catholics within the burgh and its wider environs throughout the 1690s.[84] For instance, David Eadie (mentioned above) was investigated by the privy council alongside another erstwhile town bailie in 1699 for travelling to France, for which he was imprisoned and then banished as a 'trafficking papist'.[85] Absconding to France without the relevant passes was an act declared illegal by numerous council proclamations and acts of parliament throughout the decade.[86]

Cruickshank's provostship was fraught with controversy and corruption. Concerns had been raised about his embezzling the burgh's finances and he was religiously at odds with many in the town.[87] He nonetheless managed to gain favour in four consecutive elections, from 1693 to 1696 inclusive. Opposition came to fruition before the burgh council election of 1696, though, in the form of a 'solemne protestatione', which was unsuccessful since he was able to win the election for yet another term.[88] However, his tenuous control over the burgh finally ended in 1697, when he retired. Prior to doing so, he employed remarkably conspicuous illegal means to pack the burgh council electorate and choose his son-in-law, John Johnston, as his successor.

In protest at Cruickshank's preferment of Johnston, the electorate staged a walkout and therefore abstained. Cruickshank, in complete disregard for electoral precedent, employed unqualified proxies in an alternative electorate which numbered just nine, when it should normally have consisted of at least 19.[89] Their 'partiall and maisterfull' practices were discussed in the privy council chamber on 25 November in private litigation brought against Cruickshank by two of Aberdeen's bailies, John Allardyce and Thomas Mitchell.[90] The evidence against Cruickshank and Johnston stated that after the boycott, their sham election

---

[82] *RPCS*, 3rd ser., xvi, 349–55.

[83] *RPCS*, 3rd ser., xvi, 432.

[84] NRS, CH2/1/4, p. 25, Aberdeen presbytery minutes, 1697–1702, 20 Apr. 1697; NRS, PC1/51, pp. 463–4; NRS, PC4/2, f. 10, privy council minutes, 1696–1699, 17 Mar. 1696.

[85] NRS, PC1/52, p. 3; NRS, PC 2/27, f. 241.

[86] See, for example, RPS, 1698/7/161; NRS, PC 12/1698, privy council misc.: royal letters, 28 Apr. 1698.

[87] Aberdeen City Archives (hereafter ACA), CA/1/57, pp. 573–4, Aberdeen town council minutes, 1682–1704, 29 Apr. 1696; Munro, *Memorials*, 191–2.

[88] NRS, PC2/27, f. 49; ACA, CA/1/57, pp. 592–606.

[89] ACA, CA/1/57, pp. 593–600.

[90] NRS, PC2/27, f. 50v.

© 2024 *The Authors. Parliamentary History published by John Wiley & Sons Ltd on behalf of Parliamentary History Yearbook Trust.*

consisted of – among others – a boy aged around 15, a man convicted for false measures who had been banished from the town, and several servants and tacksmen abiding outwith the burgh, who were neither burgesses nor had publicly qualified themselves with the oath of allegiance or assurance.[91] Interestingly, there was also a religious dimension to the allegations against Johnston. He was described as both a Quaker and a follower of Arminian principles, who was morally opposed to capital punishment; the latter the privy council condemned as an 'opinion [which] is wtterlie inconsistant with our lawes'.[92]

Aberdeen remained a burgh fraught with religious recalcitrance in the 1690s. Merely a month prior to the quashed election, in August 1697, the privy council ordered several ministers to desist from illegal preaching in Aberdeen presbytery.[93] The executive found that there were numerous instances of local resistance to Presbyterianism and deposed ministers continuing to preach. This had been a difficulty since the Revolution. In 1694, the privy council had written to the regents of King's College Aberdeen to ensure their diligence in opposing widespread illegal preaching and to encourage legal admittance of a minister to the parish of Old Aberdeen despite resistance.[94]

There was evident turmoil in the burgh and this was reflected in the sham election of 1697. Although perhaps exaggerated for rhetorical effect, the resulting legal case brought before the privy council made claims that the 'whole commwnitie' of the burgh had suffered and thus, as a corporate urban group, required central intervention to repair the damage.[95] The intertwined local and national consequences were, 'that therby the liberties and privileges of the burgh are manifestly stollen and disposed of by the votes of the meanest and the most inconsiderable of the people to the evident hazard of the constitutione of the royall burrowes and the publict government of the natione'.[96] Just 18 months earlier, the Revolution regime faced an invasion threat and a plot on the king's life; moreover, the peace of Ryswick (which brought an end to the Nine Years' War) was only being negotiated while these burgh council elections were held. An increasingly unstable Revolution regime was shadowed by unrest in Aberdeen. While from 1688–90 a Jacobite party was firmly in control, from 1693 up to the 'pretendit electione' of 1697 a seemingly ambiguous but revolutionarily inclined and corrupt party had been the magistracy.[97]

The privy council declared the Michaelmas election of 1697 null and void, then ordered a new burgh council election to be held on 8 December.[98] The new magistracy elected consisted of both the main complainants in the libel case brought against Cruickshank, with Thomas Mitchell installed as provost and John Allardyce as a bailie.[99] For this reason, their complaint was a conclusive success, though admittedly one where there had been clear wrongdoing and the privy council was left with little choice but to annul the election. Further measures were taken to ensure no such issues might arise again: the new burgh

[91] NRS, PC2/27, ff. 50v–51; ACA, CA/1/57, pp. 593–600.

[92] NRS, PC2/27, f. 52.

[93] NRS, PC1/51, pp. 247–9.

[94] Aberdeen University Library, KINGS/4/1/7/1/5, St Machar Cathedral dispute, 1694–1710, 16 Apr. 1694.

[95] NRS, PC2/27, f. 50v; ACA, CA/1/57, p. 602.

[96] NRS, PC2/27, f. 51.

[97] NRS, PC2/27, f. 50v.

[98] NRS, PC 2/27, f. 52.

[99] ACA, CA/1/57, p. 609.

council enacted that all matters proposed by magistrates were required to be voted on prior to implementation.[100] Additionally, a privy council act stipulated that no provost could remain in office for more than two years, that the oath of allegiance be administered each year, and that a promise be made to observe all the acts of the burgh itself and of the convention of royal burghs.[101]

Interestingly, the electoral controversy also lived on in Aberdeen's civic architecture. Ruthrieston Pack Bridge, which still stands today near the bridge of Dee in the south of the city, dates from 1693–4. This was during Cruickshank's tenure and the burgh council later found that he had 'clandestinely caus[ed] [to] put up his armes on the said Bridge without any act of council albeit he contribute nothing for building therof', since it was paid for by a public fund.[102] The burgh council in 1698 removed the inscription and replaced it with a Latin one which emphasised the council rather than any individual patronage.[103] In 1705, however, the new burgh council decided to reinstate the old stone, adding in Cruickshank's office of provost to the inscription for good measure. As such, the oscillating patterns of the Aberdeen magistracy were reflected in this somewhat petty feud over the inscription on a strategic piece of infrastructure. This represented an enduring reminder of the chaos of the post-Revolution years.

Another example that is illustrative of the council's adjudication of elections comes from Jedburgh in the Scottish Borders. Following the Revolution, the election of Jedburgh's parliamentary commissioner was contested between Robert Ainslie and Adam Ainslie. The increased electorate in February 1689 numbered 128 and ultimately voted for Robert Ainslie, a former bailie.[104] Complaints soon came before parliament's committee for controverted elections, in March 1689, which found 'that those who voted for Adam Ainslie were threatened by these magistrates to have their heads broken'.[105] The committee found in favour of Adam Ainslie, declaring the former's successful election to be null and void. Adam Ainslie continued to serve as Jedburgh's parliamentary commissioner until 1700.[106]

In 1700 there was also controversy surrounding the election of the parliamentary commissioner to represent the burgh seat of Jedburgh. When a new election was held in October 1700, Ainslie's successor, Walter Scott, and some accomplices were accused of soliciting votes by bribery.[107] One of his accomplices was a Gilbert Elliot, one of the town's bailies and possibly the clerk to the privy council of the same name who was later created the first earl of Minto, since he held family lands in Roxburghshire. On 15 September 1700, the executive found Scott correctly elected as provost. In protest against the result, however, former provost, William Simpson, and some of his town councillors held their own poll the following day. This numbered just 14, while the quorum for such an election was 21 and the potential members at the election was a burgh council of around 40,

---

[100] ACA, CA/1/57, p. 608.

[101] ACA, CA/1/57, p. 608.

[102] Munro, *Memorials*, 192.

[103] Munro, *Memorials*, 192.

[104] Patrick, 'People and Parliament', 111.

[105] RPS, 1689/3/51.

[106] *Parliaments of Scotland*, gen. ed. Young, i, 8.

[107] NRS, PC2/28, ff. 12v–16.

'as has allwayes been inviolably observed in the said burgh'.[108] Their extravagant protest went further, as the former magistrates seized the keys to the tolbooth and burgh council building, in addition to circulating a proclamation around the burgh declaring a 'head court' in their name. To make matters worse for themselves, 'and to crown the work of this usurpation', the Simpsonian party on the Sunday following '[took] possession of the magistrates seatt in the church designeing therby no doubt to make alse much disturbance in the church, as they made at the election'.[109]

Notwithstanding Simpson's complaints, coupled with the evident chicanery by the Scott interest and the Court Party in government more broadly, the defenders were ultimately declared innocent. The privy council found that Scott's election was 'very legall' and that Simpson and his accomplices were guilty of 'ane gross and highneous usurpatione of the magistracy of the toune' in attempting to set up a provisional government.[110] Therefore, although there was a clear element of court-packing of the electorate and more general management by the government faced with a threat to its hegemony, the executive acted as a court of appeal. The matter here was not as such the evident management of the election but rather the 'usurpatione' of the election, the attempted formation of a provisional burgh council, and clear breaches of the traditional electoral practices and precedent. Therefore, electoral management and adjudication were not always mutually exclusive facets of the council's complex role in elections.

Even privy councillors themselves were not immune to allegations of corrupt or illegal practices in elections. The lord provost of Edinburgh (leader of the burgh council and chief magistrate) was an office that also conferred membership of the privy council. Sir Archibald Muir of Thornton served as Edinburgh's provost from 1691–2 and again from 1696–7. His successor after the 1692 burgh council election was Sir John Hall of Dunglass (d. 1695). However, Hall's 1692 election success was brought into serious doubt when allegations emerged about several abuses of the town's electoral practices. In December 1692 the privy council heard a libel case brought by nine former bailies and trades' deacon convenors in both Edinburgh and the neighbouring burgh of Leith.[111] Hall, with the help of Muir, employed illegal proxies, sidelining those who had been opposed to Muir in 1691, and managing to secure Hall's election, much to the chagrin of many fellow burgesses. Hall and Muir had engaged in 'most illegall and factious methods and manifest violatione of the sett and decreet arbitrall of the citie' to resume their office consecutively and retain their power in the burgh.[112]

Remarkably, perhaps, the privy council did not engage in a mere show trial where evidence against Hall and Muir was discounted. Instead, the executive heard the case according to the contravention of electoral traditions and precedent. Muir was denied an influence on future elections and he and his 'cabal' received an admonition from the council.[113] However, Hall continued to serve in this office until 1694. Irrespectively, the issues brought to

---

[108] NRS, PC2/28, f. 14.

[109] NRS, PC2/28, f. 15v.

[110] NRS, PC4/3, f. 8; NRS PC2/28, f. 14v.

[111] NRS, PC1/48, pp. 480–501.

[112] NRS, PC1/48, p. 481.

[113] NRS, PC1/48, p. 501.

the board were clear backlashes against the court management of elections in 1689 and provided a platform for opponents of the Williamite 'faction' to oppose the government not only of the burgh but indeed of the political nation at large.[114] Opponents of the provost articulated that, through the illegal means used in the election, Hall and his accomplices had the 'opportunity to appropriate and embezzle the common good at their pleasure'.[115] Even if a rhetorical device, there were clearly broad community disagreements and ideological differences which came to a crescendo in these elections and were imbued with the language of popular politics.[116]

The privy council did not only oversee elections to burgh councils and for parliamentary commissioners. For instance, the council heard a petition from William Cochrane of Ferguslie in February 1701 regarding the election of a collector of the cess among the commissioners of supply in Renfrewshire, of which he was a member.[117] Ferguslie served in that capacity from 1698 until 1704, when he was imprisoned for misappropriation of funds granted to him by the treasury.[118] Conforming to an act of parliament on 31 January 1701, which enacted a supply of 12 months' cess, the commissioners in the shire gathered to elect their chief collector for this taxation.[119] John Cunningham, tenth earl of Glencairn (d. 1703), was selected as the *praeses* for this meeting and had the casting vote if there was a tie. In the event, Ferguslie gained ten votes to his opponent's nine. But, disregarding normal practice, Glencairn cast his vote in favour of the latter and the result was rendered equal. This was apparently in protest at the fact that Ferguslie had voted for himself, although there was precedent for this. Thereafter, Ferguslie obtained 'a declaration and the subscriptions' from the ten commissioners who voted for him and 'was necessitat to apply to their lo[rdshi]ps to whom the determination of such questions belonged'.[120] The privy council found that voting for oneself was legal, but that Glencairn had no right to cast a vote unless it was a deciding one. It also proclaimed that, once elected, the collector could not be dismissed from office unless in the case of 'aither death or malversation'.[121] The privy council therefore resolved the issue by calling for a new election, which was held in March, and by prohibiting any of the commissioners from meeting until then.[122]

Furthermore, the privy council – in its religious capacity – also occasionally adjudicated over the rightful election of a parish minister. The abolition of church patronage in 1690 allowed the elders and heritors of a parish to choose a minister with the consent of the congregation, a process which had 'been greatly abused' under the Restoration Episcopate.[123] Karin Bowie and Alasdair Raffe argue that this was one of the most important

---

[114]NRS, PC1/48, pp. 480–1, 501.

[115]NRS, PC1/48, p. 480.

[116]Karin Bowie, *Scottish Public Opinion and the Anglo-Scottish Union, 1699–1707* (Woodbridge, 2007); Bowie, *Public Opinion in Early Modern Scotland*, chs 1–2.

[117]NRS, PC2/28, ff. 35v–36v.

[118]RPS, 1698/7/41; RPS, A1704/7/63.

[119]RPS, 1700/10/244.

[120]NRS, PC2/28, f. 35.

[121]NRS, PC2/28, f. 35.

[122]NRS, PC2/28, f. 36v.

[123]RPS, 1690/4/114.

ways in which communities and individuals could participate in popular politics.[124] The privy council upheld this congregational right in Haddington (in the synod of Lothian and Tweeddale) in 1705, when it enacted that nobody should 'interfeir with or disturb any kirk session ther lawfullie elected and confirmed by the acts of parliament in the exercise of discipline and government competent to them'.[125] Maintaining established electoral practices, upholding the integrity of elections and punishing or preventing undue interference in them were therefore clear functions of the early modern Scottish executive.

Conclusion

The Scottish privy council was an electoral adjudicator in a political system whose elections were increasingly contested. This occurred simultaneously with the post-Revolution empowering and apogee of the Scottish parliament and indeed the privy council. The council could be utilised by the court interest among its number to embolden their local or urban support bases and also to ensure that parliamentary commissioners or burgh magistracies were returned who were favourable to the regime. Equally, urban inhabitants often petitioned the council for redress following contraventions of electoral precedent or authority in burgh council elections, complaining about long-running local magistracies and abuses of power. Although these were not always considered with great vigour by the council, the fact that resident burgesses within urban locales could supplicate the council often with (at least symbolic) support of the wider populations of their locality, demonstrates an important aspect of central as well as local political representation. This highlights a participative politics and demonstrates that electoral preferences could be articulated via interaction with state bureaucratic structures, in this case the privy council.

As Christopher Whatley, Robert Rait, and Charles Terry have argued, the privy council was at times used as an instrument for crown management of elections.[126] Perhaps a more fruitful conclusion, however, would be that the privy council managed the electorate more than it managed elections themselves in the 1690s. This is borne out by the board's interventionist policies in burgh council elections compared with its organisation of and concern for proper procedure in parliamentary elections, since the former determined the electorate in the latter. By proactively and reactively interfering in burgh council elections, the privy council looked to control and manage the outcome that would in turn ensure a favourable electorate in the polls for burgh commissioners to parliament. That being said, what is imperative to this article is that the council also operated as an electoral mediator, which upheld the integrity of elections. That disgruntled groups could plead their case in front of one of the most prominent courts in Scotland demonstrates that voting was not necessarily the end of the matter. Abstention and recourse to legal action adjudicated by the privy council were therefore evidently recognised means of expressing voting preferences or opposing election results.

---

[124]Karin Bowie and Alasdair Raffe, 'Politics, the People, and Extra-Institutional Participation in Scotland, c. 1603–1712', *Journal of British Studies*, liv (2017), 801, 809–14.

[125]NRS, PC1/53, p. 345.

[126]Rait, *Parliaments of Scotland*, 309–10; Whatley, *Scots and the Union*, 328; Terry, *Scottish Parliament*, 41–3.

　　While nobles were excluded from influencing parliamentary elections, this article illustrates that there was still significant noble power and patronage in the burghs, often exercised through the privy council. However, the privy council's fundamental function as a court complicates this picture, since it tried and punished cases of electoral impropriety, fraud and controversy, even if this contradicted the interests of one of its members. Therefore, although the council was often used by the nobility (and crown) to retain or entrench their power in the burghs, it served equally as the main legal apparatus with which to pursue the overturning of electoral manipulation in those same urban centres. These issues and electoral controversy often brought the council into a difficult position, fluctuating (and at times overlapping) between a policy of management to secure burgh councils in their favour through the adjudication of matters coming under its legal appellate jurisdiction and its function as a form of committee for controverted elections. The privy council's role in elections in the 1690s was therefore far more complex than mere management of affairs and this speaks to the increasingly febrile political atmosphere in which elections were often contested.

Parliamentary History, Vol. 43, pt. 1 (2024), pp. 72–90

Tory Travails and Collegiate Confusion: The Oxford University Election of 1722[*]

NIGEL ASTON

University of York

In terms of the unreformed franchise operative in the early 18th century, the University of Oxford made up an unusual parliamentary constituency. Here it was the votes of non-resident members that could be decisive to the outcome if the seat was contested. In late Stuart and early Hanoverian Oxford, Tories were almost certain to be returned but, in the general election of 1722, the Tory vote was split between rival candidates offering a possible opening for Oxford Whigs. This essay considers the varieties of electoral behaviour inside the university at this time of exceptional political flux nationally, how the candidates confronted the practical problem of getting 'outvoters' into Oxford, and the extent to which the heads of the colleges could rely on a sufficiently stable corporate identity to have their resident members vote in an approved way. The 1722 general election again raised questions as to who exactly was entitled to vote in a university constituancy, how much illegal voting was going on, and whether it was in a candidate's best interests either to connive or draw attention to it. The eventual choices made by the Oxford electorate would signal where the university stood in the wider political picture of the early 1720s, how far it – and the varieties of toryism it contained – was prepared to endorse the legitimacy of the new Hanoverian order.

Keywords: Whigs; Tories; Jacobitism; University of Oxford; franchise; elections; academic politics; colleges; halls

In terms of the unreformed franchise operative in the early 18th century, the University of Oxford made up an unusual parliamentary constituency. Here it was the votes of non-resident members that could be decisive to the outcome if the seat was contested. That is in terms of personality rather than party, for it was nigh certain that in late Stuart and early Hanoverian Oxford it would be Tories of one hue or another who would be returned. But what if the Tory candidature was divided between a firebrand Jacobite academic and a Hanoverian accommodationist and former minister? Could that offer an opportunity for a Whig candidate to sneak in because of a split Tory vote? And how would Oxford Whigs vote if they were not running their own candidate? Such were the intriguing range of possibilities in the general election of 1722, the first after the passing of the Septennial Act of 1716. The contest for the two university seats might be said to set up an objective test of academic loyalty to the new Hanoverian order and that mattered because, in the

---

[*] I am grateful to Robin Darwall-Smith and Bethany Hamblen for their archival assistance.

eyes of its Whig detractors, Oxford was a primary agency of Jacobite malcontents stealthily, seditiously undermining the lawful dynasty in possession.

This article considers the varieties of electoral behaviour inside the university at this time of exceptional political flux nationally, how the candidates confronted the practical problem of getting 'outvoters' into Oxford, and the extent to which the heads of the colleges could rely on a sufficiently stable corporate identity to have their resident members vote in an approved way. The 1722 general election once more raised questions as to who was entitled to vote in a university constituency, how much illegal voting was occurring, and whether it was in a candidate's best interests either to connive or publicise it. And the importance of the final result, one way or another, was significant nationally because of Oxford's place alongside Cambridge as corporations in the constitutional order of the kingdom.[1] The eventual choices made by the Oxford electorate would signal where the university stood in the wider political picture of the early 1720s, how far it – and the varieties of toryism it contained – had come in from the cold and was prepared to endorse the legitimacy of a monarchical order whose title rested on statute rather than on strict hereditary succession.

The Oxford University Electorate and its Representatives

The composition of the electoral constituency of the University of Oxford in the 1720s was, in theory, straightforward: all those who were Masters of Arts or possessed higher degrees awarded by the university held the franchise; those, in other words, who were members of convocation, its governing body, and were also members of a college or hall (the vast majority). However, the Laudian statutes of 1636 had little to say about parliamentary elections apart from one section that made provision for the method of counting votes at the time of the poll, and a votive expression that elections should be free 'according to the ancient custom, by the greater part of all those voting'.[2] When university seats had been established in 1604, the letters patent talked of the franchise as bestowed upon the 'chancellor, masters, and scholars' of each university, but the consensus was a century later that the term 'scholars' had become redundant.[3] The point was open to argument. And therefore in practice there were frequent disputes about individual entitlement to the vote, the presumption being that it primarily belonged to the resident senior members of the university, usually college fellows living in Oxford, somewhere between 400 and 500 persons in total, each with two votes. But there were also many potential non-resident voters (*extranei* or independents) whose names figured on their college's buttery books for six months prior to an election.[4] These might include the chaplains of noblemen, curates, schoolmasters, MAs

[1] William Blackstone, *Commentaries on the Laws of England. Book I: Of the Rights of Persons*, ed. David Lemmings (Oxford, 2016), i, 303, 305, 313. In Blackstone's words, university MPs could be deemed to 'protect in the legislature the rights of the republic of letters': *Commentaries*, i, 115. University burgesses were exempt from the property requirement established under the Property Qualification Act of 1711: L.L. Shadwell, *Enactments in Parliament specially concerning the Universities of Oxford and Cambridge* (4 vols, Oxford, 1912), i, 337.

[2] John Griffiths, *Statutes of the University of Oxford codified in the Year 1636* (Oxford, 1888), 129, 134. See generally ch. 5, 'University representation', in Edward Porritt and A.G. Porritt, *The Unreformed House of Commons; Parliamentary Representation before 1832* (2 vols, 1903), i, 99–103.

[3] Quoted in M.B. Rex, *University Representation in England, 1604–1690* (1954), 60–1.

[4] Authoritatively discussed in L.S. Sutherland, 'The Laudian Statutes in the Eighteenth Century', in *The History of the University of Oxford* (hereafter *HUO*), v: *The Eighteenth Century*, ed. L.S. Sutherland and L.G. Mitchell (Oxford,

© *2024 The Authors.* Parliamentary History *published by John Wiley & Sons Ltd on behalf of Parliamentary History Yearbook Trust.*

without a fellowship but on the foundation in and around Oxford who might or might not be deemed to be in occasional residence. Such individuals could be understandably keen to cast their votes when feelings ran high in a contest.[5] And, as party strife intensified after the Revolution of 1688–9, so did disputes over claims by these *extranei* to vote.

The chances were that there would be no contest since potential candidates for a seat might huff and puff before accepting that they stood no chance of victory and withdrawing. Even if there was a poll, the likelihood of many Oxford MAs turning up in person to exercise their franchise was low: distance from the city, more pressing commitments nearer home, the foreknowledge that any representative for the university would be a Tory of some kind, all acted as disincentives for non-residents to bestir themselves. And therefore if a candidate for the seat, particularly one who did not have the imprimatur of the chief executive body of the university, the hebdomadal board, stood his ground and a poll resulted, his prospects of success primarily stood or fell on his capacity to cajole, persuade and whip-in potential supporters to make the journey to Oxford.

Because of the contemporary predominance of toryism in its political culture, Oxford University elections, where contested, tended to pivot on personality rather than party. And the likelihood was that a candidate had to be endorsed by one or all of the three colleges – Christ Church, Magdalen, and All Souls – most closely connected through their more numerous alumni (in the case of the first two) and some on their governing bodies to members of both houses of parliament and even individual ministers. Electors after the 1688–9 Revolution faced the crucial question that could never be finally resolved: was it in the best interests of the university to select a 'court' candidate, a man who was – or could be – an 'insider', or to opt instead for a figure whose appeal lay in his independency? During the quarter of a century before the Tory proscription of 1714–16, there was much to be said for backing a minister or one of his closest connections as one of the two university MPs. A backbencher with 'country' instincts might provide a counteracting balance for the other seat, such a man as Sir William Whitelocke (1636–1717; MP, 1703–17) of Henley-on-Thames, who had compensated for his father being a regicide by giving ample evidence of his Tory sympathies in the 1690s.[6]

Three ministers had represented the university since 1689 and brought it some *éclat*. First was the Hon. Heneage Finch, 1689–1703, James II's solicitor-general turned leading counsel for the seven bishops at their trial in 1688, and brother of the 2nd earl of Nottingham, a secretary of state early in William and Mary's joint reign. In 1695, the university electors went one better and returned another secretary of state in the person of Sir William Trumbull, a civil lawyer, ex-envoy to France (1685), lord of the treasury, and former fellow of All Souls, whose prestige was dimmed in some quarters because of his tepid toryism.[7] Both Finch and Trumbull lost their seats in the general election of 1698 when two stalwart 'country' baronets, Sir Christopher Musgrave and Sir William Glynne, topped the poll. It was a divisive result characterised by a large voting numbers (the proctors counted 716 votes

---

1986), 191–203, esp. 195–6. In the 17th century, the question of residence or non-residence in connection with the election of burgesses seems never to have been raised at Oxford: Rex, *University Representation*, 62. No official list of members of convocation existed.

[5] Porritt and Porritt, *The Unreformed House of Commons*, i, 103.

[6] W.R. Ward, *Georgian Oxford: University Politics in the Eighteenth Century* (Oxford, 1958), 26.

[7] G.V. Bennett, 'Against the Tide: Oxford under William III', in *HUO*, v, 48–50.

in total in the convocation house, divided among four candidates) and the rejection of the preferences of heads of houses.[8] However, the return of William Bromley (Christ Church, BA 1681) as an MP at a contested by-election in 1701 turned out to be a brilliant move, for Bromley proved able to maintain his principled toryism and attention to his constituents with service as Speaker of the house of commons (1710–13) and secretary of state for the northern department (1713–14), appointments that conferred lustre on the university and underscored its central place in national politics.[9]

The Awkward Adjustment to the Hanoverian Succession

Bromley lost the Secretaryship (he refused demotion to a junior post) when the Harley government was replaced following the death of Queen Anne and the intially uncontested Hanoverian succession. But, along with Whitelock, he was returned again without a poll as a burgess in the general election of 1715.[10] In being pushed to the margin, Bromley shared the fate of the university as a whole, along with the rest of the Tory party. The 1715 Jacobite rebellion gave the dominant Whigs the 'evidence' they craved to depict all Tories as Jacobites and the behaviour of former members of the Harley administration also played into their hands. Viscount Bolingbroke fled to France in March 1715, where he was soon joined in the Pretender's service by Oxford's long-serving chancellor, James Butler, 2nd duke of Ormond. Almost immediately, the university convocation elected as the duke's successor his brother, Charles, 1st earl of Arran, whom it was assumed – erroneously – was no less committed to the 'honest cause'. Tempers were running high in the university, with anti-Hanoverian rioting occurring in late May 1715 leading to a ministerial reprimand of the vice-chancellor and the de facto military occupation of the city after further gown-and-town disturbances that autumn.[11] Oxford only narrowly escaped the threat of a royal visitation during the Stanhope–Sunderland administration (1717–20). It formed part of a raft of measures designed to remodel the institutional life of the kingdom in a manner that would have rendered it legally impossible to dislodge Whig predominance in church and state.

Had the Triennial Act continued in force and a general election been held in 1718, there is no saying what commotion a contest for one of the university seats would have triggered. It would likely have lowered Oxford's standing in the eyes of ministers even further. It might even be argued that the passing of the Septennial Act did the university a favour by not affording such an obvious outlet for partisanship. It remained, of course, in the early 1720s, a firmly Tory institution, whose loyalty to George I and his government was

---

[8] Oxford University Archives (hereafter OUA), MS Conv. Reg. Bc 30, f. 186 (register of convocation, 1693–1703).

[9] ODNB, www.oxforddnb.com (accessed 25 Jan. 2023), s.v. Bromley, William (bap. 1663, d. 1732), Speaker of the house of commons

[10] Bernard Gardiner, warden of All Souls, had argued that Whitelock's age (he was 74) 'and ye compliments already payd him by ye university' ought to deter him from standing at the 1710 general election: Bodl., MS Ballard 20, f. 21. But he stood then and again in 1713 and 1715.

[11] TNA, SP 44/116/293–7, 302–3; SP 35/2/18; SP 35/3/29; Peter Rae, *The History of the Rebellion, rais'd against His Majesty King George I* (1746), 140. There were further disturbances in 1716.

never taken for granted by the crown.[12] But by that date, a mutual consensus was gradually emerging that accepted the reality of co-existence and the desirability of restraining, in the interest of political stability, the extremes of the commonwealth Whigs on one side and Jacobite Tories on the other. The university authorities had tried to present the semblance of submission from the time of the king's accession without ever quite convincing the new Whig establishment of its authenticity. And as each year passed and the Hanoverian regime consolidated itself, the awareness of what Oxford was losing in terms of crown patronage became ever-more emphatic. The trick was to persuade the king (and, if not him, the prince and princess of Wales) to recognise that moderate Tories were loyalists; the obstacle to achieving this aim was that many of the younger, junior members of the university were unabashed in displaying their dislike of the new regime, however much it embarrassed their tutors and elders.

The majority of college governing bodies, composed of Tories of one colour or another, could see that royal largesse was operative within the university after 1714, but tended to be offered exclusively to Whigs, building up the party interest as the ambitious and the calculating jostled for preferment. Christ Church was as ever the society most open to ministerial preferences. An examination of appointments made to the chapter between 1714 and 1719 makes that plain. Of the eight canonries available at Christ Church, two fell vacant in these years and both went to court Whigs: William Baker, a client of John, 1st duke of Marlborough, was named archdeacon of Oxford in January 1715, an appointment that would have been inconceivable only 12 months previously;[13] and, when the dean, George Smalridge, a Hanoverian Tory, died in 1719, his replacement was Hugh Boulter, a Whig churchman of trenchant anti-Jacobite convictions.[14]

Tellingly, Baker was a fellow of Wadham College where the Whig interest had been in evidence during the 1688–9 Revolution. It had been further consolidated over two decades by its warden from 1689, Thomas Dunster, whose death in 1719 deprived him of the advancement outside Oxford that would probably have been his.[15] Whig leanings were emerging, too, in some smaller colleges. Exeter was held in line with difficulty by the superannuated Matthew Hole, a compromise candidate as rector after a contested election in 1716, and there were active Whigs also in Jesus and New College.[16] Whig efforts to intrude their supporters could be aggressive and attracted press attention. At whiggish Merton, where the final choice of three candidates as warden was the archbishop of Canterbury's as the

[12] For details, see Ward, *Georgian Oxford*, 52–130; J.R. Wigelsworth, *All Souls College, Oxford in the Early Eighteenth Century: Piety, Political Imposition, and Legacy of the Glorious Revolution* (Leiden, 2018), 144–76, and my *Enlightened Oxford: The University and the Cultural and Political life of Eighteenth-Century Britain and Beyond* (Oxford, 2023).

[13] John Le Neve, *Fasti Ecclesiae Anglicanae 1541–1857*, viii: *Bristol, Gloucester, Oxford and Peterborough Dioceses*, ed. J.M. Horn (1996), 85.

[14] For Boulter's anti-Jacobite leanings, see his *Foundation of Submission to Our Governors Considered: A Sermon Preached at St Olave's, Southwark, 26 November, 1715* (1715), 20, in which 'James III' was denounced as the 'popish bigotted Pretender'.

[15] 'Wadham College', in VCH, *A History of the County of Oxford*, iii: *The University of Oxford*, https://www.british-history.ac.uk/vch/oxon/vol3/pp279-287 (accessed 22 June 2022). Wadham was the only college to hang portraits of William III and George I in its hall: Ward, *Georgian Oxford*, 103–4. Baker succeeded Dunster in the wardenship and left the university to become bishop of Bangor. He was also rector of St Giles-in-the-Fields, London, and chaplain to George I on his Hanover progresses.

[16] ODNB, s.v. Hole, Matthew (1639/40–1730), Church of England clergyman and religious writer.

© 2024 The Authors. Parliamentary History published by John Wiley & Sons Ltd on behalf of Parliamentary History Yearbook Trust.

college's visitor, one of the strongest Whigs in Oxford, John Holland, was elected in 1709.[17] His controversial attempt, in co-operation with others at Merton of his persuasion, to fill six vacant fellowships exclusively with other Whigs in 1716 delighted the pro-Hanoverian press – a true display of 'English Spirit' according to *The Flying Post* of 12 March. Or, as the *St James's Evening Post* expressed it: 'The Gentlemen of Merton College take all the opportunities of distinguishing themselves from the factions in the university, and of proving to the world that they are sincerely in the service of his Majesty'.[18] A minority of Oxford students were ready for more overt pro-Hanoverian militancy. The Constitution Club, a body of young Whigs, many with connections to ministers, formed by some New College students met regularly to carouse, provoke, and parade their loyalist credentials under their president, William, Lord Hartington (1698–1755), grandson of the 1st duke of Devonshire, one of the 'Immortal Seven' who had invited the Prince of Orange to England in July 1688, and son and heir of the 2nd duke, lord steward of George I's household.[19] They were aggressive, socially confident, and ready to intrude their principles in Oxford when opportunity offered, and publicise them in the London press. More importantly, as things stood, they represented the political future.[20]

Whigs were therefore gradually moving at different levels into the university mainstream but internal rivalries within the Sunderland/Walpole/Townshend administration following the death of Earl Stanhope in February 1721 counted against their sponsoring a candidate at Oxford. Another material consideration was whether the two existing burgesses, both of them Hanoverian Tories, would present themselves to serve again in the Commons. The dutiful William Bromley, one of the most senior members of the House by this date, showed no sign of wanting to retire to his Warwickshire estate. His record of upholding a committed Tory line alongside attention to his constituents spoke for itself.[21] Bromley's probity could be taken for granted. Whatever his private reservations, he accepted the dynasty in possession. As did his colleague as burgess, Dr George Clarke (1661–1735), elected at a by-election in 1717. Clarke, a fellow of All Souls College since 1680, the man of business and supremely gifted amateur of the arts,[22] was judged by most senior Oxford politicians to be *sans pareil* as a candidate. As a young man, he had represented the university in James II's 1685 parliament, and he had had abundant administrative experience since the Revolution.[23] He was good-humoured, capable and attentive to his parliamentary responsibilities. But he was another court Tory, persona grata with the Oxford academic establishment, the

[17] Holland was made chaplain to the king and a canon of Salisbury in 1716 and a canon of Worcester in 1723. G.H. Martin and J.R.L. Highfield, *A History of Merton College, Oxford* (Oxford, 1997), 237–9; B.W. Henderson, *Merton College* (1899), 153–4.

[18] *St James's Evening Post*, 31 May–2 June 1716.

[19] For its members, see Philoxon [Richard Rawlinson], *A Full and Impartial Account of the Oxford Riots* (1715), 8–9.

[20] The Constitution Club broke up in 1718, having eventually caused the Whigs more embarrassment than good publicity. Ward, *Georgian Oxford*, 57, 61, 88–90, discusses the legal proceedings brought against the club in 1716–17.

[21] Geoffrey Holmes, *British Politics in the Age of Anne* (1967), 277–8.

[22] For Clarke's architectural achievement and ambition for rebuilding Oxford, see Matthew Craske, 'George Clarke's Oxford: The Patriotic Creation of a Monumental City', *History of Universities*, xxxv, pt 1 (2022), 187–211.

[23] Judge-advocate-general, 1684–1705; secretary-at-war, 1692–1704; joint-secretary to the admiralty, 1702–5; a lord of the admiralty, 1710–14. Tim Clayton, 'Clarke: Father and Son', in *All Souls under the Ancien Régime: Politics, Learning, & the Arts, c.1600–1850*, ed. S.J.D. Green and Peregrine Horden (Oxford, 2007), 117–31.

personification of the university's responsible politics as the hebdomadal board and most heads of houses wished to project them.

But neither Bromley nor Clarke represented the whole body of Tory opinion within Oxford, especially that substantial section that considered them too accommodating to the dynastic status quo and which looked to the exiled Stuarts as the true lodestar for loyalist Oxonians. These younger MAs, squeezed out of so much of the preferment stakes because of their politics, were growing frustrated that the university authorities appeared so reluctant to acknowledge their values or allow any them any sort of representation. That this suppression could have serious consequences concerned one anonymous senior don:

> If once the young and unthinking Part of the University meet with all Success against their Gouvernours, they like a furious horse, will too soon feel their own strength, and throw off all Submission, and, consequently, Opposition and Rebelliuon will be their first Principles.[24]

The signs were already there. When George Clarke was selected by senior academics as their preferred replacement for Sir William Whitelocke on the latter's death in 1717, there had been vexation among more partisan younger dons at what they viewed as an imposition. Their champion was Dr Pierce Dod, one of the medical fellows of All Souls and no friend to the College's Warden, Bernard Gardiner, a cautious Tory and former vice-chancellor (1711–15), related to Clarke by marriage.[25] It was reported by a Harleyite Tory canon of Christ Church that Dod 'has been used to give drink to young masters. In principles he is somewhat beyond a Tory'.[26] Dod withdrew before the contest in 1717 but he had laid down a marker: unless the two burgesses and regime conformists who formed the majority of the college heads took the Jacobite inclinations of the younger members of convocation more to heart, they could expect trouble when Bromley and Clarke stood for re-election.

Enter William King

Trouble duly came in the form of the civilian lawyer and academic firebrand Dr William King, principal of St Mary Hall.[27] King had been the favourite of the earl of Arran from the time of the latter's election as chancellor in 1715. King was first named his secretary (in which capacity he had served Arran's brother, Ormond), then installed at St Mary Hall at the chancellor's behest in 1719.[28] He made little effort to conceal his committed Jacobitism

[24] This was Provost Gibson of Queen's writing in the *Weekly Journal* on 10 Feb. 1722.

[25] Gardiner naturally championed Clarke's claims to the vacant seat: Ward, *Georgian Oxford*, 112, 121–2. So too did Bishop George Smalridge, dean of Christ Church, and Arthur Charlett, master of University College: Clayton, 'Clarke: Father and Son', 123–4. Dod was determin'd to study medicine without being ordained, to Gardiner's vexation: Wigelsworth, *All Souls College*, 71–85, esp. 67, 77–80, 85.

[26] HMC, *The Manuscripts of His Grace the Duke of Portland, preserved at Welbeck Abbey* (11 vols, 1892–1931), vii, 256. Dod resumed a level of amicable association with Clarke before the 1722 Election and cast his votes for him and Bromley. ODNB, s.v. Dod, Peirce (bap. 1683–1754), physician.

[27] William King, matric. Balliol, 9 July 1701, aged 16; BCL, 1709, DCL, 1715; called to the bar, Gray's Inn, 1712; advocate of Doctors' Commons, 20 Jan. 1716. See David Greenwood, *William King, Tory & Jacobite* (Oxford, 1969), 327, who calls him 'England's most forceful polemicist for the Jacobite cause'. He was an accomplished satirist and a formidable enemy.

[28] Greenwood, *William King*, 13, 19.

and made the most of his access to Arran to influence the chancellor's patronal selections. King was no friend of George Clarke, who in 1716 had moved to halt Lord Arran from making King an assessor in the chancellor's court, and he was bent on revenge. Well before the first general election under the Septennial Act was due, this turbulent Tory was lining himself up to be the mouthpiece and the parliamentary candidate of convocation members tired of the allegedly supine submissiveness of the university establishment towards the early Georgian order. King made no secret that his objective was to oust George Clarke, to be the voice of the disregarded, and to give all franchise holders in the contest a genuine choice: he was ready with his candidature to challenge the dominant 'influence' within the university as soon as the parliament of 1722 was dissolved and a new one summoned in March 1722.[29]

The specifically Oxonian contexts of William King standing for parliament should be seen within the wider picture of exceptional political flux nationally in the early spring of 1722. The reverberations from the South Sea scandal and the death of Lord Stanhope still echoed around the political world despite the damage limitation exercise by and for the Whig party overseen by Robert Walpole, first lord of the treasury since April 1721.[30] Though he had been forced to resign in favour of his rival, the Whig *éminence grise* remained Charles Spencer, 3rd earl of Sunderland, who retained the household post of groom of the stool and the proximity to George I that it conferred. Walpole's successful protection of Sunderland in the Commons induced no sense of gratitude in the latter, who was only too aware that Walpole henceforth had parity in government.[31] A balancing act was impossible because Sunderland had no intention of allowing Walpole permanent supremacy within Whig counsels. He wanted a general election as early as possible, preferably the summer of 1721,[32] and had pressed his views on the king, just as Walpole had argued against: the later the date, the more purchase Walpole would have on treasury patronage to be put at the disposal of candidates loyal to him.[33] His view prevailed and the general election was scheduled for the spring of 1722, the latest possible date it could be held under the provisions of the Septennial Act.

It became a contest between Walpole and Sunderland for the political advantage that securing the election of candidates loyal to them personally would bring. Sunderland sought to destroy Walpole as a political power broker. If that meant giving covert support to Tory factions, even openly Jacobite Tories who were standing against Walpolean candidates, it seems to have been a price worth paying.[34] There was also another factor at play: the

---

[29]He intimated his plan in a letter of 24 Oct. 1721 to a regular correspondent, Capt. Charles Halsted, who had been arrested in Oxford in autumn 1715 as a known Jacobite: TNA, SPD35/28/89.

[30]The 1720 reconciliation between George I and the estranged prince of Wales had brought Walpole and Viscount Townshend back into the government: B.W. Hill, *Sir Robert Walpole: 'Sole and Prime Minister'* (1989), 103–4.

[31]J.H. Plumb, *Sir Robert Walpole. Vol. I: The Making of a Statesman* (1972), 362–3; Gary Bennett, 'Jacobitism in the Rise of Walpole', in *Historical Perspectives: Studies in English Thought and Society: Essays in Honour of J.H. Plumb*, ed. Neil McKendrick, (1974), 75.

[32]*Copies of Some Letters from Mr Hutcheson, to the late Earl of Sunderland* (3rd edn, 1722), 17, 18 (5 Sept. 1721).

[33]William Coxe, *Memoirs of ... Sir Robert Walpole* (3 vols, 1798), ii, 217.

[34]'It is inconceivable that Sunderland had any serious intention to assist the Jacobites, but he was alive to the advanatges that could be derived from keeping up their expectations': G.M. Townend, 'The Political Career of the 3rd Earl of Sunderland', University of Edinburgh PhD, 1985, p. 296.

Atterbury Plot was underway with the objective of restoring 'James III'. Arran knew about it, as did Sunderland, and it is distinctly unlikely that William King did not. A Jacobite surge at the polls with an armed uprising to follow could provide Tory and Whig malcontents alike with a public future that increasingly looked otherwise closed to them in the circumstances of the early 1720s.

William King was standing. The tantalising question remained: would one of the Oxford Whigs also challenge the sitting Tory MPs, in effect acting as a spokesman for members of the university unequivocally committed to the Hanoverian succession and the current Whig administration? The emergence of a formidable Whig caucus within the university was still a work in progress, with its heartlands Wadham and Merton Colleges, though growing numbers elsewhere as in Jesus and Exeter Colleges. And these were all small colleges up against the predominance of Christ Church and Magdalen, not that such a problem had deterred King. True, Whigs were beginning to enter Christ Church without yet dissipating its essential Hanoverian Tory flavouring. And in terms of external interest that might work in their favour they might look to the Harcourt family of Stanton Harcourt and, latterly, of Nuneham Courtenay. Simon, 1st Lord Harcourt, the former lord chancellor and ally of Bolingbroke, one of those several well-established Tories with deep Oxford connections who, driven by ambition or avarice, could wait no longer and, courted by Sunderland, had drifted away from the party.[35]

Despite the appearance of party unanimity, any Whig putting his name forward would have had to decide which minister would command his loyalty. The extent to which the Whig interest in Oxford was divided between supporters of Sunderland and Walpole is hard to gauge, but a split can be presumed, especially with rumours correctly circulating that Sunderland was seeking an alliance with a section of the Tory party that would form the basis of a Whig-dominated coalition in the Commons.[36] This fissure would have made it less likely for a Whig candidate to command unanimous backing from Whigs of all shades of opinion. Neither Sunderland nor Walpole, for different reasons, was encouraging and, in those circumstances, the best recourse for Oxford Whigs bent on ousting Bromley and Clarke from the Commons might appear to be tactical voting, the *politique du pire*, to hold their noses and vote for King. There was a precedent. In the election in Convocation of a Camden professor of ancient history in May 1720, the Whig vote had gone to the lawyer Sedgwick Harrison (1683–1727), despite his being 'the most open and professed Turk of this place', an ally of William King's, and having minimal

---

[35] He was rewarded with an increased pension, a step up in the peerage to a viscountcy in 1721, and with readmission to the privy council the next year: HMC, *Portland*, vii, 266–74. Harcourt did not forget his ties to the university. See HMC, *Portland*, vii, 345, 19 Jan. 1723, for Harcourt setting up as a benefactor to Oriel. For the distrust of his new allies, see BL, Egerton MS 2540, f. 283: George Clarke to Edward Nicholas, 23 June 1724: 'Our malicious Whigs, who don't love him; set about a groundless story, I dare say, that his pension is stop'd, wch I believe they wish, for they don't love him; tho' he has been so serviceable'. A.S. Foord, *His Majesty's Opposition 1714–1830* (Oxford, 1964), 68.

[36] Townend, 'Sunderland', 274, 287, 294–6. Atterbury, Shippen, Bromley and the earl of Orrery were all approached, but the negotiations came to nothing: HMC, Portland, v, 625 (22 Aug. 1721); Bennett, *Jacobitism in the Rise of Walpole*, 76–7.

qualifications as a historian.[37] Harrison, a fellow of All Souls, had been elected to the chair.[38]

With a general election looming, contests for appointment to senior academic posts might be considered dress rehearsals for the main event. Tories were, on the whole, disappointed that Sunderland had been unable to have parliament dissolved that summer (a new session began in October 1721),[39] but at least the delay gave them more time to make ready. King's standing was not a last-minute decision and it was plain to Bromley, Clarke, and their supporters that the sitting members would not have a clear run. If his campaign could be effectively organised, King was likely to mount a formidable challenge to the narrowly based, academic status quo inside the university, and he and his allies had begun the war of words some weeks before parliament was dissolved at the beginning of March 1722.

His appeal lay less in his Jacobitism (though his convictions on that score were far from off-putting to a range of electors) than his acting as a standard-bearer against the overweening influence of heads of houses in putting up candidates without any reference back to the university electorate. King stood for the rights of individual electors, for the independent voter, and that insistence held an appeal for disgruntled Tories and Whigs alike. For Tories who were tired of representation by *politiques* of the Bromley and (especially) Clarke cast, whatever they thought of him personally, King's undubitable commitment to the 'honest cause' was welcome.[40] Jacobitism had moved into the mainstream of Tory politics after 1714 (not least because of the party's exclusion from power and preferment). University voters were now given the option of backing a candidate who best matched their own dynastic preference, whether Hanoverian or Jacobite. The stakes had been raised. This also made a divided Tory vote likely, a possibility that might just be enough to induce any Whig candidate to take the second seat from under their eyes. But, as the campaign began, there was no sign of one appearing, leaving the Whig vote one to be bid for.

The Election Campaign

King's campaign was run by Sedgwick Harrison. The two men were contemporaries snd Harrison had at least won an election. Beyond that, little is known about their personal

---

[37] Quoted in Ward, *Georgian Oxford*, 123. Sedgwick Harrison, fellow of All Souls, 1706; Camden professor, 1720–27. See *Remarks and Collections of Thomas Hearne*, ed. C.E. Doble, D.W. Rannie, and H.E. Salter (11 vols, Oxford Historical Society, ii, vii, xiii, xxxiv, xlii–xliii, xlviii, l, lxv, lxvii, lxxii, 1885–1921), i, 301 (3 Nov. 1706). The other contenders were William Denison of University College and John White of Christ Church, a lawyer and former senior proctor. Harrison only delivered his second lecture in May 1724. H.S. Jones, 'The Foundation and History of the Camden Chair', *Oxoniensia*, viii–ix (1943), 12–13. See also M.L. Clarke, 'Classical Studies', in *HUO*, v, 515.

[38] 'He was a man that might have done good Things, had he minded his Studies. But being of an invidious, malicious, furious temper, he seldom spoke well of any one, but was for doing what mischief he could': Hearne, *Collections*, vi, 106. His aunt had held Queen Mary of Modena's warming pan at the birth of 'James III'. He was another antagonist of Gardiner to whom in Aug. 1720 he refused the return of college plate lodged in the bursary. See Christ Church, Wake Papers, vol. 16, ff. 162–5. Thanks to Robin Darwall-Smith for this reference.

[39] Earl of Orrery to 'James III' on 28 Oct. 1721 in Lord Mahon, *History of England* (7 vols, 1836–70), ii, Appendix xvii.

[40] Paul Kléber Monod pointedly notes that 'Oxford was perhaps the sole constituency in England where a staunch Tory could be opposed on the basis of his not being enough of a Jacobite' in *Jacobitism and the English People, 1688–1788* (Cambridge, 1989), 277.

relationship, but their mutual cooperation in 1722 appears harmonious enough.[41] Harrison had to work fast and trade on the popularity he had demonstrated in winning the Camden chair by gathering votes from both sides of the political spectrum. The general election was spread out nationally across March and April, but the university poll was scheduled for 21 March, giving both sides less than three weeks to wage their campaign. Harrison's task inside Oxford was to stir up opinion in the smaller colleges and present William King as the man who would be their champion against the hebdomadal board and the Christ Church/Magdalen bloc. To lay the emphasis thus would offset the disadvantages in King's candidature (putting his Jacobitism aside): his lack of parliamentary experience, his relative youth, and his capacity for sarcasm and intemperate rhetoric.[42]

King could expect minimal endorsement from the chancellor and the vice-chancellor. Relations between the principal of St Mary Hall and Lord Arran had grown less cordial by the early 1720s despite the latter's covert Jacobite sympathies. The college heads argued (against citable precedents) that the university's sitting MPs were entitled to sit until they gave serious offence, and did their best to secure the public backing of the chancellor. At the end of December 1721 he acceded to pressure from a majority of the heads of houses and replaced King as his secretary.[43] He latterly drew up a letter in favour of George Clarke only for it to be hastily withdrawn when it was pointed out by the pro-King faction that a peer could not legally interfere in the election of MPs.[44] Neither was much to be expected from the vice-chancellor since 1718, Dr Robert Shippen (1675–1745), principal of Brasenose College, and a particular favourite of Arran's.[45] Shippen's Jacobite links stood out dramatically.[46] Indeed, the years in office of this high-flying cleric coincided with his brother, William Shippen, scarcely concealing his efforts in the Commons and beyond to restore the Pretender, culminating in the Atterbury Plot.[47] But Robert took a different tack in the first years of George I's reign. He was only too aware, as was Arran, that the most senior leaders of the university could not be seen to give any public sanction to actions or words that could be construed as subversive. Shippen and King do not appear to have been personally close, despite their similar politics, though as vice-chancellor, Shippen had not tried to block the latter's nomination to the St Mary Hall principalship in 1719.

[41] In some manuscript verses circulated against King after the election (later published), he was represented as being Harrison's tool throughout and compared to the lead character in Dryden's comedy *Sir Martin Mar-all: A Satire upon Physicians* (1755), 60–3.

[42] Greenwood, *William King*, 27.

[43] Canon Stratford of Christ Church, a Harleyite averse to King, reported that the chancellor 'to make his dismission less disgraceful gave him leave to resign': HMC, *Portland*, vii, 712. Cf. Hearne, *Collections*, vii, 318 (18 Jan. 1722).

[44] 'A Master of Arts', *An Account of the Late Election of the University of Oxford for Members of Parliament* (Oxford, 1722), 8–12.

[45] His Oxford career is summarised in J.M. Crook, *Brasenose: The Biography of an Oxford College* (Oxford, 2008), 123–41. See also R.W. Jeffery, 'An Oxford Don Two Hundred Years Ago', unpub. MS, Brasenose College Archives, MPP 56F4/10.

[46] Cf. the designation of Robert Shippen as 'a Hanoverian Jacobite' in Crook, *Brasenose*, 127.

[47] Eveline Cruickshanks and Howard Erskine-Hill, *The Atterbury Plot* (Basingstoke, 2004), 52, 71, 157, 189. William Shippen received a personal letter dated 1 Mar. 1722 from 'James III' announcing that an attempt at restoring him without foreign aid was imminent: BL, Add MS 78796, f. 116.

Since that date, the two men had clashed over collegiate appointments,[48] though King later suggested to Hearne that what had decisively turned the vice-chancellor against him was his refusal to withdraw and make way for Shippen's brother, William, as candidate for the university seat in lieu of Clarke.[49] With the vice-chancellor the designated returning officer in parliamentary elections, King could anticipate no favours from that quarter.

Neither could King expect most college heads to do his campaign any favours, convinced as most of them were (including the Tory ones) that a resigned Hanoverianism was the only viable path to tread. They could discern clearly enough that the basis of his campaign was directed against their overweening interest. One head, the provost of the Queen's College, John Gibson (first cousin of Bishop Edmund Gibson of Lincoln), was so incensed by what King was doing that he joined the press campaign against him.[50] According to Hearne, Gibson put out a circular with references to such as 'the younger and unthinking part of the university', and 'the green understanding of youth'. Gibson scaremongered when he contended that Tory supremacy in Oxford might be overturned should a 'great man' organise the growing whig interest.[51] King's supporters saw no necessary disadvantage to their interest should that 'great man' turn out to be Lord Sunderland. For if, in this contest of the two Whig titans, Sunderland triumphed over Walpole, there was a chance that he would at least bring Tories into alliance with him in government. At best, he would secure a Stuart restoration and a revised constitutional settlement from which Oxford was likely to emerge as a beneficiary.

King and Harrison played again and again on the cavalier and patronising treatment of younger Tories within Oxford and, themselves making use of the press to that end, went public with a letter to Lord Arran printed in *The Weekly Journal* that adduced evidence for their claim. The rubric that prohibited candidates from canvassing in person and within ten miles of the university could not prevent each side from exchanging slanderous insults.[52] There were weeks of horse-trading, intrigue, intercollegiate alliances, misinformation, threats, promises and 'treating'.[53] The task of King and Harrison, in the first instance, was to persuade voters to resist college pressure to cast their franchise unanimously, and to make it clear that it was George Clarke, not William Bromley, whom they specifically sought to dislodge. Heads of houses, not all as vehemently as John Gibson, made the case for Clarke to their colleagues in the common room; such was very much the case in Lincoln, on the part of the incoming rector, John Morley, a Hanoverian Tory who detested King.[54]

---

[48] Ward, *Georgian Oxford*, 114–15. Robert Shippen appears to have been disliked by many Tories on personal grounds: Crook, *Brasenose*, 124, 130–1.

[49] Hearne, *Collections*, vii, 401 (15 Sept. 1722). Robert Shippen also wanted Bromley to stand down in favour of the Hon. Robert Digby. There would thus have been a completely new ticket.

[50] Of Westmorland extraction; fellow, 1701; provost since 1716. Gibson had already become a canon of Lincoln and was on the look-out for further preferment which he later secured. J.R. Magrath, *The Queen's College* (2 vols, Oxford, 1921), ii, 83–4.

[51] *The Weekly Journal*, 10 Feb. 1721/2, reprinted in Hearne, *Collections*, vii, 328–9.

[52] T.H.B. Oldfield, *An Entire and Complete History, Political and Personal, of the Boroughs of Great Britain* (2 vols, 1792), ii, 387.

[53] Rex, *University Representation*, 72. 'Treating' in 1722 does not appear to have been on the scale adopted in 1705 by the high-flying Tory candidate Sir Humphrey Mackworth, who had distributed his tracts across the university gratis and sent crates of wine to college common rooms: Mary Ransome, 'The Parliamentary Career of Sir Humphrey Mackworth, 1701–1713', *University of Birmingham Historical Journal*, i (1947–8), 232–54.

[54] Vivian Green, *The Commonwealth of Lincoln College, 1427–1977* (Oxford, 1979), 306.

Among others, the political weathercock George Carter, provost of Oriel,[55] the regius professor of Hebrew, Robert Clavering;[56] and John Holland, warden of Merton, all tried to gain ministerial favour by behaving as good court Whigs and lobbying for the two sitting members. This pressure was not easy to ignore for younger fellows hoping for a college living or a university post in due course. The logic of the cooking pot dictated a vote for Clarke. Their only comfort was the intimation they were offered that William Bromley, whose position most parties viewed as unassailable, was happy to have George Clarke as his colleague.[57] There seems no doubt that all sorts of intimidation and arm-twisting went on, with King and his followers deprecated as 'banditti', and potential King voters suspected of having outstanding bills to Oxford tradesmen threatened by debt collectors.[58]

Electoral victory would hang in large part on bringing out the voters. But who exactly were they? All parties could loosely agree that foundationers (that is, fellows and scholars of a college or hall who were graduates) whether resident or not and those permanently resident inside the precincts of the university (whether foundationers or not) could vote. As to those holding honorary degrees, much in practice depended on *how* they voted. It was broadly the same story for graduates who had kept their names on their college roll – but that was the limit of consensus. And when elections came, the scope for flouting these rules was large.[59] A generous interpretation, the one most likely to favour William King, was that, among the *extranei*, MAs who had allowed their names to lapse unintentionally were no less eligible. Of course, it was the college authorities who had control of the buttery books and there is evidence that heads of houses who favoured the sitting members struck out the names of graduates they considered did not meet a narrow interpretation of eligibility and were likely to vote for William King. Even at the poll, the vice-chancellor claimed the right to find fault with the qualification of individual electors via the scrutineers (scrutators in Oxford parlance) who, though sworn to secrecy, reported to him as returning officer.[60]

If King and his supporters were to beat George Clarke for the second seat, as well as winning over as many of the younger, resident MAs as they could, they had to induce those of that status who had – or thought they had – kept their names in the college buttery books but lived outside Oxford to come into the city and vote. These would be mainly Tory parsons, squires and the occasional lawyer resident within a 50-mile radius of Oxford, men with a double vote as county freeholders, and sufficiently committed to the 'honest cause', as personified in William King, that they would be in the city on 21 March. King

---

[55]Carter (d. 1727), provost since 1708, was a careful careerist, who nurtured his contact with Archbishop William Wake and Oriel's visitor (as bishop of Lincoln) Edmund Gibson. He was a royal chaplain from 1717. 'All us Whigs are against him [King] to a man', he told Archbishop Wake: Christ Church, Wake Papers, vol. 16, f. 95 (22 Dec. 1721). Carter had not been a Whig before 1714; neither were all Oxford Whigs anti-King.

[56]Robert Clavering (1671–1747); fellow and tutor of University College, 1701; canon of Christ Church and regius professor, 1715–47; bishop of Llandaff, 1725; trans. Peterborough, 1729. ODNB, s.v. Clavering, Robert (1675/6–1747), orientalist and bishop of Peterborough.

[57]University managers also looked for endorsement from Tory grandees in the county. Among major Oxford patrons contacted was the 2nd earl of Abingdon. He was asked (so said Sedgwick Harrison) in no uncertain terms to exclude his brother, the Hon. Edward Bertie, Student of Christ Church, from his will for promising to vote for King: *An Account*, 22–3.

[58]*An Account*, 17–18, 23.

[59]Sutherland, 'Laudian Statutes', 194–6.

[60]Even his opponents conceded that Shippen chose not to exercise this power on 21 Mar. 1722: *An Account*, 28.

© 2024 *The Authors.* Parliamentary History *published by John Wiley & Sons Ltd on behalf of Parliamentary History Yearbook Trust.*

and his allies in the colleges seem to have targeted these groups as best they could, and hoped for pressure on electors from relatives, parents of pupils, and lay and ecclesiastical patrons. They certainly had access to some if not all the college buttery books and it is likely that letters (though they do not appear to have survived) went out to non-residents adjudged sympathetic. The pro-King lobby drove home the point that Clarke could not be relied on to support the Church, reminding potential voters that he had voted against the Occasional Conformity Bill (still an emotive subject in English parsonages) nearly 20 years previously.[61] The result of the contest showed how vigorous their whipping-in had been, despite the narrow window of opportunity before the poll.

The Vote and the Aftermath

Voting in Convocation lasted from 9 a.m. until 4.30 p.m. on 21 March. For all his efforts, William King came third and last when the results of the poll were declared. It was not even close: Bromley had 337 votes, Clarke 278 and King came in with 159, well under 20 per cent of the total. King's side demanded a scrutiny of the votes on the next morning. The number of so-called dubious votes were 60 for Bromley, 49 for Clarke, and 36 for King. But even admitting those, the result would have left each candidate at a comparable distance with 276, 229 and 123 respectively. King's interest 'thereupon acquiesc'd' early in the proceedings of the 22nd.[62] The 'official' total showed a remarkable 774 votes cast, the highest in any Oxford University parliamentary election before 1768.[63] King's numerous adversaries in the collegiate establishment at once opted to drive home their advantage and further discredit him. The hebdomadal board ordered Joseph Bowles, the head keeper of the Bodleian, to publish the poll and this, predictably, showed that King had made few inroads into the votes of the resident foundation members and, controversially, the word 'doubtful' was inserted against the names of many of those who had voted for King.[64] The result as given in this published poll showed that the heads had carried the day for Bromley and Clarke by comfortable majorities in Brasenose, Christ Church, New College, Oriel, Queen's, University and Hart Hall.[65]

[61] Ward, *Georgian Oxford*, 125. Harrison later claimed 'our Cause was all along promoted by personal Friendships, and by such Influences only as the Justice and Necessity of the undertaking suggested': *An Account*, 33. He was stretching a point.

[62] Hearne, *Collections*, vii, 341ff. Ward, *Georgian Oxford*, 126, gave Bromley 338 votes. It has been observed that 'Scrutinies were little more than a ploy in the electoral battle, … an attempt to unsettle a victorious side with the threat of a petition … Scrutinies rarely succeeded in seating defeated candidates': Frank O'Gorman, *Voters, Patrons and Parties: The Unreformed Electorate of Hanoverian England, 1734–1832* (Oxford, 1989), 164.

[63] University of Oxford Archives (hereafter UOA), MS SP/C/5. What cannot be ascertained is the number of those with a vote who chose not to use it. King secured the exclusive vote of no less than 86 plumpers.

[64] *A True Copy of the Poll for Members of Parliament for the University of Oxford Digested into an Alphabetical Order* (Oxford, 1722). Hearne called Bowles dissimulating and an 'egregious Coxcomb and Rascal'. He noted, too, that Jones of Balliol College, one of King's allies, had colluded in publishing what Hearne called 'this very poor, blockish Paper, rendering himself thereby the Scorn of all mankind': Hearne, *Collections*, vii, 349. Whatever its defects, *A True Copy* constitutes the earliest poll-book for this constituency.

[65] At Brasenose, Shippen made sure that 21 out of 23 possible votes went to Clarke: *A True Copy*, 4–5; Crook, *Brasenose*, 136.

But King had accumulated a considerable protest vote across the university with many second votes going to him. At Balliol (championed by Joseph Hunt, the very new master),[66] King (a Balliol graduate himself), was the first choice of most resident members, whereas at Lincoln, five fellows and four MAs defied the new rector's blandishments and backed King, four of them voting only for him.[67] He also did well among Tories at Jesus, Magdalen, St John's and Trinity, while failing to gain majority support.[68] St Mary Hall, of course, was unanimously behind its principal. Most resourcefully and remarkably, King secured the vote of many committed anti-Jacobite Whigs. Exeter College (including Rector Hole) as a man backed him; so did non-court Whigs at Merton and Wadham, both pro-Hanoverian bulwarks. Even Richard Meadowcourt, the fanatically pro-Hanoverian nephew of Warden Holland of Merton and steward of the Constitution Club, voted for King.[69] This was no small achievement, one that suggested a direct or indirect approach to ministers, either via Lord Chancellor Macclesfield, a follower of Sunderland, who had recently acquired the Shirburn Castle estate in Oxfordshire (his purse-bearer, Sir John Doyly, had been seen in mingling in university circles during March),[70] or possibly through Robert Walpole himself. Or perhaps both.

The speedy publication of *A True Copy of the Poll* did not end the controversy about the eligibility of voters, for it raised as many questions as it answered. It used a set of symbols to indicate good, bad and doubtful votes without offering any technical differentiation between these loose categories, so that attaching any precise significance to them is hard. King's supporters were aghast and, within days, announced plans for a riposte that would offer, 'An exact Copy of the Poll, in the manner it was taken, … giving a full Account of the unwarrantable Proceedings of the Vice-Chancellor, and of some other Heads of Houses'.[71] With the author given as a 'Master of Arts' (it was probably Sedgwick Harrison),[72] it was eventually published in August 1722 as *An Account of the Late Election of the University of Oxford for Members of Parliament*, and made public the alleged extent of pressure, even intimidation, deployed by most college heads to ferment anti-King feeling.[73]

Given the margin of 119 votes between himself and Clarke, it might be thought that King would resume the normal course of academic life beaten but unbowed. Not so. Despite

---

[66]His predecessor, John Baron, had only died on 20 Jan. 1722. Hunt (1681–1726) later moved to promote a court interest at Balliol. Ward, *Georgian Oxford*, 116–17; Church of England Database, https://theclergydatabase.org.uk/ (accessed 24 Nov. 2023), person ID 43710.

[67]*A True Copy*, 8–9; Green, *Lincoln College*, 320.

[68]Hearne reported that at one point King had a majority of votes at Magdalen, though not President Joseph Harwar's: Hearne, *Collections*, vii, 401.

[69]ODNB, s.v. Meadowcourt, Richard (c.1695–1760), Church of England clergyman and literary critic. Meadowcourt's first patron, Earl Cowper, was acting in conjunction with opposition Tories immediately before his death in 1723.

[70]HMC, *Portland*, vii, 317–8. 2nd Bt (c.1670–1746), head of a family resident at Chiselhampton since the reign of Henry VIII. Doyly stood unsuccessfully for Abingdon at this general election. *HPC, 1715–1754*, www.historyofparliamentonline.org/ (accessed 6 May 2022), s.v. Abingdon.

[71]*The Post Boy*, 10 Apr. 1722.

[72]Michael Treadwell, 'On False and Misleading Imprints in the London Book Trade, 1660–1750', in *Fakes and Frauds: Varieties of Deception in Print and Manuscript*, ed. Robin Myers and Michael Harris (Winchester, 1989), 41–3.

[73]Hearne, *Collections*, vii, 393. According to *An Account* (2), there were 'at least six hundred new Voters who never were represented, which far Exceed the number on ther present Poll'.

intimations of expulsion if he persisted,[74] over the summer he and his embittered supporters accumulated materials to form a convincing basis on which to unseat George Clarke. Two petitions were eventually sent up to the new parliament against the election result, King's own alleging the illegal practices of the vice-chancellor, Robert Shippen.[75] Should King achieve his objective it would only be removing one Tory (Clarke) in favour of another (himself), and it therefore made little sense tactically for the upper echelons of the party to back this manouevre, especially as William Bromley was of their number. They were looking rather to challenge Whig returnees where the electoral margins were tight. The 1722 general election had seen an exceptional number of contests (154) but the Tories had been unable to capitalise on the fault-lines within the ministry and the Whigs gained more seats than they had done in 1715, leaving the Tories with a mere 170 MPs by the time the final returns were announced in April.[76] But at least there were two Tories sitting for Oxford University and in a time of political readjustment and realignment, having William King sitting in the house of commons would not make for party unity.

In proceeding to petition the Commons, King and his allies within the university were on their own. And they did so against the backdrop of two events that further transformed the political landscape. Firstly, Lord Sunderland, who had campaigned up and down the country on behalf of his followers (including some pliant Tories), died on 19 April, leaving Robert Walpole and Lord Townshend in command of the administration.[77] Then, in May, news began to break concerning the Atterbury Plot, damaging the probity and professions of the Tories in the parliamentary session that began in October.[78] It remained to be seen how, if at all, these developments would affect the outcome of William King's bid to unseat George Clarke.[79]

King decided to come up to London to support his petition in person. It was submitted on the same day (25 October 1722) as a similar one presented by Sedgwick Harrison, Robert Brynker of Jesus College (someone who had inspected the votes cast at the poll for King's side), Joseph Sanford of Balliol College, and four others from Balliol, three of them very recent graduates.[80] It did not work to his advantage. There appears to have been covert direct or indirect contact with Robert Walpole or one of his senior aides and news of this remarkable twist to events somehow became public. It was reported that Walpole had affirmed that King had solicited his interest to obtain a favourable hearing for his petition before the house of commons on condition that King advised him about senior members of the university who were disloyal and disaffected. This disclosure opened up a second front of possible collusion between William King and Robert Walpole, so much so that King published a public statement of denial in *The Evening Post* of 27 November 1722.[81] Given

---

[74] *An Account*, 34.

[75] Ward, *Georgian Oxford*, 114–15.

[76] Plumb, *Walpole*, 377–8; Jeremy Black, 'Introduction: An Age of Political Stability', in *Britain in the Age of Walpole*, ed. Jeremy Black (Basingstoke, 1984), 7.

[77] Townend, 'Sunderland', 302, 304.

[78] Ministers were aware of a plot around the time of Sunderland's decease, probably within days of George Kelly bringing the earl of Mar's proposals across from France: Bennett, *Jacobitism and the Rise of Walpole*, 83, 91.

[79] Hill, *The King's Great Minister*, 118–19.

[80] Briefly summarised in *CJ*, xx, 43. For Sanford, see Balliol College Archives, MS 459, 'Old Joe Sanford's Notebook'.

[81] *The Evening Post*, 27 Nov. 1722; Hearne, *Collections*, viii, 21–2.

Walpole's eagerness to secure details of the Atterbury Plot at this time,[82] one should not discount the strong possibility that he wanted to gather in informants wherever they were to be had. The story did King no credit within academic circles and he sensibly decided to cut his losses. Though both petitions were referred to the committee of privileges and elections, there is no evidence the committee took any action on them.[83] The election of Bromley and Clarke stood; William King had traded on his role as a marginalised man within the Oxford academic establishment but his challenge had failed.

Conclusion

What, then, does the university contest of 1722 indicate about its electorate? First, it brings into focus the surprising uncertainty in practice about entitlement to the franchise, a persistent ambiguity that both sides could try to exploit to their advantage, thereby adding an additionally cantankerous edge to the proceedings. The Oxford heads wanted a narrow interpretation of the franchise and a paper prepared by counsel on their behalf around this time argued somewhat tendentiously that the franchise was restricted to doctors and masters *actualiter creati* who had paid their fees and kept their names in the buttery books for six months prior to the election.[84] A further clarification of the basis of the university franchise looked desirable, though the obstacle was, as always, the Laudian code of 1636. Eventually, in 1759 a form of statute was drafted by the hebdomadal board for regulating membership of convocation. Objections were raised as to its legality and it was sent for counsel's opinion. The caveats were thereafter discounted and the explanatory statute was passed at the second attempt in July 1760.[85] Secondly, despite the official prohibition on campaigning within and around the city of Oxford, the scale of unofficial lobbying that went on within and between the colleges and halls was considerable, tempered and intensified as it was by personal rivalries and grudges. Thirdly, there was the appetite of the non-resident university members, whether Tory or Whig, for an electoral contest in which they could do something to register their discontent at the way the hebdomadal board and its gentry allies between them carved up the representation of the university. The window for voting was only about ten days, but the exceptional total of nearly 400 votes cast is a testimony to the determination of many graduates to put time aside and travel to Oxford and vote.

But King's defeat also confirmed how much in practice a candidate's chances depended on the backing of the hebdomadal board and the college heads. Without their endorsement, putting one's name forward right down to a contest was, unless circumstances were exceptional, hopelessly heroic. Bromley and Clarke would go on to hold their seats for life,

---

[82] G.V. Bennett, *The Tory Crisis in Church and State, 1688–1730: The Career of Francis Atterbury, Bishop of Rochester* (Oxford, 1975), 246–57.

[83] Greenwood, *William King*, 35. For the expense and organisational difficulties of petitioning, gathering names, transporting witnesses, see James Harris: 'Controverted Elections', https://ecppec.ncl.ac.uk/features/controverted-elections/ (accessed 10 June 2023).

[84] UOA, MS SP/C/6, 'Concerning the qualifications of an elector in the elections of burgesses for the University of Oxford'. It dated from 1723.

[85] Griffiths, *Statutes*, pp. xvi–xix, 310–13. The second statute passed confirmed the prohibition of university members becoming MPs for the city of Oxford. See also Wilfrid Prest, *William Blackstone: Law and Letters in the Eighteenth Century* (Oxford, 2008), 172–5; Sutherland, 'Laudian Statutes', 198–203.

Bromley for 30 years until his death in 1732 and Clarke for 17 until his in 1736. Significantly, when a contest next occurred, in the by-election to replace Clarke in 1737, the challenger was not a maverick Tory but a court Whig. Although he did not prevail, the party, in the shape of the Hon. Robert Trevor of Queen's and All Souls, was finally ready to confront Tory hegemony at the polls.[86] The Tories, it seemed, had, for the time being, learnt their lesson from the 1722 experience and closed ranks in the face of steadily increasing Whig influence in most of the colleges of which Trevor's candidature was a token.[87] And despite King's defeat, Oxford college heads could be successfully returned to parliament as a university burgess. Hence the presence in the Commons between 1737 and 1745 of Dr Edward Butler, the serving president of Magdalen College, and a former vice-chancellor (1728–32). The difference was that Butler was adjudged a 'safe' choice by his academic peers whereas King was not.[88]

Having proved unable to exploit popular disaffection with the regime in the 1722 general election and with Walpole ruthlessly using the details – such as they were – of the Atterbury Plot to consolidate his power, the Tories were vulnerable to further punitive moves by ministers. That was particularly the case in Oxford whose chancellor, Lord Arran, was implicated by association in plans for a Stuart restoration to be led by his predecessor as chancellor, his brother the duke of Ormond. Despite the odds, Walpole left him alone and Arran survived. With the 1722 plot a fiasco and Jacobitism, for the time being, a liability, Arran saw the expediency of distancing himself from treasonable politics for the sake of the university, a tacking that was reflected *inter alia* in the greater diversity of some of his nominations to the vice-chancellorship.[89] For their part, ministers talked no more of a general visitation of the English universities and redoubled efforts to offer patronage inducements to court academic goodwill and encourage further defections from Tory ranks. Thus in 1723 Bishop Gibson (with Walpole's blessing) launched a scheme under which 12 dons from each English university were to take up duties as Whitehall Preachers in the Chapel Royal for a month each. It was followed in 1724 by the endowment of regius professorships of modern history.[90]

For the remainder of the 1720s, the crown and the University of Oxford therefore tried to co-exist with such mutual grace as they could muster. And in the general election of 1727 that followed the accession of George II (from which Oxonians intially hoped for much)

---

[86] Ward, *Georgian Oxford*, 153–5. Trevor was the son of Thomas, 1st Lord Trevor, a Tory nominee as lord chief justice in 1712, who had made his peace with Walpole and served in his cabinet between 1726 and his death in 1730.

[87] As another, later defeated, candidate, the orientalist and lawyer William Jones, told John Wilkes: 'A Whig candidate for Oxford will never have any chance except at a time (if that time should ever come) when the Tory interest shall be almost equally divided': BL, Add. MS 30877, f. 90 (7 Sept. 1780).

[88] Butler stood after William Bromley the younger died suddenly within weeks of his defeating Robert Trevor. The Oxford Whigs did not field another candidate. HMC, *Reports on the Manuscripts of the Earl of Eglinton, Sir J. Stirling Maxwell, Bart., C.S.H. Drummond Moray, Esq., C.F. Weston Underwood, Esq., and G. Wingfield Digby, Esq.* (1885), 487, 490; *HPC, 1715–1754*, s.v. Edward Butler.

[89] His narrow escape is discussed in Nigel Aston, 'The Great Survivor: Charles Butler, Earl of Arran and the Oxford Chancellorship, 1715–1758', *History of Universities*, xxxv, pt 1 (2022), 359–61.

[90] For the Whitehall Preachers, see Norman Sykes, *Edmund Gibson, Bishop of London, 1669–1748* (1926), 94–6. George Clarke was shown by Arran 'a most gracious letter to him' from the king regarding the Oxford professorship: BL, Egerton MS 2540, f. 265: Clarke to Nicholas, 10 May 1724. For the king's personal interest in the professorships, see Ragnhild Hatton, *George I: Elector and King* (1978), 36.

Bromley and Clarke were returned without a contest. Oxford Whigs, meanwhile, lost no opportunity to remind ministers of their witness to the regime: the vigorous anti-Jacobite sermon preached at St Mary's church in 1723 by John Wynne of Jesus College (fellow 1718–25), published as *The Duty of Studying to be Quiet, and to do our own Business, Explain'd and Recommended* (1724), is a good instance of that reflex. As for Dr King, he turned back to college affairs, his writing, and litigation involving his family in Ireland. He would burst again onto the national scene a generation later in 1749, not with another parliamentary bid, but with one of the most notorious public orations of the century, his crypto-Jacobite *Reddeat* speech on the opening of the Radcliffe Library in Oxford in 1749.[91]

[91]'The Opening of the Radcliffe Library in 1749', *Bodleian Quarterly Record*, i (1915), 165–72.

Parliamentary History, Vol. 43, pt. 1 (2024), pp. 91–111

Pittite Triumph and Whig Failure in the Cambridge University Constituency, 1780–96[*]

DAVID COWAN

University of Cambridge

Cambridge University has been featured in a wide range of studies of the long 18th century, but few have focused exclusively on the dynamics behind its politics. This is surprising since many of the Cambridge University electors were close to leading parliamentarians. The Cambridge University constituency was contested at each of the three successive general elections from 1780 onwards until 1796. Parliamentary contests often brought Cambridge University's political tensions into focus, which is why a detailed analysis of the poll books can demonstrate how different networks within the university behaved and could define the performance of candidates for the constituency. The relationships between the chancellors, vice-chancellors, high stewards, university officers, college heads, fellows, senate members and members of parliament who collectively made up the leadership are fundamental to understanding the electorate of Cambridge University. These relationships, in terms of friendships, alliances and rivalries, also influenced political and patronage networks within the university. William Pitt the Younger's success in changing the political complexion of Cambridge University is part of the broader realignment in British politics during the final two decades of the 18th century. Under the pressure of these events, Whig unity would come to an end as new divisions between ministerialists and reformers emerged. The experience of Cambridge University can shed light on the national shifts as well as how electioneering was carried out in the university parliamentary constituencies.

Keywords: American Revolution; Cambridge University; evangelicalism; Fox–North coalition; French Revolution; party politics; poll books; William Pitt the Younger; whiggery

Introduction

The years between the general elections of 1780 and 1796 saw a process of realignment in British politics. This shifting of political identities is very clear in Cambridge University. In a period of 16 years, William Pitt the Younger went from coming bottom of the poll in 1780 to winning the seat unopposed in 1796. During that time, Pitt also succeeded in winning parliamentary majorities as prime minister and establishing Cambridge University as a Pittite stronghold. It is a rapid ascent to political dominance that can help historians

[*]Thank you to Matthew Grenby and the ECPPEC team for inviting me to contribute to this special issue. I would also like to thank Andrew Thompson for his support and feedback on the research.

of the long 18th century to understand the shifting electoral landscape of the 1780s and 1790s.

These elections can also help historians to appreciate how the behaviour of late-Hanoverian electorates could change during periods of war and peace. In the years between the general elections of 1780 and 1796, Britain sustained a series of shocks from the revolutionary wars in America and France, as well as constitutional crises at home. This triggered significant churn in the party system, particularly in 1782–4 and 1793–4, as political polarisation intensified and old loyalties disintegrated. It is notable how the transition from war to peace and return to war affected the pace and nature of political realignment.

The response of late-Hanoverian electorates to these events can be examined in detail through the example of Cambridge University. Global political upheaval provoked strong reactions from across the ideological spectrum, setting the agenda and shaping partisan attachments in the university. For much of the reigns of George I and George II, Cambridge University had been a secure Whig seat. Over the course of the 1780s and 1790s this ideological cohesion collapsed and gave way to fresh political identities.

The Cambridge University Electorate

During the 18th century, the universities of Cambridge, Oxford, and Dublin had their own parliamentary constituencies. These constituencies were established in 1603 and would exist until their abolition in 1950. These constituencies provided a limited means for people outside of the propertied elite to participate in national politics. Instead of property, eligibility for these constituencies was largely defined by education. Members of the senate, which was the governing body of the university, held the right to vote. This required holding a doctorate or Master of Arts from the university and paying the significant sum of £4 or £5 a year to be kept on the college books, or being registered as *commorantes in villa*, which meant being unattached to a college but residing in the town.[1] Certain senate members were excluded from voting, including bishops, peers and minors. The members of parliament were elected on a first-past-the-post voting system until 1918 when it was changed to single transferable vote. The electorate included around 500 people during the later 18th century. To put this in perspective, the borough of Cambridge had an electorate of around 150 men whereas the county of Cambridgeshire had an electorate of around 3,000.[2]

Voting took place in person, but electors did not proclaim their decision in front of others. Instead, electors wrote their vote on slips of paper which were then handed to the vice-chancellor, acting as the returning officer. College heads, fellows and other senior members of the university who resided in Cambridge voted regularly; the ambitious clergymen among them needed to play an active role in advancing the political interests of their patrons. Denys Winstanley put it best when he wrote that unless a striving clergyman 'was skilled in seeing which way the political wind was likely to blow and steering his course accordingly, he had little chance of obtaining the preferment he coveted'.[3] Stagecoaches

[1] Peter Searby, *A History of the University of Cambridge: Vol. 3: 1750–1870* (Cambridge, 1997), 52.
[2] *HPC, 1754–90*, www.historyofparliamentonline.org/ (accessed 2 Mar. 2023), s.v. Cambridge University.
[3] D.A. Winstanley, *The University of Cambridge in the Eighteenth Century* (Cambridge, 1922), 34.

were used to transport the electorate of MAs who lived across Britain. This was especially important for the large colleges, principally Trinity, St John's and King's.

The chancellor, college heads and aristocratic patrons could influence the results by corresponding with friends and allies to help canvass for their preferred candidates, but no single individual could ever enjoy absolute control over the constituency due to the size and variety of its electorate. This made political and religious networks very important for the university's elections. Personal contacts did much to shape college behaviour and broader electoral patterns. Daniel Cook's 1935 unpublished thesis, 'The Representative History of County, Town and University of Cambridge, 1689–1832', and *The History of Parliament, 1754–1790* (of 1964) provided accounts of these parliamentary contests.[4] However, the true meaning of these electoral results is enhanced when viewed within the context of the university's networks and political controversies during the period.

Cambridge University was also a staunchly Anglican constituency. The university was controlled by the Church of England for the spread of Christian morality and training of clergymen. Dissenting and nonconformist sects were excluded from graduating due to the requirement to subscribe to the 39 Articles of the Church of England. Subscription was again a requirement for anyone wishing to progress up the university hierarchy to become a fellow or professor. Half of those who graduated went on to be ordained. Overall student numbers fell during the 18th century due to this emphasis on clerical education and exclusion of non-Anglicans.[5] It was the practice of the time for young elite men to leave university without completing their degrees if they were not intending to become clergymen or pursue a profession. Most fellows were also more preoccupied with their professional prospects within the Church of England hierarchy than with educating students or exploring disciplines outside of theology.

Despite these limitations, Cambridge University was a sizable and competitive constituency with a highly educated and politically aware electorate. College heads and fellows were active in parliamentary contests, influencing colleagues and members of the senate behind the scenes as well as speaking and writing publicly about current events. It was the custom for the chancellor to propose candidates for the constituency when vacancies arose, but their wishes were not always adhered to. An examination of these parliamentary contests reveals useful insights into the behaviour of late-Hanoverian electorates.

The analysis of these general election results that follows is based on the 1780 and 1784 poll books printed by local newspaper publisher Francis Hodson, and the 1790 poll book produced by the university printer John Archdeacon, as well as the useful visualisations provided by the 'Eighteenth-Century Political Participation and Electoral Culture' (ECPPEC) project.[6] These poll books were based on the votes collected by the university registry, lists on the boards of colleges, and conversations with the candidates' friends. To establish the scope of each candidate's support, the election results have been broken down to the college level to reveal who came first and second in each college to

---

[4]Daniel Cook, 'The Representative History of the County, Town and University of Cambridge, 1689–1832', University of London PhD, 1935.

[5]Searby, *History of the University of Cambridge*, 12.

[6]*The Poll for the Election* (Cambridge, 1780); *The Poll for the Election … by John Beverley* (Cambridge, 1784); *The Poll for the Election … by John Beverley* (Cambridge, 1790). For visualisations of how the voters split their votes, see ECPPEC, https://ecppec.ncl.ac.uk/case-study-constituencies/cambridge%20university/election/Sept-1780/ (accessed 28 Aug. 2023).

understand if there was a bias towards the ministry or opposition of the day. Voting patterns are highlighted to show how many voters backed a unified ministry or opposition ticket, split their vote, or stuck with a specific candidate. Voter loyalty between these elections is also examined to demonstrate how many voters switched their allegiance from one candidate or party to another, or consistently backed a specific candidate or ticket.

The presence of three candidates standing in both 1780 and 1784, as well as two candidates standing in 1784 and 1790, illuminates how voter behaviour shifted over the course of this period. Pitt was the only candidate to stand in all three elections. Although the 1796 general election was not contested, it is included because it marked the beginning of a decade in which Pitt and Lord Euston were unchallenged for the university's representation. The fact that no opposition candidate was put up is itself an important sign of how successfully Pitt and his supporters came to dominate Cambridge University politics.

The poll books contain limited information about the individual electors. College affiliation, title and surname were provided with occasional reference to first names or initials. Where an elector's name appeared with a consistent title, surname and college affiliation in two or three consecutive poll books, it is assumed that this is the same individual. For instances of electors with a shared surname or who had a change of title (for example, from Mr to Dr), volumes of *Alumni Cantabrigienses* and Emden's A *Biographical Register of the University of Cambridge* have been consulted to clarify who these electors might have been. Electors who could not be identified have been excluded from the analysis of voter loyalty between elections.[7] This has meant eliminating six possible electors from those who took part in the 1780 and 1784 elections and five possible electors from those who participated in the 1784 and 1790 elections. Such small samples being removed has not affected the patterns revealed by the analysis.

There are also records of 'objected votes' in the 1784 and 1790 poll books, but no reason was provided in the poll books to explain the objections. These electors are all excluded from the changes in the total university vote. However, electors with objected votes are still included in the analysis of voting patterns and voter loyalty between the 1780, 1784 and 1790 general elections. This maintains a consistent approach towards all three poll books and still provides insight into the political decisions being made by the Cambridge University electorate. The number of 'objected votes' in the 1784 and 1790 general elections was also small and does not significantly alter the overall results.

Cambridge University under the Duke of Grafton

Cambridge University in the decade leading up to the 1780 general election was experiencing significant political discord, much like the rest of Britain. New ideological disputes over the role of the crown and the Church had burst open during the peace that followed the Seven Years' War, especially as the crisis in America started to unfold and brought about renewed global conflict.[8] Despite the claims made in Namierite historiography, late-Hanoverian Cambridge University was not a stagnant intellectual space and there was, in

---

[7] *Alumni Cantabrigienses*, ed. John Venn and J.A. Venn (10 vols, Cambridge, 1922–53); *A Biographical Register of the University of Cambridge*, ed. A.B. Emden (Cambridge, 1963).

[8] John Gascoigne, *Cambridge in the Age of the Enlightenment: Science, Religion and Politics from the Restoration to the French Revolution* (Cambridge, 2002), 187.

fact, a great deal of political activity taking place. This misrepresentation is largely due to the influence of Henry Gunning, a prominent Cambridge reformer and esquire bedell of the university, who recorded anecdotes from his youth in *Reminiscences* (1854), providing amusing stories and settling old scores.[9] As a Whig stronghold under George I and George II, Cambridge University was a key battleground for the new political forces at work, creating fresh challenges and opportunities.

Reformers found significant support among Cambridge University's academics for limiting executive power, revising the parliamentary franchise, extending religious toleration and abolishing the slave trade. The combination of Whig doctrine, natural theology and Enlightenment thought led many to reassess the meaning of the Glorious Revolution as they approached its centenary in 1788–9.[10] John Jebb, a fellow of Peterhouse, led Cambridge University's reformers in support of national causes as well as reforms of the university itself. After leaving the university, Jebb worked with Dr Richard Watson, a fellow of Trinity, and Christopher Wyvill, a graduate of Queens', to organise a reform demonstration with John Wilkes in March 1780 at the Senate House Yard with a petition signed by 1,000 freeholders.[11]

However, there were many who remained loyal to the court and the ministry under Lord North, leading to divisions within the university. Bishop Keene of Ely, a former master of Peterhouse, had been a client of the duke of Newcastle, much like Dr Watson, but stood by the government. His son, Benjamin Keene, stood as MP for Cambridge in 1776 to oppose the 'violent Whigs'.[12] In 1780, Richard Farmer, the master of Emmanuel, used his term as vice-chancellor to propose an address in the senate to support the continuation of the war. Lord Rockingham, leader of the main opposition party, encouraged resistance in the senate, but the government sent its supporters with MAs to help vote through the address. Dr Watson would later recall the 'ministerial troops … from the Admiralty, Treasury & etc.' arriving to vote.[13]

The spread of reformism benefitted from the inability of the chancellor, the duke of Grafton, to stamp his authority on Cambridge University politics. As First Lord, the duke of Grafton was initially well-placed to exercise significant influence when he was elected chancellor in 1768. Once his ministry fell in 1770, it became increasingly difficult for Grafton to enjoy the same level of power as his predecessor, the duke of Newcastle, who had successfully masterminded patronage networks across the British establishment. After resigning as lord privy seal in 1775 over his support for reconciliation with America, Grafton's break with the court was complete. Denied royal favour and opposed to the North ministry, the rest of the university subsequently struggled to benefit from the patronage of George III and his ministers. This made it difficult for Grafton to control the representation of the university.

---

[9]Henry Gunning, *Reminiscences of the University, Town, and County of Cambridge from the year 1780* (2 vols, 1854). These reminiscences went up to 1820. The work of D.A. Winstanley, who followed a Namierite narrative of Cambridge University politics under the duke of Newcastle, has done the most to cement this perception in the historiography and is often echoed in histories of the Cambridge colleges.

[10]Gascoigne, *Cambridge in the Age of the Enlightenment*, 189.

[11]Searby, *History of the University of Cambridge*, 411.

[12]Gascoigne, *Cambridge in the Age of the Enlightenment*, 215.

[13]Searby, *History of the University of Cambridge*, 411.

As an ally of the opposition factions, Grafton was keen to promote candidates who would adopt a similar line in the house of commons, further alienating the government. Richard Croftes, a former client of the duke of Newcastle, was Grafton's preferred candidate for the opening that appeared in the university's parliamentary representation in 1771. Croftes had also backed the Grafton ministry against Wilkes during the Middlesex election affair in 1769, proving his loyalty to the chancellor. This selection met with some resistance within the university, even from Grafton's allies. The bishop of Lincoln wrote to Lord Hardwicke on 5 February 1771 that 'sending down so young a man, and so little known, has given much offence'.[14] Dr Watson declared that he and his colleagues had 'no particular objections to him as a private man … but we by no means think him of consequence enough in life to be the representative, or of ability sufficient to support the interest of the University of Cambridge'.[15] Nevertheless, Croftes defeated the independent candidate put up against him, and continued to serve an undistinguished career in the house of commons.

Cambridge University would not be contested again until a by-election in 1779, when the sitting MP, Charles Manners, acceded to the dukedom of Rutland. Political feeling in the university had been heightened, and divided, by the revolutionary war in America. Manners was a Rockingham Whig and a staunch critic of the North ministry's America policy, thus earning the admiration of Lord Chatham and his son. His family's interest in Cambridge's town and county seats, as well as involvement in the reform movements, earned Manners significant influence in future contests. With support from the duke of Grafton, Manners was replaced by James Mansfield, who had been a scholar and a fellow at King's in the 1750s, prior to an illustrious legal career, becoming a king's counsel in 1772.

Mansfield beat two other candidates in 1779 for the seat, including John Townshend, a Rockingham Whig who was a member of the Devonshire House set and a close friend of Charles James Fox. These social and political advantages allowed Townshend to appeal to the university's younger anti-government electors. Townshend was also related to an earlier MP for the university. The other candidate, Lord Hyde, who was much closer to Lord North, backing the ministry as MP for Christchurch, came bottom of the poll. Lord Hyde's patrons included Edward Hooper and Lord Granville. Despite Hyde's loyalty to the government, Lord North wrote: 'I do not like to put the King to the expense of £3,000 to bring in so uncertain a supporter as Lord Hyde'.[16] Both Townshend and Lord Hyde would stand for the constituency again in the following year's general election.

After his successful election, Mansfield aligned himself with the government. His patron, Lord Carlisle, was a firm supporter of Lord North, but Mansfield had been slow to embrace the ministry, having previously turned down the offer of the Morpeth pocket borough in favour of judicial office. Mansfield was later appointed as Solicitor-General on 1 September 1780, several days before the general election was held in Cambridge University. This was a sure sign that between support from the government and the fellows, Mansfield's re-election was secure, whereas the other seat held by Croftes remained in contention.

It was in this environment that Pitt, aged 14, began his undergraduate career at Cambridge University in 1773. Pitt took his MA without examination in 1776 but stayed in Cambridge for an additional three years despite being admitted to Lincoln's Inn in

---

[14] *HPC, 1754–1790*, s.v. Croftes, Richard of Saxham, Suff.

[15] *HPC, 1754–1790*, s.v. Croftes, Richard of Saxham, Suff.

[16] *HPC, 1754–1790*, s.v. Villiers, Hon. Thomas of The Grove, Watford, Herts.

1777. A Cambridge education left an indelible mark on Pitt's intellect, through the whig interpretation of history and philosophy, as well as an appreciation for the classics and mathematics.[17] There was also a crucial social aspect to this experience, as Pitt formed lifelong friendships with people who would later serve in his ministries. Given this strong personal attachment to Cambridge University, in addition to the prestige and status of the seat, it seemed only natural that Pitt should wish to represent it in parliament.

The American War and Pitt's First Election

As the war in America continued to rage, the political atmosphere in Cambridge University was extremely volatile. The 1780 general election saw five candidates stand for the seat with the government and the opposition competing fiercely among the fellows and the senate for votes. The poll was held on 9 September. While the chancellor put his support behind the opposition candidates, the vice-chancellor backed the ministerial candidates, reflecting the divided loyalties of the university during a moment of acute crisis. Croftes, who continued to be aligned with the opposition but had never won the affection of the university, and Mansfield, with ministerial backing, stood for re-election. Lord Hyde stood again as a supporter of the North ministry and Townshend put himself forward with support from the Rockingham Whigs. Besides the government, the Rockingham Whigs were the most organised group trying to exercise influence in the election. Sympathetic to the American colonists and supportive of reformist ideas, the Rockingham Whigs appealed to the North ministry's opponents in the university despite their more restrained policy goals.

Lord Shelburne's opposition grouping, to which Pitt was closest, was more radical in its aims, but also limited in its organisation. As a result, Pitt did not receive the blessing of the Rockingham Whigs. The duke of Rutland, however, provided advice and assistance to Pitt, including a list of MA graduands. Pitt started campaigning in 1779 and went so far as to write 400 letters in one week to canvass for support.[18] Ultimately, Pitt came bottom of the poll with 142 votes. For a relatively unknown 21-year-old candidate, this is still a respectable showing, and the duke of Rutland was able to secure the pocket borough of Appleby for Pitt so that he could enter parliament in January 1781.

Examining Pitt at the outset of his career can help clarify the future direction of the political grouping that emerged from his premiership and the volatility of British politics in the early 1780s. At first, Pitt was closely aligned to the opposition and supported many prominent reformers, but he called himself an 'independent Whig' to stay free of party loyalties and reflect the intellectual debt to his father's Country principles. Although Pitt certainly adopted many of the political assumptions of court whiggery, he still maintained a strong belief in the independence of propertied men and the value of public virtue over private interest.[19] This rejection of party and emphasis on virtue would be a distinctive part of Pitt's electoral appeal just a few years later in very different circumstances.

[17]John Ehrman, *The Younger Pitt: Volume I, The Years of Acclaim* (London, 1969).

[18]Searby, *History of the University of Cambridge*, 412.

[19]Jennifer Mori, 'The Political Theory of William Pitt the Younger', *History*, lxxxiii (1998), 234–48.

College	Hyde	Pitt	Townshend	Mansfield	Croftes	Total votes
Peterhouse	2	6	4	16	6	34
Clare Hall	8	9	10	6	7	40
Pembroke Hall	4	16	7	4	3	34
Corpus Christi	8	3	9	9	7	36
Gonville and Caius	7	5	9	13	11	45
King's	11	2	14	41	3	71
Queens'	12	6	8	17	10	53
Catharine Hall	6	3	9	7	2	27
Jesus	3	3	6	6	4	22
Trinity Hall	4	1	1	5	1	12
Christ's	12	5	10	21	3	51
St John's	59	19	73	37	51	239
Trinity	36	50	54	64	31	235
Emmanuel	21	11	10	10	5	57
Sidney Sussex	5	1	9	4	2	21
Magdalene	4	0	3	9	2	18
Commorantes in villa	4	2	1	8	2	17
Total Votes	**206**	**142**	**237**	**277**	**150**	**1012**
Total Vote Share (%)	**20.4**	**14**	**23.4**	**27.4**	**14.8**	

Figure 1: Table of 1780 General Election Results[20]

The 1780 election results also showed how the Whig identity forged after 1715 in Cambridge University had become highly fractured. Without the common threat of Jacobitism to the revolution settlement and the Protestant succession, the Whig label had lost its distinctive meaning. Many clients and protégés of the duke of Newcastle had turned against each other. Reformers were denounced as 'violent Whigs' by supporters of the government and, in turn, argued that their critics were apostates to true Whig principles. The American War exacerbated these new dividing lines, with both sides claiming to be defending the true tenets of whiggery. This ideological split was demonstrated by the election of Mansfield for the government, topping the poll, and Townshend, for the opposition, in second place (Figure 1).

Cambridge University's split representation was made more likely by the number of candidates standing, by the fluid nature of the party system, and by the volatile political scene created by the war in America. Although Townshend and Mansfield came top of the poll overall, the results from individual colleges reveal the political fault-lines within the university electorate. Pitt's fifth place did not stop him from achieving a solid victory in his alma mater of Pembroke Hall, where he voted for Townshend and himself, or coming second in Clare Hall and Emmanuel. By contrast, Croftes came second in Peterhouse and Caius, failing to top the poll in any of the other colleges. After several years as one of

---

[20] *The Poll for the Election* (Cambridge, 1780).

Chart of 1780 General Election Voters

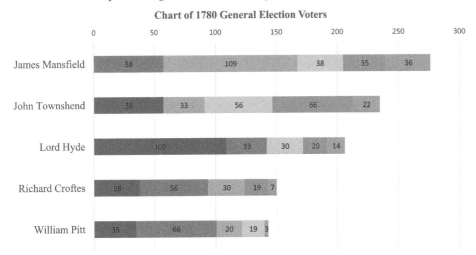

Figure 2: Chart of 1780 General Election Votes[21]

the university's parliamentary representatives, Croftes experienced a complete collapse of confidence from the electorate.

Support for Lord Hyde helps to indicate where support for the government was strongest during this time. Lord Hyde only managed to come top of the poll in Emmanuel, but came second in several colleges. Whereas support for the opposition candidates was spread out across the colleges, the government-backed candidates achieved a higher level of concentrated support. Queens', Trinity Hall, Christ's, and Magdalene all placed Mansfield and Lord Hyde at the top of the poll. By contrast, only Clare Hall and Pembroke Hall put opposition candidates in first and second place. The remainder of the colleges were split.

This becomes even more apparent when looking at the voting patterns of individual electors (Figure 2). The largest bloc was the 109 electors who voted for the government ticket of Mansfield and Lord Hyde. The next largest bloc was the 66 electors who voted for an opposition ticket of Pitt and Townshend, each of whom represented a major opposition faction. Significantly for the next general election four years later, 58 electors split their vote between Townshend and Mansfield, who would then be standing on a shared platform. Another major bloc was the 56 electors who voted for the anti-ministry ticket of Townshend and Croftes, which illustrates how the latter candidate's several years as one of the university's MPs barely provided enough support for him to come ahead of Pitt in the poll. College opinion was divided but there were clearly many electors who decided to choose a side in the fight between the government and the opposition.[22]

[21] ECPPEC, https://ecppec.ncl.ac.uk/case-study-constituencies/cambridge%20university/election/Sept-17 80/ (accessed 17 Aug. 2023).

[22] Most of Pitt's voters had Townshend for their other choice, and Pitt had very few plumpers: ECPPEC, https://ecppec.ncl.ac.uk/case-study-constituencies/cambridge%20university/election/Sept-1780/ (accessed 17 Aug. 2023).

Most of the electorate that voted used both of their votes, but there was some 'plumping' for a single candidate. The largest instance of single candidate plumping was the 36 electors who gave their vote just to Mansfield, most of whom were based in his alma mater of King's, and the 22 electors who plumped for Townshend, most of whom were in his alma mater of St John's. Croftes and Lord Hyde were also Johnians and won around 50 votes each from the college, pushing Mansfield into fourth place. These are strong indicators of the strength of college loyalty for personal followings in the university.

The Realignment of Cambridge University Politics

The ministerial instability of the years that followed the 1780 general election brought Cambridge University's MPs closer together. After losing office in 1782 when the North ministry fell, Mansfield opposed the Rockingham and Shelburne ministries that followed. The Fox–North coalition brought about Mansfield's brief return to office. Although he regularly contributed to debate in the house of commons, Mansfield was by no means a speaker who provoked enthusiasm. In 1781, the *English Chronicle* described him as 'a man of keen but not elegant parts – he speaks with point, labour and precision, but without any of those graces which give energy to talents and make eloquences pleasing, as well as instructing'.[23] Lord Hyde, by contrast, abandoned Lord North after 1782 and refused to back the coalition, eventually becoming a supporter of the Pitt ministry.

Townshend pursued a rather different course in the house of commons during these years. Sir Nathaniel Wraxall wrote of Townshend: 'Though not endowed with eminent parliamentary talents, he possessed an understanding highly cultivated, set off by the most pleasing manners'.[24] Townshend continued to be a vocal critic of the American War and supported Sir James Lowther's 1781 motion to end the conflict. When Lord Rockingham formed his second ministry in 1782, Townshend was appointed as lord of the admiralty. As a loyal supporter of Fox, he resigned from the ministry when Lord Shelburne assumed office and opposed the 1782 peace preliminaries that paved the way for a negotiated settlement between Britain and an independent America. Through the formation of the Fox–North coalition, Townshend returned to the admiralty and became a ministerial colleague alongside Mansfield.

The formation of the Fox–North coalition also precipitated an intense constitutional clash when George III decided to dismiss the ministry over its proposed East India Bill. George III turned to Pitt to form a fresh ministry, which came to be known as the 'mince-pie administration' as its survival beyond Christmas was seen as highly unlikely by its detractors. To continue in office after suffering a series of parliamentary defeats, Pitt advised George III to dissolve Parliament on 25 March 1784 so a general election could be called. Pitt was quick to start canvassing Cambridge University again. Mansfield and Townshend stood for re-election on a shared platform as opponents of Pitt. The duke of Grafton was not close to Pitt, but he was deeply opposed to the Fox–North coalition.

Pitt ran an active campaign with support from George Pretyman, his former tutor at Pembroke Hall, who acted as his private secretary and won over leading moderate and

---

[23] *HPC, 1754–1790*, s.v. Mansfield, James.

[24] *HPC, 1754–1790*, s.v. Townshend, Hon. John.

College	Pitt	Euston	Townshend	Mansfield	Total votes
Peterhouse	7	5	8	7	27
Clare Hall	17	15	9	6	47
Pembroke Hall	18	17	0	0	35
Corpus Christi	12	7	4	4	27
Gonville and Caius	21	17	7	7	52
King's	14	7	31	36	88
Queens'	18	11	9	11	49
Catharine Hall	8	6	11	6	31
Jesus	12	4	13	7	36
Trinity Hall	4	4	1	3	12
Christ's	16	19	21	11	67
St John's	76	48	91	45	260
Trinity	85	107	51	21	264
Emmanuel	25	19	12	15	71
Sidney Sussex	10	5	8	1	24
Magdalene	11	13	1	2	27
Commorantes in villa	5	3	4	3	15
Objected Votes	–8	–8	–3	–4	–23
Total Votes	**351**	**299**	**278**	**181**	**1109**
Total Vote Share (%)	**31.6**	**27**	**25.1**	**16.3**	

Figure 3: Table of 1784 General Election Results[25]

evangelical Anglican clergymen to help canvass support. The duke of Rutland again provided support to Pitt, but this became intertwined with a broader political struggle in the borough and county. Through his agent John Mortlock, who stood for the borough seat vacated by Keene, Rutland tried to assert his influence in Cambridge's parliamentary representation. Cambridge brewer William Ewin wrote to Lord Hardwicke, whose family exercised its interest in the university and county seats:

> let Mr Pitt send down the Purse of the Exchequer which is the emblem of his office – and hang it in the Senate House and we should as naturally put our vote into it as Catholicks dig their fingers into the Pan of Holy Water – with this difference that we should mark our foreheads with P in room of the X.[26]

Lord Euston, the chancellor's son, stood alongside Pitt. They had been friends since their time as undergraduates and, despite his father's poor reputation in the university, Lord Euston was able to ride on Pitt's coattails. He had considered standing in 1780, but would not have been of age to be eligible as a candidate. Instead, he was elected MP for Thetford in 1782 and supported the Shelburne-led opposition alongside Pitt. The two MPs would

[25] *The Poll for the Election … by John Beverley* (Cambridge, 1784).

[26] Searby, *History of the University of Cambridge*, 412.

© *2024 The Authors.* Parliamentary History *published by John Wiley & Sons Ltd on behalf of Parliamentary History Yearbook Trust.*

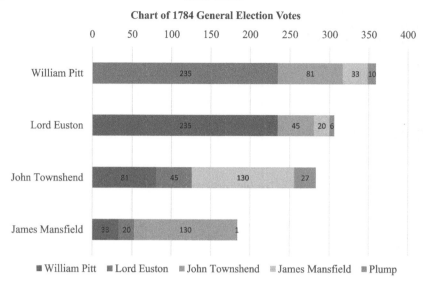

Figure 4: Chart of 1784 General Election Votes[27]

remain allies for much of the following two decades. With royal backing and strong clerical support, Pitt and Euston were elected and secured Cambridge University for the crown against Fox and Lord North in the constitutional crisis of 1782–4. It is hard to imagine this political turn without the impact of the loss of the American colonies, the blow to British confidence that followed from such a traumatic break, and a strong demand for stability after an extended period of ministerial changes. However, the decisive Pittite victory in 1784 was not absolute (Figure 3).

Townshend succeeded in winning the highest number of votes in Peterhouse, Catharine Hall, Jesus, Christ's, and St John's. He managed to come second in King's and Sidney Sussex. Townshend's vote share had also increased marginally by 1.7 per cent. It was a solid performance that demonstrated the presence of a significant segment of university opinion that remained unconvinced about Pitt and sympathetic to the Fox-led opposition. Pitt personally switched his vote from Townshend to Euston in 1784, recognising how the party dividing lines had shifted as a result of the constitutional crisis. Mansfield's reversal of fortunes was far more dramatic. His vote share plunged by 11.1 per cent and he came at the bottom of the poll in Clare Hall, Christ's, St John's, Trinity and Sidney. Mansfield came top of the poll only in King's. This poorer showing from Mansfield was strongly linked to Townshend's performance, with both candidates coming third and fourth in a significant number of colleges.

Cambridge University's political transformation in the wake of Pitt's triumph can be seen in a set of results with much greater consistency and polarisation among the electorate (Figure 4). As might be expected, the largest bloc was the 235 electors who voted for Pitt and Lord Euston. Every elector in Pembroke Hall voted for Pitt and Euston. Coming second, a

[27] ECPPEC, https://ecppec.ncl.ac.uk/case-study-constituencies/cambridge%20university/election/Apr-17 84/ (accessed 17 Aug. 2023).

bloc of 130 electors voted for Townshend and Mansfield with much of this support again coming from King's and St John's. Interestingly, a bloc of 81 electors split their votes between Pitt and Townshend, especially in St John's. Very few electors plumped for a candidate but, once again, Townshend's personal following led to 27 electors voting solely for him, which is higher than the six electors who plumped for Euston or the single plump for Mansfield.

There was certainly some change in the composition of the Cambridge University electorate between 1780 and 1784, as new members entered the senate and old members died or moved away. However, among the electors who voted in both elections, some patterns emerge. For example, 28 of the electors who voted for Lord Hyde and Mansfield, the ministerialist candidates in 1780, switched to Pitt and Euston in 1784, whereas 16 other electors switched to Townshend and Mansfield. Of the 1780 Pitt and Townshend electors, 17 of them switched to Pitt and Euston. Much of the vote switching was wide-ranging and varied across colleges. Only a small minority of electors chose to vote for the same candidates in both elections, with 14 electors choosing to back Townshend and Mansfield both times and nine electors standing by Pitt and Townshend even when these two candidates had clearly diverged from one another.[28]

Although three of the four candidates in 1784 had stood for the same constituency in the previous general election, this high level of vote switching indicates how different the political circumstances had become. Diffuse groupings based around the North ministry and the Rockingham-led opposition in 1780 had been replaced by a sharp divide between the Pitt ministry and the Fox-led opposition. The end of the conflict in America also created the space for this shift in the party system as Pitt could craft a ministry that appealed to both supporters and critics of the war. As Max Skjönsberg has noted, there 'was a clearer dichotomy between an opposition party and a broad-bottom Treasury party, and at least the semblance of a two-party framework'.[29] But the end of the American War also diminished the importance of party labels. Both sides claimed to be true Whigs, and Pitt firmly rejected party labels entirely, portraying himself as serving the public interest.[30]

An ambivalence towards party labels worked to Pitt's political advantage. The 'independent Whig' of 1780 was clearly an opponent of the North ministry and its conduct of the war in America, but he was also free of association with the fallen Fox–North coalition. As a non-partisan servant of the crown, Pitt could appeal across the political spectrum in 1784 with his promise of peace and order. Supporters of the court interest, such as the master of Emmanuel, could rally behind Pitt as the new standard-bearer of constitutional and ecclesiastical stability. Fellows like Dr Watson at Trinity and William Paley at Christ's, on the other hand, believed Pitt could be a useful ally in their reform campaigns. By winning the Cambridge University seat, Pitt also enjoyed a major boost to the national image of independence and purity that he had carefully cultivated since becoming Prime Minister. Pitt was no longer dependent on a patron for his parliamentary seat, but had won a large and competitive constituency, a powerful symbolic victory in his struggle against the cynicism and corruption he identified with the Fox–North coalition.

---

[28]See Pitt's vote: ECPPEC, https://ecppec.ncl.ac.uk/case-study-constituencies/cambridge%20university/ election/Apr-1784/ (accessed 17 Aug. 2023).

[29]Max Skjönsberg, *The Persistence of Party: Ideas of Harmonious Discord in Eighteenth-Century Britain* (Cambridge, 2021), 284.

[30]Mori, 'Political Theory of William Pitt'.

After his election in 1784, Pitt carried out regular visits to the university, but was limited by his prime ministerial duties in London. On 27 May 1790, following the death of Lord Hardwicke, Pitt was elected high steward by the senate, an honorary position as deputy to the chancellor, reflecting his status in the university and his eclipsing of the duke of Grafton. Despite not being able to devote much time to his constituency responsibilities, Pitt could rely on Pretyman as an invaluable manager of the university seat. By no means a political reactionary, Pretyman had voted in the senate against the 1775 loyal address backing the war in America and was supportive of the opposition factions. He was on friendly terms with reformist clergymen such as Gilbert Wakefield, a fellow of Jesus during the late 1770s, though these relations would become fractured in the 1790s. Appointed dean of St Paul's and bishop of Lincoln in 1787, Pretyman was a powerful advisor to Pitt on ecclesiastical appointments, helping advance the careers of Pittites in the university to help consolidate the party's strength.

Another important ally in Westminster and the university, the duke of Rutland, became lord lieutenant of Ireland in 1784 and lord privy seal. Notably, the duke of Grafton had been offered the office of lord privy seal first but declined the office. Rutland's patronage network included his cousin Robert, a future MP for the borough of Cambridge, and John Mortlock, who served several times as mayor of Cambridge. These supporters had to back Pitt and reform in return for favours from the duke. When Rutland died, he left £3,000 to Pitt.[31] The duchess dowager of Rutland and Lord Hardwicke played a role in the social life of the town by donating money to the poor. Alongside these managers, Pitt could rely on the support of individual college heads. Farmer, who had been master of Emmanuel since 1775, became a close friend of Pitt's and would twice turn down the offer of a bishopric. Under his mastership, Emmanuel was a hub of social activity for the university. In September 1784, the college celebrated its bicentenary with a luxurious feast which featured prominent guests such as the future archbishop of Canterbury Charles Manners-Sutton, Pretyman, and Pitt himself. Around 140 guests enjoyed pineapples, puddings, turtle soup and plenty of wine. Lord Westmorland, an alumnus and minister under Pitt, sent 12 bucks from his deer park to the college.[32]

Pitt could count on support from Queens', and its political transformation during this period would mirror the broader development of the Pittites.[33] For decades, Queens' had been well recognised for being one of the strongest Whig colleges in the university. Its president from 1760 to 1788, Robert Plumptre, had backed reformist causes but was also loyal to the Yorke family, especially as he held a living belonging to Lord Hardwicke. Despite failing to unite the college fellowship, Plumptre still worked with Lord Hardwicke to secure Pitt's election in 1784. His successor as president in 1788, Isaac Milner, brought a very different approach to the college. As a fellow of Queens', Milner embraced Pitt in 1784 but, unlike Plumptre, he was never friendly towards reformist causes such as ending subscription to the 39 Articles. Milner was also selective in his choice of fellows, putting pressure on

---

[31] ODNB, www.oxforddnb.com (accessed 2 Mar. 2023), s.v. Manners, Charles, fourth duke of Rutland.

[32] Amanda Goode, '"Sumptuous and substantial feastynge" – the Emma Jubilee of 1784', posted 13 Dec. 2021: https://www.emma.cam.ac.uk/members/blog/?id=546 (accessed 2 Mar. 2023).

[33] John Twigg, *A History of Queens' College, Cambridge, 1448–1986* (Woodbridge, 1987).

fellows to resign, moving college livings, and appointing tutors from inside and outside of the college to promote his views. Milner's patronage extended beyond Queens' as he intervened in the election of Trinity Hall fellows, pushing for the evangelical Joseph Jowett against the Foxite Francis Wrangham. This led to the college being dubbed 'a Fief of Queens'.[34] Milner also used his influence to advance the careers of other evangelicals.[35] The most famous conversion aided by Milner was of William Wilberforce in 1784, and he encouraged evangelical parents to start sending their sons to Queens'. This religious and political transformation of Queens' into a bastion of evangelicalism and loyalism was intimately connected in Milner's project to remake the college and university in his image.

Pittite strength was also generated by St John's, albeit in a different style from at Queens'. Instead of re-electing the Johnian Townshend, the college swung strongly towards Pitt and Euston.[36] Pitt directed royal favour towards the college by appointing Richard Beadon, a former fellow of St John's and master of Jesus from 1781 to 1789, as bishop of Gloucester, and the Hon. William Stuart, the son of Lord Bute, as bishop of St David's in 1794 and then archbishop of Armagh in 1800. Although the rise of evangelicalism and loyalism in the university intersected in some colleges, this was not the case in St John's. The college remained committed to mainstream Anglicanism and was not welcoming towards its evangelical alumnus Wilberforce. William Craven, a fellow of St John's who would become master of the college in 1789, delivered sermons that deliberately clashed with the sermons of the evangelical cleric Charles Simeon at Holy Trinity, and another fellow, Herbert Marsh, also opposed evangelicalism in his sermons while still defending Pitt's policies.

More broadly, reformist energy within the university began to fade among moderates after the 1784 general election. Of greatest importance to Cambridge University were the attempts to repeal the Test Act and the Corporation Acts in 1787, 1789 and 1790. Dr Thomas Edwards, a fellow of Jesus and formerly of Clare Hall, launched the campaign. An attempt by Dr Edwards to abolish subscription to the 39 Articles, which had found major support in 1772, did not even reach the senate for debate. Jesus provided a powerbase for the university's most ardent reformers. Robert Tyrwhitt was very influential among these reformers after supporting the 1772 anti-subscription petition. He resigned his fellowship in 1777 because of his unitarian beliefs, but continued to live in the college until he died in 1817. William Frend and Wakefield, fellows of Jesus, carried on the reformers' torch, combining religious and political change. After converting to unitarianism, Frend lost his tutorship but continued as a fellow at Jesus.

The campaign provoked a hostile reaction from Cambridge clergymen who felt increasingly threatened by the rise of dissent and potential danger to the Church of England. Evangelicals became popular targets of reformist attacks. In response, Pretyman and other moderate Anglicans preached against repeal in their sermons. Although Pitt was not a deeply religious individual, he was still influenced by Bishop Sherlock's *Vindication of the Corporation and Test Acts*, originally published in 1718 but republished in 1787 in response to the campaign. Winning the university seat in 1784 had proven Pitt's independence, but it had also tied him closely to a fundamentally Anglican constituency that expected the rights and

---

[34] Gascoigne, *Cambridge in the Age of the Enlightenment*, 231.

[35] Gareth Atkins, *Converting Britannia: Evangelicals and British Public Life, 1770–1840* (Woodbridge, 2019).

[36] Peter Linehan, *St John's College, Cambridge: A History* (Woodbridge, 2011).

College	Pitt	Euston	Dundas	Total Votes
Peterhouse	10	8	6	24
Clare Hall	24	24	9	57
Pembroke Hall	28	27	1	56
Corpus Christi	15	13	5	33
Gonville and Caius	20	19	2	41
King's	28	23	26	77
Queens'	19	20	9	48
Catharine Hall	10	8	7	25
Jesus	20	20	9	49
Trinity Hall	7	6	2	15
Christ's	26	24	9	59
St John's	108	99	43	250
Trinity	122	130	51	303
Emmanuel	40	37	8	85
Sidney Sussex	12	5	17	34
Magdalene	15	14	1	30
Commorantes in villa	6	6	2	14
Objected Votes	−7	−6	−3	−16
Total Votes	**503**	**477**	**204**	**1184**
Total Vote Share (%)	**42.5**	**40.25**	**17.25**	

Figure 5: Table Of 1790 General Election Results[37]

privileges of the Church of England to be defended. Disappointing his early reformist supporters, including figures such as Frend, Pitt voted against repeal and stood by the majority of his constituents.

When the general election was called for June 1790, the French Revolution was in its infancy and had not yet resulted in the overthrow of monarchy. However, events in France were still in people's minds as they considered their vote. To challenge Pitt and Euston, the Fox-led opposition put up Lawrence Dundas as their candidate (Figure 5). A graduate of Trinity, Dundas was standing for his first parliamentary election. On the 22 March 1790, *The Times* reported:

> After a very great expense Mr Lawrence Dundas will probably fail in his election views for Cambridge. What the opposition can mean by sending Mr Dundas to Cambridge, under the auspices of Lord John Townshend, to oppose the prime minister and the eldest son of the chancellor of the University, is beyond our comprehension. We cannot reconcile it to any principles either of common sense or common gambling.[38]

---

[37] *The Poll for the Election … by John Beverley* (Cambridge, 1790).

[38] *HPC, 1754–1790*, s.v. Dundas, Sir Lawrence, 1st Bt, of Kerse, Stirling and Aske, nr. Richmond, Yorks.

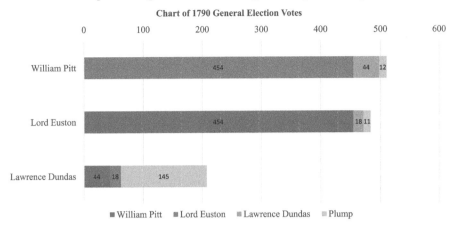

Figure 6: Chart of 1790 General Election Votes[39]

Facing an inexperienced opposition candidate, Pitt and Euston triumphed in the general election. Dundas would enter parliament as MP for Richmond, his father's pocket borough. Pitt and Euston came first and second in every college except for King's and Sidney, where Dundas succeeded in beating Euston for second place. Euston only managed to come first in Queens' and his alma mater of Trinity. With 51 votes, Dundas trailed well behind Pitt and Euston in his old college, despite its Foxite sympathies. The advantages of incumbency and a smaller field of candidates in 1790 allowed Pitt and Euston to increase their shares of the vote, respectively, by 10.8 per cent and 13.25 per cent.

The electorate was also far more polarised in 1790 than in 1784 (Figure 6). The biggest blocs of electors by far were the 454 Pitt and Euston supporters and the 145 Dundas plumpers. For such a substantial number of electors not to use both of their votes was a strong sign of how much they opposed the Pitt ministry and hoped to elect a Foxite representative. Peacetime had cemented the political identities forged during the 1784 general election. A modest bloc of 44 electors split their vote between Pitt and Dundas, with 18 electors splitting between Euston and Dundas. Plumping for Pitt or Euston was even lower at 12 and 11 electors. This reveals a very clear contest between the ministry and opposition.

However, the scale of Pitt and Euston's victory and the polarisation between the two sides masks how the political scene had shifted since the previous general election. The most stable bloc was the 139 electors who voted for Pitt and Euston in both elections. But significant numbers of other electors switched to Pitt and Euston, including the 21 electors who backed Pitt and Mansfield, 27 electors who chose Pitt and Townshend, 16 electors who chose Townshend and Mansfield, and 13 voters who chose Euston and Townshend. There was travel in the other direction as well, with various groups of vote splitters opting to split their vote again or plump for Dundas. The opposition was able to cling on with 28 Townshend and Mansfield voters plumping for Dundas and 13 Townshend plumpers deciding to split their vote between Pitt and Dundas.

[39] ECPPEC, https://ecppec.ncl.ac.uk/case-study-constituencies/cambridge%20university/election/June-17 90/ (accessed 17 Aug. 2023).

The French War and Pitt Unchallenged

As France descended further into political violence, there was significant backlash against the Revolution in the university that made Pitt's position unassailable. A loyal address to George III was passed in the senate with much greater ease than in 1775, subscriptions were raised to help French refugees, and a loyalist association against 'Republicans and Levellers' was founded. In the town, 112 publicans pledged to report any incidents of sedition they witnessed in their establishments. Demonstrations were held, resulting in the windows of reformers being smashed. On 31 December 1792, Thomas Paine was burnt in effigy at Market Square and on 25 January 1793 Great St Mary's rang its bells silently for the death of Louis XVI.[40] The following month, France declared war on Britain.

It was in this febrile environment that Milner seized the opportunity to dominate his college and stamp the government's authority on the university. Elected vice-chancellor for 1792–3, Milner invited senate members to the lodge of Queens' on 4 March 1793 and decided to put Frend on trial for publishing seditious material. The action that sparked the trial was Frend's publication of *Peace and Unity Recommended to the Associated Bodies of Republicans and Anti-Republicans* (1793). His support for the French monarchy's overthrow and extensive religious reform caused outcry in the university. Dr Thomas Kipling, fellow of St John's, was appointed as prosecutor after having worked with Dr Henry William Coulthurst, fellow of Sidney, to block Dr Edwards's 1787 repeal campaign. By choosing the public means of the vice-chancellor's court for dealing with Frend, Milner and Kipling were demonstrating the confidence of the university and the ministry in their actions.

Fellows at Jesus and Trinity supported Frend but were unable to prevent his banishment from the university in May 1793. The senate and the king's bench upheld the verdict, forcing Frend to leave Cambridge for London, where he became involved in the London Corresponding Society. By contrast, Kipling would later be appointed as dean of Peterborough in 1798, proving how people's careers could be advanced or abruptly cut off by political controversy during the 1790s. Milner, having already been appointed dean of Carlisle in 1792, hoped that his efforts to drive out reformers from the university would eventually lead to the mastership of Trinity, which was a crown appointment, or to a bishopric. Elevation to higher office never came, but Milner had undoubtedly played a leading role in tightening the Pittites' grip on the university.

The Seditious Meetings Act 1795 did not apply to lectures and talks at the universities of Oxford and Cambridge provided they had the approval of the chancellor, vice-chancellor or other university officers. The trial of Frend and Pitt's repressive legislation certainly made the university less safe for reformers, but there was also genuine widespread fear of French invasion and domestic unrest. St John's, which had already been favourable towards Pitt, turned increasingly anti-reform and became a nursery for the next generation of Pittites such as Lord Castlereagh, Lord Goderich, Lord Aberdeen, and Lord Palmerston. This reflected the broader shift among moderate clergymen who had previously been supportive of reform but were now profoundly opposed to the French Revolution.

A notable development in this trend was the position of Trinity in university politics. The fellowship had been more sympathetic to Fox than Pitt since the 1780s. Overtaking St John's

---

[40] Searby, *History of the University of Cambridge*, 416–17.

as the largest college, Trinity was a powerful source of support for the Fox-led opposition. The duke of Grafton exercised his diminished influence largely through reformers in Trinity such as Dr Watson and the master, John Hinchcliffe. Trinity also produced young Foxite talent such as Thomas Erskine and Charles Grey. Acting on Farmer's advice, Pitt appointed Thomas Postlethwaite as master in 1789, but the reformist fellowship led by James Lambert and Thomas Jones still controlled college business. This led to the election of fellows such as John Tweddell who had previously praised the French Revolution in Trinity Chapel.

Underneath this apparent Foxite dominance, the college was beginning to change. Pitt looked to another generation to convert Trinity from a Foxite outpost into a Pittite stronghold.[41] Daniel Peacock, a fellow of Trinity, was in the minority when he wrote a 1794 pamphlet defending the constitutional order and rejecting the claims of the French Revolution.[42] William Mansel, also a fellow of Trinity, became an active supporter of Pitt and was involved in the prosecution of Frend. When Postlethwaite died in 1798, Pitt would appoint Mansel as master, an office he would hold until 1820. Spencer Perceval, the future Pittite prime minister, was a pupil of Mansel and repaid his old mentor by advising that he be appointed to the bishopric of Bristol in 1808.

Outside of the colleges, reformers were able to enjoy alternative forms of institutional support after the French Revolution began. The Cambridge Society for Constitutional Information had been founded by the Baptist Revd Robert Robinson of the Stone Yard Chapel in memory of the Glorious Revolution, but members eventually turned their attentions towards France. The *Cambridge Intelligencer* was set up at Bridge Street by Benjamin Flower as an organ of reformer opinion, printing its first issue on 20 July 1793. Flower was a unitarian and heir to a Hertfordshire brewing company who worked with Frend and Wakefield to publish articles in support of peace with France, parliamentary reform and religious toleration. By the mid-1790s the paper was selling over 2,000 copies a week.[43] Reliant on its Cambridge location and writers, the paper was mainly read outside of the city, reaching across provincial Britain.

Despite the perseverance of a reformist minority in the university, Pitt found his position strengthened to the point that no opposition candidate was put up against him in the 1796 general election. Cambridge at the university, borough and county levels was firmly behind the Pitt ministry and its prosecution of the war against France. When Lord Euston and the Cambridgeshire MPs, General Adeane and Charles Philip Yorke, supported Pitt against Grey's peace motion, the *Cambridge Intelligencer* remarked that they hoped the MPs would 'meet with a proper reward from their injured and abused Constituents'.[44] All three parliamentarians would be re-elected in 1796.

Formalities were still observed and commented on, however. The *Cambridge Intelligencer* provided the following account of this 'little electioneering amusement' in its 28 May 1796 edition:

[41] Edward Hicks, '"Christianity Personified": Perceval and Pittism', University of Oxford DPhil, 2018.

[42] Daniel Peacock, *Considerations on the Structure of the House of Commons; and on the Plans of Parliamentary Reform agitated at the Present Day* (London, 1794).

[43] M.J. Murphy, *Cambridge Newspapers and Opinion, 1780–1850* (Cambridge, 1977), 120.

[44] British Newspaper Archive, *The Cambridge Intelligencer*, 31 Jan. 1795 (accessed 3 Aug. 2022).

© *2024 The Authors.* Parliamentary History *published by John Wiley & Sons Ltd on behalf of Parliamentary History Yearbook Trust.*

The Members of the University met at the Senate-house, and re-elected the man who has totally apostatized from the sentiments he professed when he was first elected, and who, we doubt not, will in a short time, be considered, by the people at large, as the greatest curse the Almighty ever permitted to plague a nation. Lord Euston who has supported his measures, and whose guilt is aggravated, when we consider the contrast which the conduct of his noble Father, the Duke of Grafton, presents to his view, was likewise re-elected. Neither Mr. Pitt nor Lord Euston made any speech on the occasion. A boy, who was asked the reason, said well enough, "they did not intend opening their mouths till dinner time".[45]

Pitt would not be challenged for the university again for the rest of his life, and reformist activity continued to decline in the years that followed. The *Cambridge Intelligencer* eventually ceased publication in 1803 following the imprisonment of Flower and Wakefield for libel. This marked the final nail in the coffin for the Cambridge reformers and the triumph of Pitt.

Conclusion

For the first time since the days of Edward Finch and Thomas Townshend during the Whig Supremacy in 1727 to 1768, Cambridge University's representation was dominated by two individuals for over two decades. This represented the impact of the dramatic events following the Seven Years' War and the arrival of a new consensus based on loyalty to the Hanoverian constitution. Defeat in the American War strengthened the sense of the crown and the Church being under threat, making Cambridge University a less hospitable place for reformers and providing fertile territory for the emerging Pittites to grow and flourish during the upheaval of the 1790s. When Pitt's second ministry was formed in 1804, Lord Euston found himself gravitating towards the opposition. However, the two university MPs would remain firm friends and allies in parliament. Euston continued to be elected for the university until 1811 when he succeeded his father as duke of Grafton.

Pittite influence continued to be felt in the town and county as well through the Manners and Yorke interests. Charles Philip Yorke would serve as MP for Cambridgeshire until 1810 while Lord Charles Manners, second son of the duke of Rutland, was MP for Cambridgeshire until 1830. The duke of Rutland's cousin, General Robert Manners, represented the borough of Cambridge from 1791 to 1820. This indicates that Pitt's transformation of the university's political identity had an impact on the broader locality. It also shows how the Pittites' origins were distinctively whiggish. The fortunes of the Manners and Yorke families can be seen as symbolic of the gradual transition of 'old corps' whiggery towards anti-revolutionary Pittism.[46] Circumstances had changed dramatically, but the fundamental belief in the Glorious Revolution settlement and the Hanoverian succession endured.

When Pitt died in 1806, Cambridge University played a leading role in crafting the Pittite mythology that would generate statues, birthday celebrations, clubs and scholarships

---

[45] British Newspaper Archive, *The Cambridge Intelligencer*, 28 May 1796 (accessed 3 Aug. 2022).

[46] J.J. Sack, *From Jacobite to Conservative: Reaction and Orthodoxy in Britain, c. 1760–1832* (Cambridge, 1993).

across the country over the following decades.[47] This included the transformation of Pitt into an ideal model of Christian and conservative statesmanship. The bishop of Lincoln delivered the commemoration day sermon on 17 December 1806 in Trinity College Chapel, marking Pitt's death, and would later write a biography of his former pupil. When Pitt died, there was only one vote in the senate against a grace to honour his memory. A public meeting was held in Trinity Lodge and agreed on commissioning a statue for the Senate House. A sum of £7,400 was raised with excess funds creating Pitt Scholarships in Classical Learning in 1813 and the Pitt Press in 1833. Prominent subscribers included Lord Hardwicke, Spencer Perceval, Lord Euston, Wilberforce, Lord Palmerston, Lord Castlereagh and the duke of Rutland. Reinventing Pitt as a religious conservative, despite his reformist views on Catholic emancipation, was critical to the continued cohesion and strength of the Pittites in Cambridge University after his death.

The triumph of Pitt and the breakup of whiggery could not have occurred without the ebb and flow of political intensity formed by the nation's journey from war to peace to war again. A divisive conflict against fellow countrymen in the American colonies triggered a breakdown of political loyalties. This was reflected by a fragmented and wide field of candidates in the 1780 general election and the constitutional crisis of 1782–4. With the return to peace, Pitt won the broad support of the university, among reformers and courtiers alike, with a promise of stability. Pitt's peacetime leadership of the nation was rewarded with the office of high steward and token opposition in the 1790 general election. War with France and the violent aftermath of the Revolution consolidated and expanded the Pittite coalition to the point that no opposition stood against Pitt for the 1796 general election. Cambridge University was at the heart of the national polarisation of politics between Pittites and Foxites that emerged from the fracturing of the old Whig party. Ultimately, Pitt was able to navigate these alternating periods of war and peace and turn it to his advantage, building a robust political grouping that would continue to flourish long after his death.

---

[47]J.J. Sack, 'The Memory of Burke and the Memory of Pitt: English Conservatism Confronts Its Past, 1806–1829', *HJ*, xxx (1987), 623–40.

Parliamentary History, Vol. 43, pt. 1 (2024), pp. 112–128

Reading against Reform: The Bristol Library Society and the Intellectual Culture of Bristol's Elections in 1812[*]

JOSHUA J. SMITH

University of Stirling

This article pioneers a new methodological approach to the study of electoral politics by combining an analysis of the politics of reading, library association and the reading habits of electors in an English urban constituency in the early 19th century. By integrating an examination of reading practices and intellectual context into our analysis of electoral contests, political history scholars can go further in their examination of the unreformed electoral system and attempt to gauge the motivations behind voting habits and partisan identification in this period. Using electoral voting data and the records of an urban subscription library, this article explores the interrelation between the Bristol Library Society and Bristol's electoral politics, as well as conducting an analysis of which books were being borrowed and read by electors in a politically tumultuous year. Although few in number compared with the total size of Bristol's electorate, Bristol Library members were among some of the most politically and culturally influential individuals in Bristol society and were active participants in electoral contests in the city, either as candidates, campaigners, civic officials or voters. An analysis of their voting habits reveals that the library's membership reflected the Tory political hegemony that became pronounced in the city's civic politics. Moreover, an analysis of their reading habits in 1812 reveals an interest in political texts that were conservative and anti-Gallic in tone, that were representative of the political climate in Bristol in 1812, and which contributed to the defeat of candidates for reform in its electoral contests.

Keywords: anti-Jacobin; Bristol; civic politics; club; Edward Protheroe; extra-parliamentary party; libraries; reading; Samuel Romilly; voting

Combining an analysis of library records with voting records, this article will exhibit a new methodological approach to the study of electoral politics in Georgian Britain. Library records, particularly borrowing records, represent an underutilised source in the study of the political motivations of Britons in the unreformed electorate. An appreciation of the intellectual and reading context in which votes were cast enables us to deepen our analysis of political motivations and stimuli. The structural elements of politics, including networks of sociability and association, go a long way to explain the outcomes of electoral contests, yet

[*]My thanks to Dr Emma Macleod and Professor Katie Halsey for their comments on earlier drafts of this article. I am also grateful to the 'Eighteenth-Century Political Participation & Electoral Culture' project (hereafter ECPPEC) for sharing 1812 voting data for Bristol with me early. This work was supported by the Arts and Humanities Research Council [AH/R012717/1].

a study of reading habits, along with providing a greater appreciation for the local contexts in which elections were fought, can help to explain the formation of political opinions and voting intentions. This article cross-references electoral data from the October 1812 general election in Bristol with the borrowing records of the Bristol Library Society to examine the reading habits of the city's civic class quantitatively, so as to consider the potential influence reading played upon the formation of the intellectual climate in which this electoral contest was fought.[1] Though an exclusive establishment, the Bristol Library Society formed a key associational crutch to the maintenance of intellectual, cultural and political networks in the city, with its members consisting of some of Bristol's senior civic and political individuals. The borrowing records of this group reveal that they read a selection of books which shared a sense of anxiety at the safety and solidity of the British state, seemingly threatened by internal saboteurs and the belligerence of first Revolutionary and then Napoleonic France. Whether this reading of anti-French texts, many of which looked back to the early 1790s and the heady days of Revolutionary terror, shaped the political sentiments of these readers, or their political sentiments shaped their reading habits, the reading of these texts is representative of a strand of anti-Gallicanism which pervaded the electoral contest in Bristol in October 1812.

Since the late 1980s, a host of historical scholarship on the state and nature of the unreformed electoral system has rescued it from misinterpretations of whiggish history and the so-called 'reform perspective', the denigration of 18th-century society as 'unreformed' by 19th-century reformers.[2] The electoral system pre-1832 was not overwhelmingly venal, corrupt or stagnant; its electors were not the mindless pawns of regional magnates; and the system as a whole was not immune to change or limited reform.[3] In rectifying these misconceptions, political historians have increasingly stressed the vibrant and dynamic nature of Georgian politics, particularly at a local level.[4] In doing so, they have sought to define 'political awareness' in the Georgian voting public. Frank O'Gorman describes the 'political awareness' of the voter as emerging from his social and political environments and relationships, his image of himself and others, and his ideals, expectations and objective realities.[5] In

---

[1] In combining an analysis of electoral polling data with additional sources, this article follows a similar methodological approach to John Phillips's and James Bradley's studies of electoral behaviour: John Phillips, *The Great Reform Bill in the Boroughs: English Electoral Behaviour, 1818–41* (Oxford, 1992), 37–44; J.E. Bradley, *Religion, Revolution, and English Radicalism: Nonconformity in Eighteenth-Century Politics and Society* (Cambridge, 1990), 39–46.

[2] For the use of this phrase, see Joanna Innes and Arthur Burns, 'Introduction', in *Rethinking the Age of Reform: Britain 1780–1850*, ed. Arthur Burns and Joanna Innes (Cambridge, 2003), 4–7. For a defence of this 'Whig interpretation of history', see Annabel Patterson, *Nobody's Perfect: A New Whig Interpretation of History* (New Haven, 2002), 1–35.

[3] Frank O'Gorman, *Voters, Patrons, and Parties: The Unreformed Electoral System of Hanoverian England, 1743–1832* (Oxford, 1989), 2–4; *Rethinking the Age of Reform*, ed. Burns and Innes; *The Many Lives of Corruption: The Reform of Public Life in Modern Britain c.1750–1950*, ed. Ian Cawood and Tom Crook (Manchester, 2022).

[4] For some examples, see Phillips, *Great Reform Bill*; Gordon Pentland, *Radicalism, Reform and National Identity in Scotland, 1820–1833* (Woodbridge, 2008); Katrina Navickas, *Loyalism and Radicalism in Lancashire, 1798–1815* (Oxford, 2009).

[5] The concept of 'political awareness' is rarely explicitly defined but often discussed as a necessary requirement for 'public opinion' in this period: J.A.W. Gunn, *Beyond Liberty and Property: The Process of Self-Recognition in Eighteenth-Century Political Thought* (Kingston, Ontario, 1983), 263–315; H.T. Dickinson, *The Politics of the People in Eighteenth-Century Britain* (Basingstoke, 1995), 221–54; J.E. Bradley, 'The British Public and the American Revolution: Ideology, Interest and Opinion', in *Britain and the American Revolution*, ed. H.T. Dickinson (1998), 153–4.

turn, electoral behaviour 'arises out of such powerfully held social, political, and even moral, standards and beliefs'.[6] Setting aside the omission that 'political awareness' is defined only in respect to voters, and not those who did not have the vote but exercised political influence through other means, this definition also underplays the importance of ideas in motivating and shaping political engagement.[7] One may go further in this instance and assess the role that reading played in the incubation or circulation of ideas among a politically engaged public.

The study of political print and print culture has formed a major aspect of this reassessment of the unreformed political system, although the significance of the reception and reading of such material rarely merits much discussion.[8] Political biographies, for example, regularly record their subjects' interactions with books and reading material, but typically do not undertake an analysis of their reading in any great depth.[9] On the other hand, those political figures who were known particularly for their voracious reading have been studied within the field of the history of reading.[10] These, like other studies of political reading, have focused on the individual, often exceptional reader, at the expense of the political reading habits of a collective.[11] By basing our analysis of political reading habits on library records, rather than individual reading records, it is possible to expand an analysis of the significance of reading to electoral politics to that of a whole community of readers.

For much of the 18th and 19th centuries, the Bristol Library Society served as Bristol's foremost cultural and intellectual institution, as well as its largest and most popular lending library.[12] Founded in 1772, by the 1810s it boasted a membership of almost 300 and a

---

[6] O'Gorman, *Voters, Patrons, and Parties*, 225.

[7] H.T. Dickinson, *Liberty and Property: Political Ideology in Eighteenth-Century Britain* (1977), 1–10.

[8] Stuart Andrews, *The British Periodical Press and the French Revolution, 1789–99* (Basingstoke, 2000); J.E. Cookson, *The Friends of Peace: Anti-War Liberalism in England, 1793–1815* (New York, 1982), 84–114; Kevin Gilmartin, *Print Politics: The Press and Radical Opposition in Early Nineteenth-Century England* (Cambridge, 1996); Kevin Gilmartin, *Writing against Revolution: Literary Conservatism in Britain, 1790–1832* (Cambridge, 2006); M.O. Grenby, *The Anti-Jacobin Novel: British Conservatism and the French Revolution* (Cambridge, 2001); Ian Haywood, *The Revolution in Popular Literature: Print, Politics and the People, 1790–1860* (Cambridge, 2004); Jon Mee, *Print, Publicity and Popular Radicalism in the 1790s: The Laurel of Liberty* (Cambridge, 2016); J.J. Sack, *From Jacobite to Conservative: Reaction and Orthodoxy in Britain c. 1760–1832* (New York, 1993), 8–29.

[9] For an exception to this, though not strictly a biography, see David Bebbington, *The Mind of Gladstone: Religion, Homer, and Politics* (Oxford, 2004).

[10] K.J. Hayes, *The Road to Monticello: The Life and Mind of Thomas Jefferson* (Oxford, 2008); K.J. Hayes, *George Washington: A Life in Books* (Oxford, 2017); R.C. Windscheffel, *Reading Gladstone* (Basingstoke, 2008).

[11] Stephen Colclough, *Consuming Texts: Readers and Reading Communities, 1695–1870* (Basingstoke, 2007), 96–117; Mark Towsey, *Reading History in Britain and America, c.1750–c.1840* (Cambridge, 2019), 57–65; Julieanne Lamond, 'Representative Readers: Political Agency, Reading History, and the Case of Matthew Charlton', *Library & Information History*, xxxvii (2021), 219–33. For a similar approach for a different context, see Geoff Baker, *Reading and Politics in Early Modern England: The Mental World of a Seventeenth-Century Catholic Gentleman* (Manchester, 2010).

[12] Paul Kaufman's analysis of borrowings from the Bristol Library between 1773 and 1784, conducted in the 1950s, is still regularly cited by scholars: *The Minute Book of the Bristol Library Society, 1771–1801*, ed. Max Skjönsberg and Mark Towsey (Bristol Record Society, lxxv, 2022), xii n. 14; Paul Kaufman, *Borrowings from the Bristol Library, 1773–1784: A Unique Record of Reading Vogues* (Charlottesville, 1960). See also Kathleen Hapgood, 'Library Practice in the Bristol Library Society, 1772–1830', *Library History*, v (1981), 145–53; Kathleen Hapgood, *The Friends to Literature: Bristol Library Society 1772–1894* (Bristol, 2014); Max Skjönsberg, '"This Revolution in the Town": Richard Champion and the Early Years of the Bristol Library Society', *Library & Information History*, xxxvii (2021), 149–67.

© 2024 The Authors. Parliamentary History *published by* John Wiley & Sons Ltd *on behalf of Parliamentary History Yearbook Trust.*

collection that numbered 7,709 books and 270 pamphlets.[13] Critically, as a proprietary subscription library, ownership and management of the library was vested in its membership, in the form of annual regular meetings and an elected committee. This system of associational management, termed 'subscriber democracy' by Robert Morris, blended democratic and constitutionalist elements with an emphasis upon rights, regulations and conventions.[14] Hierarchies within the library represented those from without, and committee positions were generally filled by civic elites, church ministers (both Anglican and dissenting), merchants, and medical and legal professionals.[15] This was library politics as local politics writ small. These individuals, and the library's wider membership, formed an influential civic class who were deeply involved in Bristol's cultural and political life.[16]

The Bristol Library was a particularly established example of the subscription library, a form of library association that was widespread throughout the British Isles and North America by the first decade of the 19th century.[17] The surviving records of these libraries provide us with an insight into the associational networks and power relations that underpinned such communities. Among these, the Bristol Library Society is unique for the scale of its borrowing records, which run from 1773 until 1857 and offer an unparalleled insight into the reading habits of an urban community in the 18th and 19th centuries.[18]

Bristol was an urban community with its own distinct and vibrant political culture.[19] It was a prestigious electoral prize, the largest urban electorate outside of London and home to around 5,000 eligible voters at the start of the 19th century. It was, however, an expensive and difficult parliamentary constituency to control.[20] Its electoral politics in the 18th century was 'intensely oligarchical', with its political class formed of a collection of families and individuals who managed the civic administration of the city, were actively

---

[13] *A Catalogue of the Books belonging to the Bristol Library Society* (Bristol, 1814), viii (hereafter *Catalogue* (1814)).

[14] R.J. Morris, 'Clubs, Societies and Associations', in *The Cambridge Social History of Britain, 1750–1950*, ed. F.M.L. Thompson (3 vols, Cambridge, 1990), iii, 412.

[15] Bristol Archives (hereafter BA), 32079/153, minute book of annual general meetings, 2 Dec. 1772–28 Mar. 1870. For biographical sketches of the library's committee members in the 18th century, see *Minute Book*, ed. Skjönsberg and Towsey, 253–65.

[16] Jonathan Barry, 'Bristol Pride: Civic Identity in Bristol, *c.* 1640–1775', in *The Making of Modern Bristol*, ed. Madge Dresser and Philip Ollerenshaw (Tiverton, 1996), 40–2; Martin Gorsky, *Patterns of Philanthropy: Charity and Society in Nineteenth-Century Bristol* (Woodbridge, 1999), 113–61; Mark Harrison, *Crowds and History: Mass Phenomena in English Towns, 1790–1835* (Cambridge, 2002), 57–89; Steve Poole and Nicolas Rogers, *Bristol from Below: Law, Authority and Protest in a Georgian City* (Woodbridge, 2017), 85–110.

[17] There are estimated to have been over 350 subscription libraries active across the British Isles and North America by 1800: *Minute Book*, ed. Skjönsberg and Towsey, xii. For an overview of the growth of the subscription library movement, see David Allan, *A Nation of Readers: The Lending Library in Georgian England* (2008), 63–77; William St Clair, *The Reading Nation in the Romantic Period* (Cambridge, 2004), 246–54; K.A. Manley, *Books, Borrowers, and Shareholders. Scottish Circulating and Subscription Libraries before 1825* (Edinburgh, 2012), 17–45. For an overview of the different types of libraries active in this period and its nomenclature, see Katie Halsey, 'Types of Libraries', https://borrowing.stir.ac.uk/types-of-libraries/ (accessed 26 Mar. 2023).

[18] Bristol Central Library (hereafter BCL), B7453–7529, registers of the Bristol Library Society.

[19] See Peter Brett, 'The Liberal Middle Classes and Politics in Three Provincial Towns: Newcastle, Bristol, and York – *c.* 1812–1841', University of Durham PhD, 1991; Harrison, *Crowds and History*, 205–20; Phillips, *Great Reform Bill*, 65–105; Poole and Rogers, *Bristol from Below*.

[20] *HPC, 1790–1820*, www.historyofparliamentonline.org/ (accessed 14 Nov. 2022), s.v. Bristol; 'Bristol', ECPPEC, https://ecppec.ncl.ac.uk/case-study-constituencies/bristol/ (accessed 26 Mar. 2023).

involved in the city's two political clubs and were also socially prominent among Bristol's other clubs and societies, particularly the Bristol Library Society.[21]

These structural elements of politics in Bristol, and networks of sociability and patronage were clearly important in determining electoral contests, and the Bristol Library Society, could be an important element in the creation and maintenance of such networks.[22] Yet to understand fully why electors would cast their votes in a specific manner requires an appreciation of the local intellectual or ideological context. Subscription libraries contributed to this through the circulation of texts within a politically engaged and socially and economically secure population. The electoral significance of this has not been examined by either library or political historians of pre-Reform Britain. Analysis of library borrowing records and electoral polling data provides an opportunity to link together the intellectual climate in which elections took place with the act of voting itself, and to go further in our analysis of the political vitality of the unreformed political system. Bristol's size as a political constituency, the extent of its subscription library (and its surviving records), and the feverish nature of Bristol's politics in 1812, which witnessed two electoral contests, make it a prime candidate for such an analysis. Bristol Library members were directly involved in nearly all facets of Bristol's electoral activity in 1812, as candidates, canvassers, civic officials, voters and street participants. Voting data for the 1812 general election provides the opportunity to analyse the votes and political affiliations of the members of the subscription library quantitatively and to cross-reference this data with their record of reading for that year.[23] While local circumstances were a significant factor in deciding Bristol's electoral contests, the reading habits of library electors were thoroughly international. The phantom of France and the legacy of Revolutionary terror loomed large in the material borrowed from the Bristol Library and this reflected, or possibly accentuated, discourses in the election such as a customary mistrust of external political figures and an anti-Gallicism that contributed to the defeat of the insurgent Whig candidate.

Before we can proceed to an analysis of this intellectual culture, it is necessary to provide some background to both of Bristol's electoral contests of 1812 in order to understand better the context within which each election was fought and read. Bristol's oligarchical, dynastic politics was built upon a series of interwoven networks between members of different associational organisations; these included the city's two political clubs, the Tory Steadfast Society and the Whig Independent Club, as well as charitable or voluntary associations such as the Colston Society, the Society of Merchant Venturers, the Bristol Library Society and the centre of local civic governance in the corporation.[24] Securing the political support of the members of these sociable institutions, in addition to Bristol's large electorate,

---

[21] Poole and Rogers, *Bristol from Below*, 85.

[22] Skjönsberg, 'Richard Champion', 151.

[23] *The Bristol Poll-Book* (Bristol, 1818). This electoral data has been digitally transcribed: 'Oct. 1812 Bristol', ECPPEC, https://ecppec.ncl.ac.uk/case-study-constituencies/bristol/election/Oct-1812/ (accessed 24 Mar. 2023).

[24] For an overview of Bristol's civic governance prior to its reform in the 1835 Municipal Corporations Act, see Graham Bush, *Bristol and its Municipal Government, 1820–1851* (Bristol, 1976), 17–28; Harrison, *Crowds and History*, 62–4. See also *Politics and the Port of Bristol in the Eighteenth Century: The Petitions of the Society of Merchant Venturers, 1698–1803*, ed. W.E. Minchinton (Bristol Record Society, xxiii, 1963), xi–xviii; Barry, 'Bristol Pride', 25–47; Steve Poole, 'To be a Bristolian: Civic Identity and the Social Order, 1750–1850', in *Making of Modern Bristol*, ed. Dresser and Ollerenshaw, 76–95; Gorsky, *Patterns of Philanthropy*; Poole and Rogers, *Bristol from Below*, 85–101.

made contested elections particularly expensive. It was for this reason that its two respective factions frequently agreed to split the representation of the city between them, as occurred between 1754 and 1774, and again between 1784 and 1812.[25] This infrequency of contests was a source of much discontent. It was only a challenge to the city's established political clubs that forced a ballot in March 1812, when the incumbent Tory MP, Charles Bragge (1754–1831), opted not to stand for re-election at Bristol and the Steadfast Society selected Richard Hart Davis (1766–1842), a local West India merchant and the MP for Colchester since 1807, to be his replacement.[26] Although the Whig club decided not to challenge for the seat of the 'Blues', Henry 'Orator' Hunt (1773–1835), active in Bristol's radical politics since 1807, was determined to force a contest. The resulting 15 days of polling in July saw an election that was 'extraordinarily violent', as Hunt's and Davis's armed supporters skirmished in the streets.[27] Hunt was ultimately well beaten, 1,907 votes to 235, but his chief success lay in keeping the polls open for so many days, thus gaining for himself a national platform and forcing Davis's Tories to spend over £14,000 in campaign expenses.[28]

A further electoral contest was assured to take place at the next general election, which occurred in October that year, with Hunt again choosing to challenge Davis. Divisions between Bristol's Whigs now produced a contest for the second parliamentary seat with the resignation of the long-term incumbent, Evan Baillie (1741–1835). In December 1811, the Whig Independent Club had invited Sir Samuel Romilly (1757–1818), the prominent lawyer and legal reformer, to stand as his replacement. Romilly's candidature, and his support for the abolition of slavery, were strongly opposed by certain Whig families of the West India interest, such as the Protheroes, Ameses and the Baillies. They proposed a candidate of their own, Edward Protheroe (1774–1856), in his stead.[29] Although his candidacy was rejected by the Whig club, Protheroe opted to stand for election anyway, promising to be the 'enemy of tyranny and corruption whether exercised by a Court, an Aristocracy, or a Club'.[30]

John Phillips writes that the 1812 general election illustrated the 'complex cross-currents of Whiggery in Bristol' and saw the establishment of a general pattern of Whig division that repeated itself in further electoral contests in 1818, 1820, 1826 and 1830.[31] Much of this division owed itself to differences over the abolition of slavery, which, as a political issue, was able to cut across partisan lines and serve as a unifying force among Bristol merchants.[32] There was also a great degree of political distance between the two 'Whig' candidates

---

[25] Phillips, *Great Reform Bill*, 75.

[26] The following account of Bristol's politics in 1812 is drawn from *Bristol Poll-Book*, i–lxiv; Brett, 'Liberal Middle Classes', 86–99; *HPC, 1790–1820*, s.v. Bristol; Harrison, *Crowds and History*, 209–20; Phillips, *Great Reform Bill*, 83–6; Poole and Rogers, *Bristol from Below*, 307–11.

[27] John Belchem, *'Orator' Hunt: Henry Hunt and English Working-Class Radicalism* (2012), 26–30; Poole and Rogers, *Bristol from Below*, 307.

[28] Despite it being some 16 years since Bristol had last faced a contested election, and despite the length of the poll itself, the total of recorded votes represented less than half of the total electorate. This may be due to no official Whig candidate standing for election, although without a surviving poll book, it is impossible to say for sure. Violence during the period of polling may also have played a role: *HPC, 1790–1820*, s.v. Bristol; Harrison, *Crowds and History*, 215; Poole and Rogers, *Bristol from Below*, 308–9. Turnout was also low at the general election in October.

[29] Samuel Romilly, *Memoirs of the Life of Sir Samuel Romilly* (3rd edn, 2 vols, 1841), ii, 229–30.

[30] *Bristol Poll-Book*, xxvi.

[31] Phillips, *Great Reform Bill*, 83.

[32] John Latimer, *The Annals of Bristol in the Eighteenth Century* (Bristol, 1893), 476–7.

© 2024 *The Authors.* Parliamentary History *published by John Wiley & Sons Ltd on behalf of Parliamentary History Yearbook Trust.*

which reflected schisms within the Whig party at a local and national level. Romilly was a proud and vocal abolitionist, who was also supportive of parliamentary reform and Catholic emancipation. In contrast, Protheroe, as a banker and West India merchant, had accrued much of his wealth through his family's plantations in Jamaica, St Vincent and Trinidad, and was publicly evasive on both parliamentary reform and the repeal of penal laws against both Dissenters and Catholics.[33] A supporter of Romilly's, and a library member, described his politics as that of a 'neutral and negative whiggism': he was certainly politically closer to the Grenvillite wing of the parliamentary Whigs than its Foxite group.[34] Arguably, the divisions between Bristol Whigs which first arose at the election of 1812 were the same political differences that had led the Portland Whigs to join with William Pitt in 1794, and would lead William Grenville and his followers to split from Charles Grey's Whigs in 1817.[35] An analysis of the borrowings from the Bristol Library can help to explain why the intellectual and political climate in Bristol proved to be so unfavourable to Romilly and his politics.

The disarray within the Whig camp assured Davis's safe re-election in October 1812 and ceded a great deal of political control to Bristol's Tories, enabling them to decide to which Whig candidate they wished to lend their second votes.[36] On the third day of the poll, Davis and Protheroe openly united in what was akin to a joint electoral ticket.[37] For his part, without the institutional support of Bristol's Whig club, Protheroe was reliant upon Davis's aid to be elected. This resulted in him being mocked in satirical prints and would cause further trouble in subsequent contests.[38] Protheroe's politics were certainly closer to Davis's than Davis's politics were to Romilly's. Davis proudly pronounced himself a Tory who saw 'the encroaching and overbearing licence of the people' as the most prominent danger to the constitution.[39] Davis's and Protheroe's similar backgrounds, as West India merchants and Bristol Library members, may also have played a role.[40] Beginning on 6 October, the polling lasted for ten days. Romilly retired on the eighth day, having received 1,678 votes; Hunt received 444, with the two victorious candidates, Davis and Protheroe, receiving 2,901 and 2,432 votes respectively.[41]

[33]Legacies of British Slavery, https://www.ucl.ac.uk/lbs/person/view/27337 (accessed 16 May 2023), s.v. Protheroe senior, Edward; Phillips, *Great Reform Bill*, 84. Hunt, in his opening address, said of Protheroe, 'that after listening to him with great attention, he could not discover what his politics were': *Bristol Poll-Book*, i.

[34]C.A. Elton, *An Account of the Entry of Sir Samuel Romilly into Bristol* (Bristol, 1812), 28–9, quoted in Brett, 'Liberal Middle Classes', 93; *HPC, 1790–1820*, s.v. Protheroe, Edward. See also Mitchell, *The Whigs in Opposition*, 19–20, 109; Peter Jupp, *Lord Grenville, 1759–1834* (New York, 1985), 420–39.

[35]Mitchell, *The Whigs in Opposition*, 109; J.J. Sack, *The Grenvillites, 1801–29: Party Politics and Factionalism in the Age of Pitt and Liverpool* (1979), 163–9; Frank O'Gorman, *Emergence of the British Two-Party System, 1760–1832* (1982), 21–6; Jupp, *Lord Grenville*, 443–9; W.A. Hay, *The Whig Revival, 1808–1830* (Basingstoke, 2005), 17–18.

[36]Phillips, *Great Reform Bill*, 83.

[37]Romilly, *Memoirs*, ii, 275.

[38]British Museum, 1868,0808.8026, Charles Williams, 'Two candidates for the city of B——l general election Octr, 1812' (1812); Phillips, *Great Reform Bill*, 86–8.

[39]*Parliamentary Register* (ser. 1, 41 vols, 1803–20), xxxix, 594, quoted in *HPC, 1790–1820*, s.v. Davis, Richard Hart; Phillips, *Great Reform Bill*, 85. Davis was also a vocal opponent of religious toleration, including Catholic emancipation and the abolition of slavery: Romilly, *Memoirs*, ii, 283–4.

[40]Protheroe had been a library subscriber since 1802, while Davis subscribed in 1805: BA, 160, cash book, 2 Dec. 1772–24 Apr. 1871, p. 25.

[41]'Oct. 1812 Bristol', ECPPEC.

Bristol Library members were active participants in Bristol's electoral politics in 1812 and were well placed to affect the political climate of the city. They were directly involved in the politicking, whether as candidates (Davis and Protheroe) or as campaigners. As chair of the Steadfast Society, library committee member Thomas Daniel (1762–1854) was central to Tory electioneering efforts throughout the year and a was hugely influential figure in Bristol society.[42] Protheroe's candidature was aided financially and logistically by his two younger brothers, Henry (1777–1840) and Philip (1779–1846), who were both library members.[43] Romilly received support from the alderman John Noble (d. 1828) and Charles Abraham Elton (1778–1853), a member of the mercantile gentry whom Hunt later accused as being among 'the foremost to abuse and belie me' during the October 1812 election.[44] Bristol Library members were also involved in the management and organisation of the electoral process as magistrates, sheriffs and barristers.[45] Finally, library members were also among the some 5,000 electors of Bristol who cast their votes in both July and October 1812.

In the absence of other sources, the Bristol Library's registers provide an accurate record of who could access the library in 1812. These reveal that between January and December 1812, 229 borrowers made a total of 3,097 borrowings.[46] This total offers a useful sample of names of Bristol's civic class to compare against those of voters appearing in the 1812 poll book. Using other records and biographical information it has been possible to identify 79 individuals who borrowed from the library in 1812 and who voted in the general election in October.[47] Of the 4,389 individuals who voted in the election, these 79 library electors make up just less than 2 per cent of the total Bristol electorate for 1812.[48] Without a full list of the library's members (the practice of publishing membership lists of the society was discontinued in 1798) and a full electoral roll for Bristol, it is impossible to conclusively determine how many library members were able to vote in 1812.[49] Burgess books detail

---

[42] BA, SMV/8/2/2/2, White Lion committee book, 1805–26; ODNB, www.oxforddnb.com (accessed 23 Mar. 2023), s.v. Daniel, Thomas; Bush, *Bristol and its Municipal Government*, 25–6, 84; Harrison, *Crowds and History*, 81.

[43] Romilly, *Memoirs*, ii, 230; John Latimer, *The Annals of Bristol in the Nineteenth Century* (Bristol, 1887), 52.

[44] Harrison, *Crowds and History*, 72–8, 210–12. Nevertheless, Hunt would also describe Elton as being one 'of the very best men amongst the gentry of Bristol': Henry Hunt, *Memoirs of Henry Hunt* (3 vols, 1820–2), iii, https://www.gutenberg.org/cache/epub/8463/pg8463.html (accessed 28 Oct. 2023). See also *Bristol Poll-Book*, xiii; ODNB, s.v. Elton, Sir Charles Abraham. Romilly's nomination in October 1812 was seconded by Elton's father, Revd Sir Abraham Elton (1755–1842), who had served on the Library Society's committee in the 1770s: Romilly, *Memoirs*, ii, 271–2; *Bristol Poll-Book*, xxxvii–xxxix; *Minute Book*, ed. Skjönsberg and Towsey, 258.

[45] These included Benjamin Bickley (1763–1846), George Hillhouse (1778–1848) and Abraham Hilhouse (1787–1867) as sheriffs, and Edmund Griffith (d. 1835) as steward of the sheriff's court: Alfred Beaven, *Bristol Lists: Municipal and Miscellaneous* (Bristol, 1899). For the electoral process in Bristol, see Harrison, *Crowds and History*, 209.

[46] Borrowings for the year 1812 were recorded in two consecutive borrowing registers: BCL, B7483, f. 31, Oct. 1811–Aug. 1812; B7484, f. 32, Aug 1812–July 1813. Borrowings were recorded and tallied by title, although members were able to borrow multiple volumes at a time. There were 292 total subscribers in 1812 (not including life members who would not have paid an annual subscription), meaning that 78 per cent of the library membership were active borrowers: BA, 160.

[47] These are chiefly *Minute Book*, ed. Skjönsberg and Towsey; BA, 153; BA, 32079/155, minute book of committee, 31 Mar. 1789–10 Mar. 1807; BA, 32079/156, minute book of committee, 24 Mar. 1807–22 Mar. 1823; BA, 160; *Index to the Bristol Burgess Books: Volumes 1 to 21, 1557–1995* (Bristol, 2005). For four borrowers it has been impossible to determine their identities from multiple individuals of the same name listed in the poll book and they have been excluded from the following analysis.

[48] 'Oct. 1812 Bristol', ECPPEC.

[49] *Minute Book*, ed. Skjönsberg and Towsey, app. 2.

© 2024 *The Authors.* Parliamentary History *published by John Wiley & Sons Ltd on behalf of Parliamentary History Yearbook Trust.*

who may have been eligible to vote as freemen, but freeholders (worth 40 shillings or more) could also vote in Bristol's elections.[50] A significant proportion of this electorate lived beyond Bristol and would not have been eligible for library membership, which was available only to those that lived in or close to the city.[51] Nor was the vote open to the library's 12 female borrowers in 1812.[52] Although Bristol's electorate was large, by the 19th century it represented just less than a quarter of the city's wider population, or around one in five males. Moreover, increases in the size of the electorate had failed to keep pace with urban population growth meaning that, as a proportion of the wider population, the size of Bristol's electorate had declined over time.[53] There was a symmetry here with the Bristol Library, whose own membership, although gradually increasing until 1821, also failed to keep pace with population trends.[54]

Nevertheless, this tally of 79 library electors underplays the number of those who could vote in 1812. Electoral turnout in 1812 (66 per cent) was markedly lower than it had been at elections earlier in the 18th century, and there are a number of library members who borrowed books and were eligible to vote but are not recorded as doing so.[55] Likewise, there are a number of eligible voters who are not recorded as library borrowers and either could have or did vote in October 1812.[56] Despite being a small proportion of the overall electorate, this list of 79 library electors includes individuals who would have been well known among Bristol's civic society, including Joseph Cottle (1770–1853), Thomas Daniel, John Eagles (1783–1855), Philip John Miles (1774–1845), John Noble and James Cowles Prichard (1786–1848).[57] As political campaigners, organisers and pamphlet-writers their influence went far beyond the act of voting. As a collective group, they were instrumental actors in the discourses which shaped electioneering in Bristol in 1812.[58] As borrowers, they were a representative group in terms of the number of borrowings they made and were about no more or less likely to borrow books than non-voting library members.[59] In a

---

[50] *HPC, 1790–1820*, s.v. Bristol; Poole and Rogers, *Bristol from Below*, 92.

[51] See, for example, the refusal to transfer a library share to a gentleman living in Weston-super-Mare: BA, 32079/157, minute book of committee, 1 Apr. 1823–20 Dec. 1836, 15 July 1828.

[52] These included Ann Span (1777–1844) and the inventor Sarah Guppy (d. 1852): Legacies of British Slavery, s.v. Bartlet, Ann, https://www.ucl.ac.uk/lbs/person/view/2146630841 (accessed 24 May 2023); ODNB, s.v. Guppy, Sarah.

[53] Poole and Rogers, *Bristol from Below*, 92.

[54] BA, 32079/153, pp. 90–2; BA, 160; Hapgood, *Friends to Literature*, 17–19.

[55] For example, turnout in 1754 was 84 per cent: Poole and Rogers, *Bristol from Below*, 92. It is curious why Bristol's turnout in Oct. 1812 was so low considering that preparation for a general election had been underway for over a year. Although it was noisy and boisterous, there was also no repeat of the electoral violence of July: *HPC, 1790–1820*, s.v. Bristol. Library members who borrowed books and were not recorded as voters in 1812, despite being eligible, included the independent Whig candidate Edward Protheroe, along with his younger brother Philip, Evan Baillie, John Paine Berjew (1748–1833), Lowbridge Bright (1741–1818), William Gibbons (1782–1848) and Nathan Windey.

[56] Even if they did not borrow books, such individuals may have used their library membership to read in the library building. These included the Tory candidate Richard Hart Davis, as well as Schaw Grosett (d. 1820), Charles Joseph Harford (1764–1830), John Peace (1785–1861) and Henry Protheroe.

[57] ODNB, s.v. Cottle, Joseph and Eagles, John; *HPC, 1820–32*, s.v. Miles, Philip John; ODNB, s.v. Prichard, James Cowles.

[58] For examples, see *Bristol Poll-Book*, i–lxiv; Brett, Liberal Middle Classes', 86–96.

[59] Seventy-nine (34 per cent) elector borrowers out of a total of 229 borrowers, responsible for 1,102 (36 per cent) borrowings out of a total of 3,097.

similar manner of proportionality to Bristol's electorate and its total population, the library's electors account for just over a third of its active borrowers in 1812. This group is also generally representative of voting habits of the Bristol electorate in 1812 more widely. Votes by library electors were cast in five different ways: 43 voters voted for Davis and Protheroe; 19 'plumped' for Davis, using only one of their votes and voting for one candidate, with nine doing the same for Romilly; seven voters split for Romilly and Davis; and only a single voter ignored the Whig divide and voted for Romilly and Protheroe. There were no plumpers for Protheroe and no votes at all for Henry Hunt.

That no Bristol Library members voted for Hunt is not a complete surprise. Hunt succeeded in securing only a tenth of the votes he had achieved earlier in July and his voters were principally those involved in small crafts and trades that were not well represented among the Bristol Library's membership.[60] His standing at the general election in 1812 was partly performative, especially while the split within the Whig camp made the prospect of an electoral contest inevitable, and his polling at the July by-election demonstrated that he had little chance of success. Yet Hunt was an 'expert in the politics of exposure' and his goal at both elections in 1812 had been to extend the length of the poll, raise his public profile and expose the tactics employed by Bristol's political factions.[61] Hunt's chief target in all this was the city's corporation, which was widely viewed as a symbol of corruption and remained a target of much popular loathing.[62] Despite close links between the Bristol Library and the corporation, there were also critics of it among the library's membership, most notably the author and newspaper proprietor John Mathew Gutch (1776–1861); however, no other members wished to align themselves openly with Hunt in this cause, mindful perhaps of the social opprobrium that might come with such an association.[63]

The voting habits of Bristol Library members roughly correspond to those of the wider electorate, except in a few key respects. Library voters were slightly more likely to vote for the two successful candidates, Davis and Protheroe, than the wider electorate (54 per cent to 48 per cent). They were also slightly less likely to plump for Romilly (12 per cent to 17 per cent).[64] These who did so included Unitarians of Lewin's Mead Chapel, Bristol's leading nonconformist centre, including its minister, Revd John Prior Estlin (1747–1817), and two influential members of its congregation, Richard Bright (1754–1840) and Charles Abraham Elton.[65] A far greater divergence in voting habits comes in the percentage of library members who plumped for Davis versus that of the wider electorate (24 per cent to 8 per cent), with far more choosing to pin their political colours firmly to the flag of the 'blue' interest.[66] In terms of electoral strategy, plumping for Davis accomplished very

---

[60] Poole and Rogers, *Bristol from Below*, 309–10.

[61] Romilly, *Memoirs*, ii, 264; Harrison, *Crowds and History*, 213–17; Poole and Rogers, *Bristol from Below*, 310.

[62] Gorsky, *Patterns of Philanthropy*, 64–6; Harrison, *Crowds and History*, 219; Belchem, 'Orator' Hunt, 30–1; Poole and Rogers, *Bristol from Below*, 308–10.

[63] *Minute Book*, ed. Skjönsberg and Towsey, xv; Hapgood, *Friends to Literature*; Bush, *Bristol and its Municipal Government*, 22–3; ODNB, s.v. Gutch, John Mathew. Following the July by-election, the Steadfast Society published the names, occupations and parishes of the 235 men who had voted for Hunt: *A List of the Persons who Voted for Mr Hunt at the Late Election* (Bristol, 1812), cited in Harrison, *Crowds and History*, 215 n. 59.

[64] Figures taken from Phillips, *Great Reform Bill*, 85–6.

[65] *The Bright–Meyler Papers: A Bristol-West India Connection, 1732–1837*, ed. Kenneth Morgan (Oxford, 2007), 122–3; ODNB, s.v. Estlin, John Prior.

[66] My calculations.

little. The divided contest between the Bristol Whigs ensured that his position was never truly threatened, and Bristol's Tories enjoyed the luxury of being able to choose whichever Whig candidate they wished to share the representation of Bristol.[67] Although Davis was politically closer to Protheroe, there were still many differences between the candidates. While Protheroe prevaricated on the issue of Catholic Emancipation and supported peace negotiations with France, Davis was staunchly anti-Catholic and supported the full prosecution of the war effort.[68] It might have been that even Protheroe's 'mild' Whig principles proved too much for those library members who identified themselves solely with the Tory interest. Certainly, members of the Tory political club, the Steadfast Society, were well-represented within the library's membership. At the Steadfast meeting held on 24 June 1812, convened to establish Davis's election committee for the July by-election, five of the 13 attendant members were also library members. This did not include other prominent Tories who were not in attendance, including Edward and Thomas Daniel, George Daubeny (1775–1851) and James Tobin (1736–1817).[69] This was a group of individuals united by their political beliefs, associational participation, merchant backgrounds and service in the corporation.[70] This contingent within the library was representative of a wider Tory dominance in Bristol's civic politics, which became more pronounced in 1812 when the party secured a majority membership within the corporation.[71] Indeed, it was two library members who were instrumental in this development, when the shipbuilding brothers George and Abraham Hilhouse were appointed in 1812.[72]

Recognising this political complexion of the library is significant not only for our understanding of where the library was situated within Bristol's political spectrum, but also for how the library collection was used by its members. Though non-partisan, the Bristol Library was not an ideologically or a politically neutral borrowing space, and this reading context shaped how individuals used the subscription library, the intellectual and ideological significance of borrowing from the Bristol Library and the political texts within it. The Bristol Library was not the only source of reading material available to electors in 1812, even if studies of comparative urban readers suggest they were more likely to get most of their reading material from subscription libraries.[73] Bristol was home to a number of different library types, including circulating, scientific and medical libraries.[74] It also had a lively newspaper culture, with publications of various political shades.[75] Electors may also

[67] Nearly 90 per cent of Protheroe's votes were doubled with a vote to Davis: Phillips, *Great Reform Bill*, 86.

[68] Phillips, *Great Reform Bill*, 85; *HPC, 1790–1820*, s.v. Protheroe, Edward and Davis, Richard Hart.

[69] Those library members present included Thomas Cole, Thomas Eagles (1746–1812), Gabriel Goldney (1766–1837), Charles Ridout (d.1815) and Richard Vaughan (1767–1833): BA, SMV/8/2/2/2, 50. There were at least 32 library members in the Steadfast Society during the 18th century: *Minute Book*, ed. Skjönsberg and Towsey, xxxvi.

[70] Harrison, *Crowds and History*, 78–82.

[71] Harrison, *Crowds and History*, 64; Brett, 'Liberal Middle Classes', 94.

[72] Latimer, *Bristol in the Nineteenth Century*, 37; Bush, *Bristol and its Municipal Government*, 34.

[73] Colclough, *Consuming Texts*, 98.

[74] This information is taken from Robin Alston's 'The Library History Database: British Isles to 1850', currently held offline by the Institute of English Studies, University of London. It can be accessed via the Wayback Machine at https://web.archive.org/web/20090523101524/ http://www.r-alston.co.uk/library.htm (accessed 20 Jan. 2023).

[75] Phillips, *Great Reform Bill*, 87; Brett, 'Liberal Middle Classes', 142–7; Keisuke Masaki, 'The Development of Provincial Toryism in the British Urban Context, c.1815–1832', University of Edinburgh PhD, 2016, pp. 24–78.

have read books from their own libraries or read texts in situ, either in the open street, a shop window, a public space as a pasted flyer, or via a shared pamphlet. Elections were, of course, a prime theatre for the creation of political reading material and its dissemination to those who did and did not have the right to vote.[76]

The social, cultural and structural dynamics of the Bristol Library Society also shaped the ways that its collection was used by Bristolians and may have influenced their voting behaviour and the wider intellectual climate. Just as a back catalogue of an individual's reading and their ideological frameworks (their social, political and religious beliefs) shaped the way they interacted with a new book, so too did the associational context from which a book was borrowed speak to the reading experience.[77] Moreover, the arrangement of books in the library, into class and subject headings, acted as both an aid to reading and a shaper of reading practices in shepherding readers towards similar material.[78] This, coupled with the acquisition practices of the Bristol Library, under the careful management of the elected committee, was designed to foster a space and collection of books for polite, cultured education that was worthy of the city's urban elite.[79] This was not intended to be a narrow, prejudiced or partisan type of learning. On political topics the library sought to purchase a range of literature which, by 1812, still included many works that were a legacy of the 'pamphlet wars' of the 1790s, including works by Edmund Burke, John Bowles, John Gifford and Arthur Young, but also by Joseph Priestley, Mary Wollstonecraft and Daniel Stuart.[80] This afforded Bristol readers a great degree of choice, but the structures within the library would have been significant in shaping reading patterns. For example, filed under 'Metaphysic, Ethic, and Logic', Wollstonecraft's *Vindication of the Rights of Woman* (1792) was kept both intellectually and physically separate from other political works, being stored in a different press within the library, away from the political pamphlets.[81] It is important to recognise the potential of these influences upon borrowing and reading habits, and in turn upon voting habits and the intellectual climate in which the contest was fought.

In addition to its broad range of pamphlets from the 1790s, the Bristol Library seems to have never undergone a political 'purge' of books as may have occurred elsewhere.[82]

---

[76] Harrison, *Crowds and History*, 211.

[77] Christy Lindsay, 'Reading Associations in England and Scotland, c.1760–1830', University of Oxford DPhil, 2016, 20–2. This method, alive to the significance of the associational context to the reading of a text, builds upon the methods of reader-reception theorists, particularly Wolfgang Iser's 'horizon of expectations': Wolfgang Iser, *The Act of Reading: A Theory of Aesthetic Response* (1980). In a similar method, though principally examining the circulating library and the private library, James Raven argues that by 'recovering a sense of the internal arrangements of these libraries, we gain more clues about the cultural significance of reading': James Raven, 'From Promotion to Proscription: Arrangements for Reading and Eighteenth-Century Libraries', in *The Practice and Representation of Reading in England*, ed. James Raven, Helen Small and Naomie Tadmor (Cambridge, 1996), 196.

[78] The annotated 1798 catalogue of the Bristol librarian John Peace includes a diagram of one of the inner rooms of the library, with the books arranged into 26 presses and six subjects: BCL, B8453.

[79] *Minute Book*, ed. Skjönsberg and Towsey, xxvi–xxx.

[80] *Catalogue* (1814). For more on this debate and its pamphlets, see Emma Macleod, *A War of Ideas: British Attitudes to the Wars Against Revolutionary France, 1792–1802* (Oxford, 1998).

[81] *Catalogue* (1814). A work could be filed under multiple headings, although only in the case of large multi-volume works.

[82] See, for example, John Galt's description of the removal of the works of 'tainted authors' from the library at Greenock: John Galt, *Autobiography* (2 vols, 1833), i, 38–43. For further examples, see Manley, *Books, Borrowers, and Shareholders*, 100–2; K.A. Manley, 'Infidel Books and "Factories of the Enlightenment": Censorship and

Indeed, these instances have led some reading scholars to conclude that certain years saw a major reordering in subscription library collections as anti-Jacobin invective succeeded in engendering the removal of suspect texts from library shelves.[83] Despite a large contingent of Bristol's Tories among its membership, and despite being headed by a cautious and conservative vice-president in Samuel Seyer (1757–1831), no authors were blacklisted from the Bristol Library Society, nor were any works removed from circulation for political motives.[84] The library even stocked the work of the arch-Jacobin himself, Thomas Paine, having both parts of his attack upon institutional religion in *Age of Reason* (1796). These had been purchased at a committee meeting on 18 October 1796.[85]

For a library user in 1812, somewhat chronologically distanced from the 'pamphlet wars' of the 1790s, this literature and these authors might have lost some of their political charge. Certainly, few of these works were being regularly taken out of the library in 1812, with library members instead preferring newer publications. Nevertheless, Wollstonecraft's *Rights of Woman* was borrowed by one voter in 1812, John Brent Cross, on 27 November.[86] Cross was an apothecary on Dove Street and had close connections to members of Bristol's medical community and others interested in it, including James Cowles Prichard, Richard Smith (1772–1843), George Fisher (d. 1821) and James Storr Fry (1767–1835), all of whom were library members.[87] The borrowing register shows that Cross borrowed *Rights of Woman* for almost a full month and read it alongside Walter Scott's *Marmion* (1808) and *Lady of the Lake* (1810), Elizabeth Hamilton's *Letters of a Hindoo Rajah* (1796), and the 4th earl of Chesterfield's *Works* (1777–78) and *Letters to his Son* (1774).[88]

Cross's reading was varied and, as it came after the general election, could not have swayed his choice of vote which, like the majority of library electors, was for Davis and Protheroe.[89] His borrowing of a politically contentious text comes seemingly at odds with his own political views.[90] It may be that he read *Rights of Woman* for a practical purpose,

Surveillance in Subscription and Circulating Libraries in an Age of Revolutions, 1790–1850', *Book History*, xix (2017), 171; Loveday Herridge and Sue Roe, 'Reading Sheffield: Sheffield Libraries and Book Clubs, 1771–1850', in *Before the Public Library: Reading, Community, and Identity in the Atlantic World, 1650–1850*, ed. Mark Towsey and K.B. Roberts (Leiden, 2017), 187; *A Country Carpenter's Confession of Faith* (1794), cited in St Clair, *The Reading Nation*, 257.

[83] William St Clair dates this as 1794, with Stephen Colclough and others suggesting 1798 as significant: St Clair, *The Reading Nation*, 257; Richard Cronin, *The Politics of Romantic Poetry: In Search of the Pure Commonwealth* (Basingstoke, 2000), 61–82, cited in Colclough, *Consuming Texts*, 110–11; H.J. Jackson, *Marginalia: Readers Writing in Books* (New Haven, 2001), 78; Andrews, *British Periodical Press*, 72–82.

[84] For an exemplar of Seyer's politics, see his description of the political situation of Bristol in Nov. 1820: BA, 44954/1/1, calendar of events in Bristol, 1820–27, 28–9.

[85] *A Catalogue of the Books belonging to the Bristol Library Society* (Bristol, 1798); *Minute Book*, ed. Skjönsberg and Towsey, 213. However, Paine's work is not listed in later catalogues published in 1814 and 1834.

[86] BCL, B7484.

[87] 'Oct 1812 Bristol', ECPPEC; Michael Whitfield, *The Dispensaries: Healthcare for the Poor before the NHS* (Bloomington, 2016).

[88] BCL, B7484.

[89] 'Oct 1812 Bristol', ECPPEC.

[90] In 1818 and 1830, Cross voted for the candidates proposed by Bristol's Tory and Whig clubs, while in 1835 he was listed as a Conservative candidate to be city alderman. 'June 1818 Bristol', ECPPEC, https://ecppec.ncl.ac.uk/case-study-constituencies/bristol/election/June-1818/ (accessed 26 Mar. 2023); 'Aug 1830 Bristol', ECPPEC, https://ecppec.ncl.ac.uk/case-study-constituencies/bristol/election/Aug-1830/ (accessed 26 Mar. 2023); Beaven, *Bristol Lists*, 42.

and for its insights on female education. In this regard, his borrowing of Chesterfield's *Letters to his Son* two days before he chose to return Wollstonecraft may be significant. In another respect, Cross's reading of Elizabeth Hamilton's two novels, *Memoirs of Modern Philosophers* (1800) and *Letters of a Hindoo Rajah*, which bookended his borrowing record for 1812, may have encouraged him to seek out a work of 'modern philosophy' himself.[91] Perhaps his reading of Hamilton's anti-Jacobin critique furthered his own disparagement of Wollstonecraft's text.[92] As it did for others, this kind of reading could have reaffirmed Cross's sense of identity, enabling him to situate better his political views or provide him with the means to better develop them.[93] The associational context in which Cross borrowed these texts would also have been significant among fellows of similar politics within an association which stressed order and process.[94] Without library or reading records, and barring the survival of other sources, the individual idiosyncrasies which determined both reading or voting habits remain intangibly distant. Even with these borrowing records, it is difficult to say whether either the act of reading or voting pre-empted the other. Yet it does point to a potential motivator for electoral behaviour, in this case an anti-Jacobin strand in Bristol's politics in 1812, that would otherwise be left unknown. Moreover, this is an analysis which can be undertaken at both a qualitative and quantitative level, with the latter further contextualising the social and intellectual setting within which this electoral contest was decided.

The 1812 election saw in Romilly an external political figure vying to be chosen as Bristol's parliamentary representative. In 1774, when Edmund Burke had stood for election in the city, he and his supporters had gone to great efforts to interact with its social and cultural networks, and Burke himself had joined the Library Society as a life member and had donated several books to it.[95] Romilly made no such similar attempts.[96] No doubt, the width in political views between Romilly and some of Bristol's conservative Whigs was significant, but just as significant may have been a bibliographical climate of anti-Gallicism which made Bristol an unfavourable constituency for a man of his political views and heritage.

In 1812, voters made a total of 1,102 borrowings from the Bristol Library, which were representative of the general borrowing trends of the wider library membership.[97] 'Travel' was far and away the most popular borrowed subject, accounting for 21 per cent and 22

---

[91] Cross borrowed Hamilton's *Memoirs* on 14 Jan. 1812: BCL, B7484.

[92] It may be significant that he chose to return both *Rights of Woman* and the first volume of *Hindoo Rajah* on the same day (26 Dec. 1812): BCL, B7484.

[93] Bebbington, *Mind of Gladstone*, 15–40; Windscheffel, *Reading Gladstone*, 234–9; Towsey, *Reading History*, 63–5; Lamond, 'Representative Readers', 225–7.

[94] Allan, *Nation of Readers*, 75, 106–7; David Allan, 'Politeness and the Politics of Culture: An Intellectual History of the Eighteenth-Century Subscription Library', *Library & Information History*, xxix (2013), 159–69.

[95] Skjönsberg, 'Richard Champion', 149–58; *Minute Book*, ed. Skjönsberg and Towsey, xxxv–xxxvi.

[96] Poole and Rogers, *Bristol from Below*, 309.

[97] BCL, B7483 and B7484. To enable an analysis of library borrowing by subject, each borrowed text was given one of eighteen different subject categories (belles lettres; drama; education; fiction; fine arts; history; law; lives; medicine; natural philosophy; periodicals; philosophy & morality; poetry; politics, society & political economy; practical arts/useful knowledge; theology and travel). These subject categories were jointly formulated by the projects 'Books and Borrowing, 1750–1830: An Analysis of Scottish Borrowers' Registers' (https://borrowing. stir.ac.uk/) and 'Libraries, Reading Communities & Cultural Formation in the 18th-Century Atlantic' (www. liverpool.ac.uk/history/research/research-projects/history-libraries/).

© *2024 The Authors.* Parliamentary History *published by John Wiley & Sons Ltd on behalf of Parliamentary History Yearbook Trust.*

per cent of total borrowings by all library members and library electors respectively. Indeed, for library members and library electors, the four most popular borrowed subjects (travel, history, periodicals and lives) accounted for 54 per cent of all borrowings made.[98] The popularity of travel writing was not a trend restricted to Bristol; records from comparative libraries elsewhere in the British Isles suggest that it was generally popular.[99] No doubt, travel writing's popularity as a library borrowing came in part from the broad category of works it could encompass.[100] Yet the most popular borrowed political works also had an international, outward-looking dimension and a fixation with French domestic politics. The works of political and social theorists were borrowed by voters, including works by Voltaire, Adam Smith, Edmund Burke, Richard Price, Thomas Malthus and Mary Wollstonecraft, but not in large numbers. Instead, library electors were more likely to take out a work such as Joseph Weber's *Memoirs of Marie Antoinetta* (1805–12), edited by the leading anti-Jacobin, Robert Charles Dallas, which included an analysis of *Several Important Periods of the French Revolution*. Of almost equal popularity was Theodor von Faber's translated *Sketches of the Internal State of France* (1811), which was widely reported as having been suppressed by Napoleon in Europe.[101] Not all works offered a negative depiction of Napoleonic France, however. Anne Plumptre's *Narrative of a Three Years' Residence in France* (1810) was both a work of travel writing and political 'polemic', providing a first-hand account of Napoleon's reign, recognising his legitimacy to rule and advocating peace with him.[102] Yet Plumptre's narrative was swimming against the political and bibliographic tide among the Bristol Library's borrowers. Indeed, anti-Jacobin and anti-Gallic sentiment crossed over into other seemingly apolitical subject categories. The most popular novelist for library electors in 1812 was Elizabeth Hamilton, with her *Letters of a Hindoo Rajah* and *Memoirs of Modern Philosophers* being borrowed a total of 11 times. In both, Hamilton set her sights against the levelling tendency of French principles, as well as the 'new philosophy' of British writers such as Wollstonecraft, William Godwin and Mary Hays.[103]

French domestic politics, even events occurring some two decades earlier, continued to appear prominently in the reading material of Bristol readers in 1812. The resultant anxiety from such a reading syllabus would have been heightened by a number of features of the October general election. As had been the case in 1774, a competitive contest in the city had been forced by an outsider standing for election. The violence and disorder that had

[98] The top four most popular borrowed subjects for all library members: travel, 650 (21 per cent of total); history, 372 (12 per cent); lives, 342 (11 per cent); periodicals, 314 (10 per cent). For library electors: travel, 247 (22 per cent); history, 121 (11 per cent); periodicals, 119 (11 per cent); lives, 109 (10 per cent).

[99] 'Travel' was as popular at subscription libraries in Scotland, including the Leighton Library and the Wigtown Subscription Library. Borrowing records from both, in addition to 16 other historic libraries in Scotland, will be published as part of the 'Books and Borrowing' project. Paul Kaufman's analysis of borrowings from the Bristol Library in the 18th century also found 'travel' to be the most popular subject: Paul Kaufman, 'Some Reading Trends in Bristol 1773–84', in Paul Kaufman, *Libraries and Their Users: Collected Papers in Library History* (1969), 31.

[100] Nigel Leask, 'Eighteenth-Century Travel Writing', in *The Cambridge History of Travel Writing*, ed. Nandini Das and Tim Youngs (Cambridge, 2019), 93–107; Nigel Leask, *Stepping Westward: Writing the Highland Tour c. 1720–1830* (Oxford, 2020), 7–11; Carl Thompson, *Travel Writing: The New Critical Idiom* (2011), 44–52.

[101] Theodor von Faber, *Sketches of the Internal State of France* (1811), v–vi; *British Critic*, xxxviii (July 1811), 59–60; *Critical Review*, 3rd ser., xxiii (August 1811), 403–4.

[102] Adriana Craciun, *British Women Writers and the French Revolution: Citizens of the World* (Basingstoke, 2005), 179–83.

[103] Grenby, *Anti-Jacobin Novel*, 69–99.

© 2024 *The Authors. Parliamentary History* published by *John Wiley & Sons Ltd* on behalf of *Parliamentary History Yearbook Trust*.

accompanied the July by-election typified the dangers of electioneering in a city which had forgotten the conventions and structures which managed electoral proceedings.[104] Its results showed that Hunt had little chance of electoral success, but Romilly, backed by the Whig club, was a serious electoral prospect.[105] His political views, support for parliamentary reform, for religious toleration and, above all, for the abolition of slavery, placed him at odds with many of Bristol's merchant dynasties and raised the resultant electoral stakes yet further.[106] His candidature had already proven deeply divisive, forcing a conclusive split within the city's Whig faction that would not be fully healed until 1833.[107] Romilly blamed his defeat on the union of Davis and Protheroe against him, but Henry Hunt considered him to have been failed by his public supporters: 'The fact was, that these hypocritical Whigs would rather have sacrificed Romilly a hundred times, and have elected the devil himself, than they would have voted for Hunt'.[108] Hunt was overstating his chances of success, but to many political commentators, Romilly and his views were dangerous and foreign.

Writing after the conclusion of the contest, Robert Southey, a former resident of Bristol and a library member himself, warmly welcomed Romilly's defeat.[109] Despite not even knowing the names of the successful candidates, Southey considered Romilly's character, as a 'philosophical lawyer', to be cheap and his politics to be dangerous, based upon 'pseudo-philosophy' rather than on any rational judgement of man and society. Taken together, these 'would assuredly tend to make this country a province of France'.[110] Romilly's Huguenot ancestry gave this latter remark a slight xenophobic barb and his family heritage was continually referenced, particularly by his Whig opponents, to stress his status as an outsider, not only to Bristol's politics but England more generally.[111] Romilly sought to tackle from the outset the claim that Bristol was set to elect a 'foreigner' to represent it in parliament by stressing his own Englishness in a speech he made during his first arrival into the city in April 1812.[112] Nevertheless, references continued to be made to his French roots in comparison to the local connections of his opponent. At a political dinner attended by Protheroe, toasts were made to 'A natural *Bristol* whig, and may it never be scratched by *London* or *French* fashions'.[113] The same allusion was drawn by Henry Protheroe, albeit in a less than subtle manner, when, during the course of the election, he frequented public houses,

[104] Harrison, *Crowds and History*, 218–19.

[105] *HPC, 1790–1820*, s.v. Bristol; Poole and Rogers, *Bristol from Below*, 309–10.

[106] Phillips credits the issue of slavery with the realignment of Whig identity in Bristol away from party labels after 1826: Phillips, *Great Reform Bill*, 90–4. Arguably, however, it was largely a solidification of trends that were first openly raised in 1812.

[107] Phillips, *Great Reform Bill*, 93.

[108] Romilly, *Memoirs*, ii, 275–82; Hunt, *Memoirs*, iii.

[109] Southey was writing to the wine merchant Charles Danvers (c.1764–1814), who was himself a library member and borrower in 1812. For more on Southey's membership of the Bristol Library, see *Minute Book*, ed. Skjönsberg and Towsey, xlvi.

[110] 'The Collected Letters of Robert Southey: Part Four: 1810–1815', ed. Ian Packer and Lynda Pratt (2013), http://romantic-circles.org/editions/southey_letters/Part_Four/HTML/letterEEd.26.2165.html#back6 (accessed 23 Mar. 2023).

[111] ODNB, s.v. Romilly, Sir Samuel; Brett, 'Liberal Middle Classes', 94.

[112] *Bristol Poll-Book*, xxi.

[113] C.H. Walker, *An Independent Address to the Electors of Bristol* (Bristol, 1812), 11–12, quoted in Brett, 'Liberal Middle Classes', 94 (emphasis in original).

© 2024 The Authors. *Parliamentary History* published by *John Wiley & Sons Ltd* on behalf of *Parliamentary History Yearbook Trust*.

scattering money and vocally damning 'French principles'.[114] A general anti-Gallicism played a role in accentuating political differences between Whig candidates in Bristol in 1812, with Protheroe able to stress his occupation as a merchant and his participation within the political and social networks of the city, including the corporation and the Library Society, to his advantage. The borrowing records of the Library Society also demonstrate that library electors were reading a selection of works that were anti-Gallic in either their tone or analysis. Whether these reading trends were directly influential in determining voting trends is another matter. Yet the popularity of anti-Gallican texts throughout 1812 at least implies that this general milieu preceded the elections of that year, rather than resulting from them. It also demonstrates the persistence of anti-Jacobin lines of argument in the reading literature and political contests of the 1810s and beyond.[115] Critically, as only an analysis of quantitative reading records can show, this literature, and its arguments, were making their way directly to voters through the managed and ordered medium of the subscription library.

Combining an analysis of library records with traditional political sources opens up new avenues for research into the cultural and intellectual climate of the unreformed political system. Recent digital humanities projects, whether concerned with 18th-century voters or readers, that make data available and cross-searchable will enable researchers to more easily undertake this cross-analysis of different data sets.[116] In turn, this will allow political historians to go further in their examination of the overall vitality and the independence of electors in the unreformed electorate by using reading records to examine the local intellectual climate in which political allegiances were forged and votes were cast. The application of this methodology for the study of Bristol in 1812 sheds new light upon the cross-currents of local and national politics at play in the city which had lasting legacies on its electoral politics. While the Bristol Library was not a decisive player in the city's politics, both the library and its members were deeply integrated within the social and political networks that decided elections. The library's membership in 1812 reflected the political complexion of the city as it would remain for the next three decades, with the Tory club maintaining near hegemonic political control.[117] Coinciding with this, and representative of the reading material chosen by Bristol's library electors in 1812, was a political climate that was insular and anti-Gallican, and that made Bristol an unfavourable environment for reformist and radical politics.[118]

---

[114]Latimer, *Bristol in the Nineteenth Century*, 52.

[115]See, for example, the opposition to the 'egalitarian school' in a political essay written by William Gladstone at Oxford in 1831: Bebbington, *Mind of Gladstone*, 15–x27.

[116]Examples include ECPPEC, 'Books and Borrowing', and 'Libraries, Reading Communities & Cultural Formation'.

[117]Phillips, *Great Reform Bill*, 73–83; Brett, 'Liberal Middle Classes', 84–5.

[118]Harrison, *Crowds and History*, 240; Poole and Rogers, *Bristol from Below*, 1.

© 2024 *The Authors*. Parliamentary History *published by John Wiley & Sons Ltd on behalf of Parliamentary History Yearbook Trust*.

Parliamentary History, Vol. 43, pt. 1 (2024), pp. 129–147

'No distinction exists as to religion, profession, or sex': Imperial Reform and the Electoral Culture of the East India Company's Court of Proprietors, 1760–84

BEN GILDING

As contemporaries frequently pointed out, and often in disparaging terms, the governing institutions of the British East India Company contained an almost unprecedented 'democratical' element. By this, they were referring to the Company's General Court of Proprietors, its sovereign deliberative body, composed of all East India stockholders. Ownership of certain proportions of stock conferred the rights to participate in debate, to vote on policy, and to elect on an annual basis the directors who governed the day-to-day affairs of the Company. These electoral rights were granted solely by virtue of stock-ownership and made no distinctions based on sex, social status, nationality or religion. This article examines the ways in which women, non-Britons and religious minorities, in particular, took advantage of the opportunities for political participation opened up by the politicisation of the East India Company's general court in the 1760s, as well as the ways in which this was discussed and debated by contemporaries both in parliament and the press. Tracing the political activities of Mary Barwell, William Bolts and Joseph Salvador provides a unique window into a variety of ways in which the Company offered an alternative venue for political activity for groups often otherwise excluded from the formal politics at Westminster. In doing so, it also shows how the democratic elements of the Company's general court played a significant role in shaping the reform of the East India Company between 1767 and 1784, a process which ultimately led to their curtailment.

Keywords: East India Company; empire; democratic culture; gender; religious minorities; Jews; stockholding; lobbying; xenophobia; misogyny

Historians have long identified the East India Company's General Court of Proprietors as an alternate forum for political activity in 18th-century Britain.[1] This deliberative body, composed of all East India stockholders, was renowned for its democratic elements and was often referred to derisively as a 'Little Parliament'.[2] Benjamin Franklin used these same words, albeit with more positive connotations, to describe the colonial assemblies of North America.[3] There are numerous other parallels between the East India Company's general

---

[1] Lucy Sutherland, *East India Company in Eighteenth-Century Politics* (Oxford, 1952); C.H. Philips, *The East India Company, 1784–1834* (Manchester, 1961); H.V. Bowen, *Revenue and Reform: The Indian Problem in British Politics, 1757–1773* (Cambridge, 1991).

[2] *Autobiography and Political Correspondence of Augustus Henry, Third Duke of Grafton,* ed. Sir William Anson (1898), 237.

[3] *The Papers of Benjamin Franklin,* ed. L.W. Labaree (20 vols, New Haven, 1970), xiv, 62–71: Benjamin Franklin to Lord Kames, 25 Feb. 1767.

court and the American legislative assemblies in the period following the Seven Years' War, not least among which was the shared experience of struggling against the efforts of successive British governments to draw a revenue from the colonies in the face of an expanding national debt. In contrast to other colonial assemblies, however, the East India Company's headquarters (or East India House) was based in London, on the site now occupied by the Lloyd's Building on Leadenhall Street. When issues of representation arose, as they did in other colonial contexts, in response to issues of jurisdiction within the developing imperial constitution, the membership of the so-called 'parliament of Leadenhall-street' was attacked for its 'democratical' elements.[4] One prominent reformer even described it, in no sympathetic terms, as 'the most Democratic Body that ever existed'.[5] In particular, contemporaries criticised the fact that anybody could purchase stock and that ownership of any amount of stock entitled one to attend and even participate in debates. As one contemporary chronicler observed: 'no distinction exists as to religion, profession, or sex'.[6]

Huw Bowen's work has shed a great deal of light on the East India Company's governing institutions as well as the social composition of its stockholders.[7] The themes developed in this article owe a debt to his statistical data derived from the Company's stock ledgers. While Bowen has provided calculations of the proportion of stockholders who were women and estimates of the numbers who resided outside of Britain, this article sheds light on the ways in which the Company's general court offered opportunities for political participation among otherwise politically marginalised sections of the populace. By analysing the ways in which women, non-Britons and religious minorities engaged with the Company's governing institutions, as well as the contemporary commentary this caused, this article highlights a distinct period of the East India Company's metropolitan history, one that was both peculiarly political and democratic. Numerous individuals from these groups took advantage of the opportunities offered by the Company's politicisation, but this article focuses on the contributions of three key figures. The activities of Mary Barwell, as a political and financial manager of her family's East Indian fortune, William Bolts, as a foreign-born and disgruntled Company employee turned whistle-blower, and Joseph Salvador, as a wealthy merchant and financier with a large investment in the Company's stock, represent three very different ways in which individuals could participate in the Company's politics.

Although this article seeks to trace participation in the politics of the East India Company, including its annual elections of directors, it is important to be clear about the available evidence. The Company kept excellent records about the results of each ballot and election. However, in contrast to many parliamentary elections for which we have surviving poll book data, the Company did not make any record of which stockholders exercised their right to vote, or for whom or what they voted. Nonetheless, despite the lack of individual voting records, we know anecdotally that many women, non-Britons and religious

---

[4] *Cobbett's Parliamentary History of England* (36 vols, 1806–20), xix, col. 156: speech of Richard Rigby, 16 Apr. 1777.

[5] BL, Add. MS 38398, ff. 114–15: [John Robinson], 'Considerations on East India Affairs'.

[6] Peter Auber, *Analysis of the Constitution of the East India Company* (1826), 349.

[7] H.V. Bowen, *Business of Empire: The East India Company and Imperial Britain, 1756–1833* (Cambridge, 2006); H.V. Bowen, '"Dipped in the Traffic": East India Stockholders in the House of Commons 1768–1774', *Parliamentary History*, v (1986), 39–53; H.V. Bowen, 'Investment and Empire in the Later Eighteenth Century: East India Stockholding, 1756–1791,' *Economic History Review*, xlii (1989), 186–206; H.V. Bowen, 'British Politics and the East India Company, 1766–1773', University of Wales PhD, 1986.

minorities who possessed the right to vote in the Company's elections did so. Looking beyond the act of voting, however, we can also trace the participation of stockholders in other forms of activities related to Company elections and politics more generally, including lobbying, debating and various forms of campaigning, such as attending public meetings and drafting publications for the pamphlet and newspaper press. Such activities are revealing of the unique and 'democratical' political culture of the East India Company and the ways in which a diversity of stockholders found opportunities for political manoeuvring within its institutional framework, even while they were debarred from formal participation in other political arenas.

The political and democratic elements of the Company's constitution, alongside financial and political mismanagement, troubled contemporaries deeply and became intertwined with the process of imperial reform. The resulting clashes between Company and government between 1767 and 1784 led to repeated legislative measures to amend the parts of the Company's constitution that were deemed to be too democratic. Thus, despite the continuation of the general court as an institution and the maintenance of the Company's nominal independence after 1784, it can be said that the hyper-politicised and democratic electoral culture of the East India Company's general court between roughly 1760 and 1784 marks a distinct period in the Company's history. It also offered a unique, albeit fleeting, window of political opportunity in the third quarter of the 18th century.

The English East India Company was established by a crown charter in 1600. Recent research has largely revised the erroneous presumption that the Company's early history was characterised by relatively tranquil commercial activity and has instead highlighted the political, judicial, military and diplomatic aspects of the Company's activities in Asia, resulting in its designation as a 'Company-State'.[8] It remains the case, however, that the Company underwent its most significant revolution in the decades following Robert Clive's reconquest of Calcutta in 1757 and the subsequent arrangements with the nawabs of Bengal and the Mughal emperor. It was from this period that the East India Company began to acquire territorial sovereignty over large swathes of the Indian subcontinent, distinguishing it from the settlements and factories over which it had formerly exercised jurisdiction. By the treaty of Allahabad in 1765, the Company had become de facto governor of the province of Bengal and had obtained access to its lucrative land revenues. This not only completely altered the structure of the Company's trade, turning its employees from enterprising merchants into extractive governors, but it also drew the attention of the British public and parliament to an unprecedented degree. Although many contemporaries were troubled by the idea that a company of merchants could obtain sovereignty over large and populous territories, far more seem to have been interested in the financial opportunities offered by the Company's new circumstances. The government wanted to draw a revenue from the Company and many private individuals saw the Company's new situation as an unprecedented opportunity for investment and speculation. Throughout much of the 18th century, meetings of the Company's general court had been fairly quiet, quarterly affairs, predominantly associated with reviewing dividends and the usually uncontested annual elections of directors. From the early 1760s, however, the number of meetings rose dramatically and

---

[8]Philip Stern, *The Company-State: Corporate Sovereignty & the Early Modern Foundations of the British Empire in India* (Oxford, 2011).

the elections of directors were increasingly contested as rival groups attempted to take advantage of the Company's new circumstances in Bengal, be that for patronage, plunder or stock-jobbing.[9] The metropolitan response to news of the Company's acquisition of both substantial territories and revenues in India, therefore, resulted in the rapid politicisation of the Company's affairs.

The East India Company was led by 24 directors, who, prior to 1773, were elected annually by the stockholders. The only qualifications necessary to entitle a stockholder to a vote, both in the directorial elections and on points of Company policy, were to possess at least £500 of stock and to be above the age of majority. Those who possessed less than £500 of stock (including minors) could still attend the quarterly general courts and even participate in their debates.[10] Thus, there was nothing in the Company's constitution barring people of all faiths, women, foreigners or minors from participating in the Company's governing institutions. When these meetings became increasingly concerned with the governance of overseas territories and the constitutional relationship between the Company and the British state, these groups gained an unrivalled opportunity to participate formally in a political process to a degree that they were barred from doing at the parliamentary level. In fact, so political were these meetings that a considerable number of MPs and lords began purchasing the requisite qualification in East India stock in order to participate.[11]

If politicians were increasingly meddling in the Company's politics, to what extent can we measure the participation of other groups? In the case of female stockholders, this is complicated by the nature of the available evidence. We know, for instance, that in 1756, just before Clive's victory at the battle of Plassey, women held almost 28 per cent of the Company's stock and, although it dropped significantly over the course of the period under study, by 1783 they still held 12.5 per cent.[12] We also know that most of the women who owned stock at this time were either widowed or spinsters, and that women generally held smaller amounts of stock than their male counterparts and held it for longer periods of time.[13] Typical of this trend was Ann Coates, a widow, who in 1773 had held £500 of stock since at least 1747, and Charlotte Fielding, a spinster, who had held £100 of stock since 1753.[14] Although there is no record of attendance at general courts, it is unlikely that such long-standing female investors would have involved themselves in the heated Company politics of the 1760s. Coates, owing to the value of her stock, was entitled to a vote in the general court and may well have attended ballot days to protect her investment. Fielding, on the other hand, would have been much less likely to attend courts as the value of her stock did not entitle her to a vote. On the other end of the spectrum, we find figures like Lady Betty Germain, who owned some £25,000 of East India stock. She was so involved with Company politics that she actively participated in the practice of 'stock-splitting'. This involved parcelling out stock to trusted individuals in £500 blocks ahead

---

[9] For tables showing the increase in voters in general courts, as well as the frequency of meetings, see Bowen, *Business of Empire,* 63, 65.

[10] BL, IOR H/208, 7–10: Laurence Sulivan to Samuel Wilks, 9 Oct. 1778.

[11] Bowen, '"Dipped in the Traffic"', 39–53; Bowen, 'Investment and Empire in the Later Eighteenth Century', 195.

[12] Bowen, *Business of Empire,* 108.

[13] Bowen, *Business of Empire,* 87.

[14] *A List of the Names of All the Proprietors of East India Stock* (1773), 14, 22.

of an election or vote in order to 'create' new stockholders, who would vote as directed, before transferring the stock back to its original owner. The practice of stock-splitting first emerged on a large scale in 1763. In this same year, Lord Shelburne convinced Lady Betty to create up to 50 votes in favour of Laurence Sulivan, a prominent company director.[15] Although few stockholders could muster the resources of Lady Betty, the printed lists do suggest that women (in particular wives, sisters and mothers) were frequently the trusted recipients of these £500 parcels of stock.

Beyond the lack of official attendance records, another difficulty with assessing participation in the politics of the general court is the way the Company held its votes. They were initially determined by a show of hands, unless the result was challenged, in which case a division was held. After a division, any nine stockholders could request a ballot, which would be advertised in the newspapers and held on a subsequent day.[16] Even in the case of ballots, we only know the total numbers of votes cast on each side of a question, not individual voting records. From the 1760s, the debates of the general court were regularly printed in the newspapers. However, no evidence of women exercising their right to speak at a general court has yet been uncovered, although we know that they frequently voted on ballot days. In fact, there appears to have been a convention that women did not attend the debates, even if they voted on a subsequent day.[17] Even among men, a small minority of speakers dominated the debates and many of those were also MPs.[18] Most participants at the Company's general courts seem to have attended debates primarily to be informed of the issues at hand and perhaps even to soak in, and help create, some of the theatre of the occasion. Nonetheless, fledgling politicians and lawyers reportedly treated the Company's general court as something of a debating society. As a venue of political activity, the Company's general courts were frequently likened to a 'school of oratory', a 'probationary Theatre for young Lawyers … and a Stage for the Efforts of discontented Statesmen to make a Cats-paw of the Company'.[19] However, voting in person and speaking in debates were far from the only ways in which individuals could participate in the Company's electoral politics.

While many appeared to have but a fleeting zeal for the affairs of the East India Company, the Company was a major part of Mary Barwell's life. Her father was a former director and governor of Bengal, and her brother Richard was a leading member of the Company's civil service in Bengal. Mary was born into a tight-knit kinship network, common among families with both investments and employment in the Company, which involved her other brothers, James and Roger, and even her mother and sister.[20] During the stock-splitting

[15] Bute Archive at Mount Stuart, BU/98/8/185: Laurence Sulivan to the earl of Shelburne, 24 Feb. 1763. On Sulivan's role in the East India Company, see G.K. McGilvary, *Guardian of the East India Company: The Life of Laurence Sulivan* (2006).

[16] Auber, *Constitution of the Company*, 352.

[17] Bowen, 'British Politics and the East India Company, 1766–1773', 39–40; see also *A Letter to Sir George Colebrooke, Bart. on the Subjects of Supervision and Dividend* (1772), 27.

[18] Bowen, *Revenue and Reform*, 33.

[19] *Memoirs of the Life of Warren Hastings, First Governor-General of Bengal,* ed. G.R. Gleig (3 vols, 1841), iii, 97: John Scott to Warren Hastings, 10 Nov. 1783; Alexander Dalrymple, *Reflections on the Present State of the East India Company* (1783), 12.

[20] Margot Finn, 'The Female World of Love and Empire: Women, Family and East India Company Politics at the End of the Eighteenth Century', *Gender & History*, xxxi (2019), 7–24.

campaigns of the late 1760s, Richard Barwell, from his lucrative position as a councillor in Bengal, sent the enormous sum of £12,000 to Britain to purchase India stock to be divided among trusted friends and family, including his 'Unckle, Mr. Brown, [his] Mother, sisters and brothers'.[21] This gave the Barwells a considerable degree of influence in the Company's affairs, with the possibility of creating at least 24 votes in the general court and no doubt facilitating Richard's consistent rise to the highest stations on the Bengal establishment.

In the immediate aftermath of his father's death in 1769, it seems that Richard placed discretionary authority over his fortune and interests in Britain with his brother Roger. For high-ranking Company officials, having an agent or a party to manage one's affairs in London became increasingly necessary from the early 1760s given the factional strife that ravaged the Company's affairs. The distance, both chronologically and geographically, between Britain and India, and the frequent turnover of the Company's directors in their annual elections, meant that both news and orders were frequently out of date by the time they reached their destination. It was important, therefore, for employees serving overseas to have trusted confidants in Britain, vested with discretionary authority, to ensure that their interests were protected.[22] As Richard himself admitted, 'I cannot at this distance be particular … [t]he times must direct your pursuits on either your own or on my behalf'.[23] It was also vital that these agents received the most up-to-date information on the Company's circumstances in India to protect against misinformation and safeguard the family's fortune in East India stock.[24] However, it quickly emerged that, as agents, his brothers Roger and James were both unreliable and error-prone, frequently mixing their own personal ambitions with those of Richard.[25] His unmarried sister, Mary, on the other hand, had consistently proved herself to be both prudent and vociferous in pursuit of Richard's interests, at times rejecting the advice of family and friends, and taking the initiative in lobbying for Richard's advancement. Over the course of the early 1770s, Mary's role as Richard's 'confidant and negotiator' deepened, not just in the eyes of her grateful brother in India but also among the Company's chairmen and directors, and government ministers.[26] Mary continued to navigate between the political worlds of Leadenhall Street and Downing Street until Richard's final departure from India in 1780. During this time, she defended him from damaging allegations of corruption, secured his position as a member of the supreme council of Bengal, and continued to manage and utilise her brother's ever-increasing fortune for both political and financial ends.

Mary's financial management on behalf of her brother has been covered in detail by Amy Froide in her study of women as public investors.[27] Suffice to say that, as her brother's

---

[21] 'Two Letterbooks of Richard Barwell, 1769–73', ed. Lucy Sutherland, *Indian Archives,* vii (1953), 125: Richard Barwell to Roger Barwell, n.d. [c.1770].

[22] Ben Gilding, 'British Politics, Imperial Ideology, and East India Company Reform, 1773–1784', University of Cambridge PhD, 2020, pp. 263–314.

[23] 'Letterbooks of Richard Barwell', *Indian Archives,* vii, 131: Richard Barwell to Roger Barwell, 22 Dec. 1770.

[24] 'Letterbooks of Richard Barwell', *Indian Archives,* viii (1954), 35: Richard Barwell to Mary Barwell, 8 Dec. 1772; 39: the same to the same, 3 Mar. 1773.

[25] 'Letterbooks of Richard Barwell', *Indian Archives,* viii, 18: Richard Barwell to Roger Barwell, 27 Dec. 1771; 14: Richard Barwell to Mary Barwell, 30 Sept. 1771; 19: Richard Barwell to Mary Barwell, n.d.

[26] 'Letterbooks of Richard Barwell', *Indian Archives,* viii, 34: Richard Barwell to Mary Barwell, 8 Dec. 1772.

[27] A.M. Froide, *Silent Partners: Women as Public Investors during Britain's Financial Revolution,* 1690–1750 (Oxford, 2016), 107–17.

agent, she was gradually entrusted with managing a fortune in excess of £500,000 by the mid-1770s.[28] However, in addition to investing on behalf of her brother, Mary was also a stockholder in her own right and participated in the stock-splitting campaigns of the late 1760s. She even lent a substantial amount of her own money to others to purchase stock for splitting. When the stock price crashed in 1769, she lost a sizeable sum and was still receiving payments from Laurence Sulivan and his son over a decade later.[29] In addition to these losses, she also gave personal loans to other figures associated with the East India Company and, on several occasions, was forced to initiate legal proceedings in order to recover her substantial investments.[30]

On a political level, Mary's decision to invest the family's fortune, or at least a substantial part of it, in the banking firm headed by Sir George Colebrooke, one of the pre-eminent figures in the East India Company, turned out to be astute. While the bankruptcy of Colebrooke's firm in 1773 led to criticism of her financial acumen from her brothers in London, the decision was crucial to the success of Richard's career in Bengal.[31] The same financial crisis that brought Colebrooke's banking firm to its knees also forced the Company to request a loan from the government in order to avoid defaulting on its debts. In exchange for bailing out the Company, however, Lord North's administration demanded significant reforms of its constitution. Of particular importance to the Barwells was the North administration's insistence on replacing the governor and council of Bengal with a new supreme council consisting of four councillors and a governor-general. In the first instance, the membership of the new supreme council would be appointed by parliament. This reform significantly reduced the number of councillors in Bengal, of whom Richard Barwell was one. Lord North insisted on nominating three of the councillors who, if necessary, could form a majority capable of overruling the governor-general. Warren Hastings, an experienced Company servant who had only just been appointed governor of Bengal, was retained as governor-general. There was, therefore, only one spot remaining on the supreme council for the Company's nomination. It is a testament to the financial power of the Barwells, as well as to Mary's shrewd negotiating skills, that Colebrooke, as chairman of the Company, managed to get Richard appointed to this much-coveted position.[32]

Richard Barwell's selection as a member of Bengal's supreme council was a momentous coup for the family's fortunes and resulted in a dramatic alteration in Mary's role as her brother's agent. While Mary badgered Colebrooke for several years in efforts to reclaim the money she lost investing in his firm, Richard was surprisingly calm in the understanding that his new appointment offered him the opportunity to continue to augment his already vast fortune.[33] In the meantime, Richard's appointment by parliament transformed his understanding of the nature of his office. While a Bengal councillor, he had envisioned

---

[28] Froide, *Silent Partners,* 113.

[29] Bodl., MS Eng. hist. b. 190, f. 11: Laurence Sulivan to Stephen Sulivan, 20 Jan. 1782.

[30] 'Letters of Richard Barwell – VII', *Bengal Past & Present,* xi (1915), 299: Richard Barwell to Mary Barwell, n.d. See also Froide, *Silent Partners,* 116.

[31] Froide, *Silent Partners,* 111.

[32] Sir George Colebrooke, *Retrospection: Or Reminiscences Addressed to My Son Henry Thomas Colebrooke, esq.* (2 vols, 1898–9), ii, 35–7.

[33] 'Letters of Mr. Richard Barwell—VIII', *Bengal Past & Present,* xii (1916), 69: Richard Barwell to Mary Barwell, 30 Nov. 1774.

himself predominantly as an employee of the Company. As a member of the supreme council, however, Richard, like Warren Hastings, saw his position as a dual appointment, with responsibilities to both crown and Company. The supreme councillors were, as one contemporary astutely pointed out, the 'Servants of Two Masters'.[34] Richard was explicit in appealing to the new public nature of his office. He frequently addressed separate letters to the Company's directors and to Lord North, having been informed by Mary of the managerial role that North aimed to maintain over the Company's affairs.[35] Recognising that 'the pursuits of the Ministry' in India were to be undertaken through the 'medium of the Company', he informed John Robinson (North's treasury secretary and political manager) that he had instructed Mary 'to be wholly directed by you in all matters that shall be agitated in the Proprietors' Court'.[36] To Mary he added, 'the line I am determined to take, is implicit devotion to the Government', and enjoined her to promote their interests 'to the utmost of your power and engaging all the friends you can influence to carry them through the Proprietary Courts'.[37] Mary, as Richard's agent, was therefore tasked with conducting negotiations and coordinating efforts with both the government as well as the family's allies within the Company, a line of conduct that often found her walking a tightrope between competing interests. Her proximity to both the Company and the ministry, however, allowed Mary to fend off potentially damaging allegations of corruption in salt contracts levelled against Richard during his tenure as supreme councillor.[38] The fact that Richard weathered such charges was no doubt assisted by his (and Mary's) success in convincing Hastings's friends that he was an indispensable ally and in persuading the North ministry that he was pliable enough to take their side when push came to shove against the Company.

Richard Barwell has often been characterised as a loyal Company-man and staunch ally of Warren Hastings in his conflicts with both the North administration and the three ministerial members of the supreme council. His instructions to Mary, however, suggest that his position was far more nuanced.[39] Privately, Richard declared his willingness to support Hastings's removal from office, even if his public actions in the supreme council suggested unswerving loyalty. In secret instructions to Mary, Richard urged her to '[k]eep well with all parties, operate with … Hastings's friends, but in all questions for or against them made a point of by the Ministry, go implicitly with the Ministry'.[40] Ultimately, Richard was able to weather the storms of the supreme council's tumultuous opening decade and retire on his own terms. Much of his success in this regard can be attributed to Mary's role as his 'confidential agent'. Richard was frequently in a much stronger position, politically speaking, than his superior Warren Hastings, who had notoriously bad luck with agents who

---

[34] *Public Advertiser,* 4 Feb. 1774: 'On the East-India Affairs. A Modest Proposal'.

[35] 'Letters of Mr. Richard Barwell—IX', *Bengal Past & Present,* xii (1916), 185–86: Richard Barwell to Lord North, 30 Nov. 1774; 'Letters of Mr. Richard Barwell—IX', 189–90: Richard Barwell to John Robinson, 30 Nov. 1774.

[36] 'Letters of Mr. Richard Barwell—IX', 189–90.

[37] 'Letters of Mr. Richard Barwell—IX', 182–85: Richard Barwell to Mary Barwell, 1 Dec. 1774.

[38] 'Letters of Mr. Richard Barwell—IX', 226–27: Richard Barwell to Mary Barwell, 25 Mar. 1775.

[39] See, for instance, Amba Prasad, 'Introduction', in *Fort William–India House Correspondence* (21 vols, Delhi, 1949–85), xiv, p. xxxi; P.E. Roberts, 'Hastings and His Colleagues,' *The Cambridge History of India,* v: *British India, 1497–1858,* ed. H.H. Dodwell (Cambridge, 1929), 225–47; Robert Travers, *Ideology and Empire in Eighteenth-Century India: The British in Bengal* (Cambridge, 2007), 145.

[40] 'Letters of Richard Barwell—IX', 212: Richard Barwell to Mary Barwell, 25 Feb. 1775.

not only betrayed his trust but also misspent the resources he had allocated them.[41] Mary's efforts ensured that Richard remained a darling of the Company's stockholders during a period of government encroachment, all the while maintaining the closest relations with the North ministry.

Insofar as there was public commentary on the participation of women in the Company's general court, there was an equally mixed reaction among the wider public and politicians. One newspaper scribbler penned a sarcastic petition from the 'Committee for guarding the Rights of the Female Proprietors of India Stock'. In it, they outlined their opposition to Fox's India Bill, albeit for the rather lewd reason that the bill 'erected' 15 commissioners to oversee the Company's affairs, 'an Erection', they declared, 'so unsatisfactory and so inadequate to its Purposes'.[42] On the other hand, there were more serious and earnest calls for the female stockholders not only to vote but also to attend the debates in the general courts in order to save the Company from a 'mad' combination of 'Gentlemen proprietors' whose only concern was immediate profit.[43] In so doing, the female stockholders are generalised and positively stereotyped as being above the vices of stock-jobbing and speculation, which, as we have seen, they were not. Among the myriad appeals 'to the proprietors of East India stock' in the newspaper and pamphlet press, a number of publications were addressed to both 'Gentlemen and Ladies', or even, albeit infrequently, 'to the *Fair Proprietors*' alone.[44] These very consciously gendered addresses reveal the assumption that female stockholders were keeping informed of the debates at India House in the interest of their investments. They also reveal the extent to which the voting power of women in the general court was acknowledged, understood and actively courted by the different factions involved in the East India Company's politics.

Although some women clearly found means to thrive in the labyrinthine politics of the Company's general court, they were far from the only group to take advantage of the unique opportunities for political participation offered by the East India Company. In fact, when arranging the massive stock-splitting campaign of 1769, much of the stock was purchased temporarily from Dutch and other European stockholders.[45] In the mid-1760s, over one-third of the Company's entire stock was owned by continental Europeans, the vast majority of which was held by Dutch investors. Just as in the case of female investors, the proportion of stock owned by Dutch and other foreign investors dropped to less than one-fifth after the American Revolutionary War and never recovered to its former proportions.[46] It is difficult to ascertain just how many non-British stockholders actively participated in the Company's politics. There were certainly frequent references in the press and in private correspondence to the malign influence of foreign stockholders, particularly after the war of Austrian succession as the rivalry between the British, French, and Dutch East India

[41] Gilding, 'British Politics, Imperial Ideology, and East India Company Reform', 263–314.

[42] *Public Advertiser*, 4 Dec. 1783: 'Petition of the Female Proprietors of East India Stock'.

[43] *Morning Chronicle*, 25 May 1774: Letter 'To the Ladies Proprietors of India Stock'.

[44] *Gazetteer and London Daily Advertiser*, 5 Apr. 1764: Letter *'to the Fair Proprietors of the East India Stock'*, signed 'A Word to the Wise'. For letters signed to both 'Gentlemen and Ladies', see *London Chronicle*, 29–31 Mar. 1763; *Public Advertiser*, 9 Apr. 1763; *Lloyd's Evening Post*, 8–11 Apr. 1763, among many others.

[45] Lucy Sutherland and J.A. Woods, 'The East India Speculations of William Burke', in *Politics and Finance in the Eighteenth Century*, ed. Lucy Sutherland (1984), 344–45.

[46] Bowen, *Business of Empire*, 98, 112.

companies bubbled over into armed conflict and increasingly became an object of national concern.[47] It is challenging enough to trace foreign ownership of stock, given that it was often registered under the British addresses of agents or bankers.[48] It is even more difficult to uncover evidence of foreign stockholders having voted or spoken in the Company's general courts. If they did participate in the Company's politics, it is far more likely they did so during the annual elections of directors that took place every April. The regularity of such contests stands in stark contrast to the unpredictability of other divisions and ballots, which could be requested at the desire of nine proprietors, usually after the same number of stockholders had summoned a general court on 'special affairs' to debate the subject in question. The ad hoc nature of these meetings and the narrow time frame between debates and ballots meant that it would be logistically difficult for foreign stockholders, even those based just across the Channel in Amsterdam, to receive intelligence and embark on a journey at such short notice. Even if it could be done in extreme circumstances, it was unlikely to have been undertaken by enough stockholders to have a tangible impact on the outcome of ballots, especially when one considers that over 1,000 votes were cast in many instances in the 1760s and 1770s.[49] As a result, in spite of the contemporary rhetoric, the direct participation of foreign stockholders, as a body, upon the Company's general courts was likely to have been both infrequent and ultimately inconsequential.

One case stands out nonetheless: that of Dutch-born William Bolts. While much has been written about Bolts's extraordinary life in Asia and in the service of various European courts, much less attention has been paid to his activities as a 'foreign' owner of East India stock and his participation in the Company's general courts.[50] His origins are obscure and have been the subject of much historiographical debate. Bolts himself stated in his will that 'since the 7th of February AD 1739 [he] has been an inhabitant of various Parts of this Terrestrial Globe'.[51] However, it seems that he was born in Amsterdam to a German father. By the age of 20, he had gained considerable experience as a merchant in Lisbon and found himself employed by the British East India Company, which was desperate to recruit 'persons well experienced in business' to fill the vacancies caused by the military and political turmoil in Bengal in the late 1750s.[52] Although at various points Bolts strategically claimed to be a subject of Britain and of the elector palatine, he was often treated as an 'alien' when in Britain in the late 1760s and early 1770s, and at times even described himself as such.[53]

In British India in the 1760s, Bolts would have found himself among a diverse community of both Europeans and non-Europeans where such designations of 'foreignness' were of little significance. Bolts was among a number of non-British Europeans settled in India who were either directly or indirectly employed by the British East India Company. It was

[47]See, for instance, *London Evening Post,* 4–6 Mar. 1760; *London Chronicle,* 1–3 July 1760.

[48]Bowen, *Business of Empire,* 110.

[49]Bowen, *Business of Empire,* 62.

[50]W.G.J. Kuiters, *The British in Bengal, 1756–1773: A Society in Transition seen through the Biography of a Rebel: William Bolts (1739–1808)* (Paris, 2002); Holden Furber, 'In the Footsteps of a German "Nabob": William Bolts in the Swedish Archives', *Indian Archives,* xii (1958), 7–18.

[51]TNA, PROB 11/1485/54.

[52]*Fort William–India House Correspondence,* ii, 168: court of directors to the president and council of Calcutta, 23 Nov. 1759; BL, IOR B/75, 470: minutes of the court of directors, 10 Oct. 1759.

[53]Furber, 'William Bolts in the Swedish Archives', 16; *Morning Chronicle,* 27 May 1772.

in this context that he, like so many of the Company's other employees, became heavily engaged in what was called the 'country trade' (i.e., trade within India) which was not in breach of the Company's monopoly over trade *between* Britain and the Indo-Pacific, and indeed was seen as necessary in light of the Company's extraordinarily low salaries. Bolts seems to have been remarkably successful in this trade. He worked alongside a network of Armenian and Bengali merchants and intermediaries, and seems to have acquired strong connections in the court of the nawab of Bengal.[54] It was also through this trade and these communications networks that he fell foul of the Company's authorities, most particularly the governor of Bengal, Harry Verelst.[55] As a result, he was forcibly deported from the Company's settlements and shipped back to Britain in 1768.

In the years following his removal, Bolts sought legal redress from various authorities including the privy council and the court of chancery, and he was joined in some of these suits by his Armenian colleagues. Both before and during these suits his self-identification is revealing and fascinating. We know that when facing the threat of persecution by the Company's authorities in Bengal, he appealed to Magna Carta as a subject of Great Britain.[56] There is some validity in his claim, as he would almost certainly have been amenable to the courts of justice established by the British crown in India both before and after 1773. And it was the earlier of these courts, Calcutta's mayor's court, to which Bolts made another appeal. Owing to his high standing among the Company's employees in Calcutta, Bolts was appointed an alderman of the mayor's court in August 1766.[57] The mayor's court consisted of a mayor and nine aldermen, seven of whom had to be 'natural-born British subjects', but two other positions in Calcutta were allowed for 'foreign protestants' so long as their 'Prince or State [was] in amity with Great Britain'.[58] Although Bolts was probably appointed to one of these latter positions, in his petition to the grand jury of Calcutta in 1768, he claimed to be a 'freeman and Loyal Subject of Great Britain', likely justifying this self-identification through his continued participation in the Company's corporate institutions in Calcutta.[59] In a later publication, and one addressed to the public at large, Bolts acknowledged that he had 'not the honour of being a natural-born subject of Great Britain, yet being from his infancy bred in it, and having always lived amongst the natives of this happy country, he is in heart an Englishman and wishes to be no other, so long as the oppressed can obtain, from the English laws, justice adequate to their injuries'.[60] At the same time, his accusers, while not explicitly denying his British subjecthood, seem to have played on its ambiguity by questioning his allegiance. They accused Bolts on several occasions of collaborating with

---

[54] See the examination of William Bolts by the Commons select committee, printed in *Middlesex Journal,* 13–15 Aug. 1772.

[55] Of particular emphasis was a correspondence Bolts held in French with Jean Baptiste Gentil that was considered potentially seditious.

[56] N.L. Hallward, *William Bolts: A Dutch Adventurer Under John Company* (Cambridge, 1920), 204: petition of William Bolts to the grand jury of Calcutta, 27 May 1768.

[57] Hallward, *William Bolts,* 42.

[58] William Bolts, *Considerations on India Affairs; Particularly Respecting the Present State of Bengal and its Dependencies* (1772), 77.

[59] Hallward, *William Bolts,* 203–5; see also 93–7: petition of William Bolts to the court of directors, 19 May 1769.

[60] Bolts, *Considerations,* xi–xii.

the Dutch and even with the nawab of Bengal through a French intermediary at his court.[61] Such accusations were no doubt considerably more forceful, given the uncertainties over Bolts's subjecthood, as well as the amorphous nature of that concept in the early modern world.[62]

Upon returning to Britain, and alongside his legal proceedings, Bolts engaged in a press campaign against his former employers, exposing numerous instances of oppression and corruption, and calling into question the way that British interests in India had been managed by the Company. Although the complaints of Bolts and others were sometimes attributed to disappointed ambition, the claims, and particularly those made by Bolts against the governance of Lord Clive and Harry Verelst, were widely believed.[63] His *Considerations on India Affairs*, printed in 1772, was credited with 'opening the Eyes of the Nation' to the true nature of the Company's governance in its newly acquired territories.[64] One former Company employee reported that Bolts had 'raised the public Indignation ag[ains]t the servants of the Company' and that his accusations 'were swallowed greedily by the Public, whose Eyes are fixed on the correction of these Abuses by the Interposition of Parliament'.[65] Although Bolts's claims did not go unanswered, his relatively simple message, engaging prose and genuine attempt to appeal to the broader and largely uninformed public ensured that his work was highly influential at a time when East India Company reform was already under serious consideration.[66]

Alongside his publications in the press, Bolts also attacked the Company from within. He purchased the grand total of £5 of East India stock, which enabled him to attend the general court and participate in its debates. While this amount of stock did not entitle him to a vote, his motive in purchasing East India stock was almost certainly to defend his claims and to attack the Company and its managers rhetorically. His success in the Company's general court, however, seems to have been far more limited than his revelatory publications. Despite receiving the support of the influential Johnstone clan, with whom he was associated through his business ventures in Bengal, Bolts seems to have been far from successful in pursuing his interests in the Company's general court.[67] When his claims against the Company were made the subject of a meeting of the general court on 25 September 1771, they were thrown out after only a brief debate with various accusations made on both sides. In March 1772, after Bolts had published his most damaging allegations against the Company, his affairs came again before the general court. During an altercation with Governor Johnstone, Sir George Colebrooke, who would soon be elected to his third and final stint as chairman of the Company, remarked that Bolts was a '*bad citizen, and bad*

[61] *Fort William–India House Correspondence*, v, 360–1: president and council of Calcutta to the court of directors, 10 Dec. 1767; *Public Advertiser*, 27 Sept. 1771.

[62] H.W. Muller, *Subjects and Sovereign: Bonds of Belonging in the Eighteenth-Century British Empire* (Oxford, 2017).

[63] *Public Advertiser*, 4 Mar. 1772: letter signed 'Zoroaster'; see also *The Last Journals of Horace Walpole during the Reign of George III from 1771–1783*, ed. A.F. Steuart (2 vols, 1910), i, 72–3.

[64] *Public Advertiser*, 3 Mar. 1773: letter signed 'William Bolts'.

[65] BL, Add. MS 29133, f. 72: Ralph Leycester to Warren Hastings, 12 Mar. 1772; ff. 90–1: John Caillaud to Warren Hastings, 27 Mar. 1772.

[66] Harry Verelst, *A View of the Rise, and Progress, and Present State of the English Government in Bengal, including a Reply to the Misrepresentations of Mr. Bolts and Other Writers* (1772).

[67] Kuiters, *William Bolts*, 83; on the Johnstones, see Emma Rothschild, *The Inner Life of Empires: An Eighteenth-Century History* (Princeton, 2011).

subject'. In response, Bolts requested two forms of satisfaction, 'within' and 'out of doors', by which he meant both a public explanation of the comments in the general court and an insinuation that he would request a duel with Colebrooke in its aftermath. Colebrooke agreed, at least to the first demand, and explained that 'the reason why he made use of such epithets was, because Mr. Bolts had in that book said, that the nation would never be benefitted by her trade to Asia, till government took the whole of the management in their hands'. As for why he used the term '*bad subject'*, however, Colebrooke was even more explicit, claiming Bolts had mentioned in a plea to the court of exchequer that 'he was not born in these dominions'.[68] Later, Colebrooke also reportedly refused Bolts's challenge to a duel on the advice of his friends. Colebrooke, however, was not alone in attempting to malign Bolts and his cause by alluding to his ambiguous subjecthood. Several writers made note of Bolts's Dutch origins in an attempt to discredit his reliability as a whistle-blower.[69] In spite of these attempts, however, Bolts's revelations continued to be taken seriously by the wider public and were responsible for piling additional pressure on the North administration to reform the Company's governance.

Bolts is, however, one of the only non-Britons we find having such a considerable individual impact and participating directly in the Company's metropolitan political institutions. That he was quite unique in doing so is perhaps unsurprising given his enterprising and entrepreneurial character. After leaving Britain he went on to found the Imperial Asiatic Company of Trieste and Antwerp in 1775 with the backing of Maria Theresa, as well as planning and sponsoring several other expeditions to the Pacific and the northwest coast of America.

Bolts was a rather extraordinary case, but there were many instances of Britons exhibiting anxieties about the role foreign investors might play in undermining their imperial ambitions in India. During the famous parliamentary inquiry into the affairs of the Company in 1767, for instance, the Company's then chairman, George Dudley, was grilled on the issue of foreign investment. He admitted under questioning that the Dutch and French could divide their stock among friends in order to 'get a Majority in our General Courts and command the affairs of the Company'.[70] The particular concern at the time was that foreign investors might push for a higher dividend with no regard for the prosperity of the Company or British commerce in general. Dudley knew the Dutch had a large share of the stock but claimed that he could not provide an exact figure because the stock was so fluctuating, and that it was so fluctuating because of the stock-splitting campaigns that at times involved the temporary purchase of stock from Dutch investors. Such fears about the ability of foreign stockholders to influence collectively votes of the general court were repeated in the newspapers and even in the house of commons. George Johnstone, for instance, claimed that a 'vessel [was] freighted in Holland to bring over voters' to influence the general courts.[71] One considerably more specific newspaper report claimed that

---

[68] *London Evening Post,* 3–5 Mar. 1772. Similar reports of the debate are corroborated in seven other newspapers, and a later letter signed 'Ridens' in *Morning Chronicle,* 27 May 1772, reports that Colebrooke called Bolts '*an alien, a bad man, and a bad citizen'*.

[69] *General Evening Post,* 3–5 Mar. 1772; *Morning Chronicle,* 27 May 1772.

[70] BL, Add. MS 18469, ff. 61–2: evidence taken before the committee on the state of the East India Company. See also *London Evening Post,* 8 May 1773.

[71] BL, Egerton MS 250, ff. 4–5.

27 Dutch stockholders were brought from Amsterdam in the *Young Johannes* and that many more had arrived in the *Johanna* and other ships to vote at the directorial election of 1763.[72] Whether true or not, these claims highlight contemporary fears that foreign stockholders could influence the policy of what was increasingly being seen as a national and political rather than a private and commercial enterprise.

Given the immense sums of money laid out to create votes and the lengths people went to to secure victory in the Company's elections, the possibility that a party or faction might have courted groups of Dutch investors and encouraged them to travel to London to vote in the directorial elections cannot be entirely ruled out. But in this scenario the foreign stockholders would simply have been participating in the Company's politics, taking one side or another, rather than banding together to dictate affairs as was feared. Not all contemporary statesmen, however, were so concerned about the dangers of foreign stockholding. In 1772, Edmund Burke even floated the idea of organising a petition from the Dutch stockholders after recognising that many of them would be negatively affected by the government's plan decrease the Company's dividend.[73] However, given the prevalent fears that foreign stockholders were attempting to keep up a high dividend for private profit, and against the national interest, such a move would probably have been counterproductive to the opposition cause. A decade later, in 1784, Henry Dundas, perhaps foreshadowing the more liberal commercial policies of the government of William Pitt the Younger, shared his worries about foreign ownership of stock to the house of commons. While debating about providing further financial assistance to the Company, he argued that if the government lowered the dividend too far, it might cause the foreign stockholders to 'sell out; a circumstance that … could not but shake the credit of the Company, and materially affect that of the public'.[74] Despite this more sympathetic attitude from the government, foreign ownership of East India stock never regained the same proportions it had held in the early 1760s. Consequently, it also failed to ignite the same degree of fear among the public.

Religious minorities in Britain were subject to far fewer legal or social impediments to political participation than either women or non-Britons. They could even potentially vote in the unreformed parliamentary electoral system so long as they fulfilled the various other criteria such as age and property qualifications. They were still barred, however, from holding many public offices and were not eligible to be elected to parliament. Thus, for wealthy and influential figures such as Joseph Salvador, an important leader in London's Sephardi Jewish community, the East India Company offered a degree of direct political participation that was denied them elsewhere. Salvador was a second-generation British Sephardi Jew, his grandfather's family having moved from the United Provinces. He remained active within the Bevis Marks Synagogue throughout his life, serving as its *parnas* (head or warden)[75] for many years. He was also a founding member, secretary, and later president of the board of deputies of British Jews.[76] Like Samson Gideon before him, he emerged as a key advisor to

---

[72] *London Chronicle*, 12–14 Apr. 1763.

[73] *Correspondence of Edmund Burke*, ed. Lucy Sutherland (10 vols, Cambridge, 1960), ii, 391: Edmund Burke to the duke of Portland, (5 Dec. 1772).

[74] *Cobbett's Parliamentary History of England*, xxiv, col. 1330: speech of Henry Dundas, 4 Aug. 1784.

[75] OED, www.oed.com (accessed 30 Mar. 2023), s.v. parnas.

[76] Maurice Woolf, 'Joseph Salvador, 1716–86', *Transactions, Jewish Historical Society of England*, xxi (1968), 105, 108; see also ODNB, www.oxforddnb.com (accessed 30 Mar. 2023), s.v. Salvador, Joseph (1716–1786), merchant.

successive British governments on commercial and financial affairs, and was himself a large subscriber to government loans.[77] Unlike Gideon, who married a Christian, had his children baptised and even solicited for a peerage, Salvador sought to engage in politics while maintaining his standing within the Sephardi community, lobbying the duke of Newcastle and Henry Pelham for the introduction of the Jewish Naturalisation Act (1753) on its behalf.[78] Salvador, who was born in London, would not himself have benefited directly from this act as – had it not been repealed in December 1753 after an outburst of politically motivated antisemitism – it would have allowed foreign-born Jews to obtain naturalised subjecthood without having to receive the sacrament as a part of the process.[79]

In addition to lobbying the treasury on behalf of his fellow Jews, Salvador became increasingly entangled in the politics of the East India Company. It would be difficult, if not impossible, to calculate with any degree of accuracy what proportion of the Company's stock was held by religious minorities of various faiths and denominations. We do know, however, that Salvador was far from the only member of London's Jewish community who took advantage of the Company both as a sound place for investment and as an alternative venue for political activity.[80] While Salvador was a large investor in East India stock, he is most notable for being perhaps the most active Jewish stockholder in the Company's politics during this period. He was no mere political chancer in his dealings with the East India Company and would not have been described as one of its 'political' or 'artificial' proprietors. He had held £8,500 of East India stock since his father's death in 1754 and from 1749 had been trading with India as an exporter of coral and an importer of diamonds.[81] Salvador's participation in the Company's politics during the 1760s can therefore be understood as defending his investment as well as preserving and developing his coral and diamond trade, in which he relied on the collaboration of the Company's employees. Nonetheless, it is clear that Salvador got swept up in the politicisation of the Company's general courts in the early 1760s and became not only one of the most zealous supporters of Lord Clive, but also, it seems, participated to some degree in the stock-splitting campaigns in his favour.[82]

In the early 1760s Salvador became embroiled in the Company's factional politics, utilising his connections with government for the benefit of his allies and business partners. Salvador had long been advising the government on financial affairs and was a frequent subscriber to its annual loans. Although he received no direct emolument for his advice, he was given advance notice of important news, such as the beginning of peace negotiations in August 1762. This could enable him to adjust his investments accordingly and he could also potentially gain social capital by being the source of information for others in

[77] Huw Bowen notes that both Salvador and Gideon lent large sums of money to the East India Company during wartime in the 1750s. See Bowen, *Business of Empire*, 34.

[78] On Gideon's lobbying for a peerage, see BL, Add. MS 33055, f. 219: Samson Gideon to the duke of Newcastle, n.d.

[79] Todd Endelman, *The Jews of Britain, 1656–2000* (Oxford, 2002), 75.

[80] We know, for instance, that the 1773 list of East India stockholders named dozens of individuals from prominent London-based Jewish families, including the Mendes DaCostas, the De Castros, the Franks, and the Francos, among many others. Aaron Franks was also a frequent speaker in the Company's heated general courts of the 1760s.

[81] Woolf, 'Joseph Salvador', 104–5.

[82] Woolf, 'Joseph Salvador', 115.

the City.[83] Armed with these strong connections, Salvador sought to bring them to bear to influence the votes of the Company. Although a supporter of Clive, with whom he may have already done business in the diamond trade, initially he sought to broker an accommodation between Clive's supporters and those of Laurence Sulivan, who had begun to differ over the Indian clauses of the peace of Paris in 1762–3.[84] The problem for Salvador was that Clive's attack on the terms of peace involved a critique not just of Sulivan, who had advised the government on that account, but also of the government itself. As a result, in spite of Salvador's attempts to broker a deal where both Clive and Sulivan would sit as directors, the government, in self-defence, threw the weight of its patronage, for the first time, behind a party at East India House and even split stock, using funds in the hands of the paymaster-general.[85] This set a crucial precedent for government interference in the Company's affairs and in so doing directly undermined any semblance of stockholder-democracy in the general court, replacing it with government interest.

Sulivan's alliance with government, solidified by mutual interest, would have probably left Salvador in the wilderness of East India politics were it not for the unexpected resignation of Lord Bute as prime minister and his replacement with George Grenville in April 1763. Although designated by Bute as his successor, Grenville immediately began building an independent base of support, and Clive, with the handful of seats he controlled in the house of commons, proved an attractive acquisition. Almost immediately after Sulivan's success in the directorial elections of April 1763, we find Clive having met with Charles Jenkinson, Grenville's treasury secretary, who had previously been the means of Salvador's connection with Lord Bute.[86] Whether Salvador facilitated the initial connection between Grenville and Clive is unclear; however, we know that once it was established, and Grenville had decided to use the weight of government to support Clive over Sulivan, Salvador became a key intermediary between government and East India House. In doing so, he facilitated loans to support the Company through a post-war financial crisis and fronted the campaign for the restoration of Clive's *jagir* (or feudal grant from the Mughal emperor, worth £27,000 a year).[87]

In addition to the behind-the-scenes liaising between the Company and the government, Salvador increasingly participated publicly in the debates in the general court.[88] Such was his importance within Clive's party that it was he who introduced the motion that resulted in Clive being sent back to Bengal as governor in 1764, in a move orchestrated with the Grenville ministry.[89] He also helped to organise meetings of stockholders prior to debates in the general court to determine policy and take account of their numbers.[90] While Clive

[83]Bute Archives at Mount Stuart, BU/98/7/371: Joseph Salvador to Charles Jenkinson, 30 Aug. 1762; BL, Add. MS 38304, f. 129: Charles Jenkinson to Thomas Rous, 31 Mar. 1765.

[84]Lucy Sutherland, 'The East India Company and the Peace of Paris', *EHR,* lxii (1947), 179–90.

[85]Bute Archives, BU/98/8/192: Joseph Salvador to Lord Clive, 21 Feb. 1763.

[86]*The Grenville Papers: Being the Correspondence of Richard Grenville, Earl Temple, K.G., and the Right Hon. George Grenville, their Friends and Contemporaries,* ed. W.J. Smith (4 vols, 1852), ii, 46.

[87]BL, Add. MS 38397, f. 72: Joseph Salvador to Charles Jenkinson, 21 Oct. 1763; BL, Add. MS 38202, f. 248: Joseph Salvador to Charles Jenkinson, 22 Apr. 1764.

[88]See Bowen, *Revenue and Reform,* 33.

[89]*London Evening Post,* 17–19 May 1764.

[90]*St James's Chronicle,* 3–6 Mar. 1764; *Gazetteer and London Daily Advertiser,* 10 Mar. 1764; BL, Add. MS 38397, f. 78: Joseph Salvador to Charles Jenkinson, 8 Mar. 1764.

was in Bengal between 1764 and 1766, Salvador corresponded with him regularly, updating him on the state of his interests in Britain and offering to remit his fortune and those of his associates to Britain through the diamond trade.[91] However, by the summer of 1765, both Grenville and Jenkinson were out of office. While Clive could find favour in the governments of Rockingham and Chatham, Salvador never again attained such a close connection with government. He remained an important player in Company politics for several more years, if for little reason beyond the size of his investment in stock. However, he gradually lost whatever influence he had as his financial affairs deteriorated in the late 1760s. By the time Jenkinson returned to the treasury board, Salvador's finances were in disarray.[92] He was forced to sell off his lavish properties as well as his impressive collection of fine art. By 1771, he sold his last £500 of East India stock.[93] Thereafter, he had little association with the Company, trying in vain to rekindle his financial affairs while suffering from chronic ill-health. In 1784, Salvador retired to an estate he had purchased many years earlier in South Carolina, where he spent the final two years of his life.

Public commentary on the ownership of stock by religious minority groups, rather than being an object of direct assault in itself, was frequently blended with other criticisms, designed to discredit the institution of the general court as a political body. In the house of commons, Thomas Erskine, who would go on to be lord chancellor, declared that it was 'impolitic and absurd' for 'so immensely important' a part of the empire to be governed by 'a ballot of men and women, and foreigners, enemies to our prosperity'.[94] In the Lords, the earl of Sandwich complained that 'no great things ought to be expected from [the Company's directors], if it was but recollected from what a motley group they were elected, men, women, children, young and old, foreigners, Jews, Papists, and Protestants'.[95] Perhaps Sandwich momentarily forgot that several of these same directors sat as MPs in his pocket boroughs and that he himself was a considerable dealer in East India stock. When parliament increased the voting threshold at general courts from £500 to £1,000 of India stock, Lord Shelburne, who was not even in government, defended the measure by reportedly declaring the £500 proprietors to be '*paltry* stock-brokers, *sharping* Jews and Dutchmen'.[96] Many of the attacks against the authority of the Company's general courts, therefore, exhibited the mixture of misogyny, antisemitism and xenophobia that characterised the patriarchal, Protestant and propertied dimensions of the unreformed political system of 18th-century Britain.

It is important to note that although this article has treated women, foreigners and religious minorities as distinct categories of stockholder, there was much overlap between the groups. For instance, a considerable portion of the female owners of East India stock were Dutch. Joseph Salvador even transferred £1,000 of stock to a female relative in

---

[91] Woolf, 'Joseph Salvador,' 120–21: Joseph Salvador to Lord Clive, 12 May 1766 and Joseph Salvador to Lord Clive, 19 May 1766.

[92] BL, Add. MS 38206, f. 81: Joseph Salvador to Charles Jenkinson, 28 Oct. 1768.

[93] *Public Advertiser*, 27 July 1771; *Gazetteer and New Daily Advertiser*, 16 Jan. 1773; Woolf, 'Joseph Salvador,' 111.

[94] *Cobbett's Parliamentary History of England*, xxiii, col. 1293: speech of Thomas Erskine, 27 Nov. 1783.

[95] *An Authentic Account of the Debates in the House of Lords, on Tuesday, December 9, Monday, December 15, and Wednesday December 17, 1783 (1783)*, 121–2.

[96] *London Evening Post*, 24 June 1773.

Amsterdam who thereby fell into all three categories.[97] It is unknown whether she held stock for anything other than a financial investment. It is important, nonetheless, that women, non-Britons and religious minorities are analysed separately. Each of these groups possessed its own limitations as well as opportunities for participating in the politics of East India House, as have been traced through the political activities of figures such as Mary Barwell, William Bolts and Joseph Salvador.

The same economic and political forces that encouraged a broader and more diverse section of the British population to invest in the Company and partake in its rapid politicisation in the 1760s also ultimately resulted in government intervention. From 1763, successive governments began splitting stock, using the funds of the paymaster general and marshalling existing stockholders within their sphere of influence to vote in particular ways. In 1767, the government took direct action to limit the dividends on the Company's stock to 10 per cent, which had been driven by those deemed to be stock-jobbing to the unaffordable high of 12.5 per cent. They also attempted to limit the practice of stock-splitting by requiring stockholders to have held their stock for six months in order to be eligible to vote. However, this move simply made stock-splitting a longer and therefore riskier practice. The six-month timeframe increased the degree of trust required in the person to whom the stock was transferred and raised the likelihood that the value of the stock could fall dramatically, as it did in the midst of the splitting campaigns of 1768–9, with devastating results for the finances of many involved. In 1773, in addition to other major reforms, parliament took the drastic steps of raising the threshold of stock that qualified a proprietor to vote in general courts from £500 to £1,000 and increasing the terms of office of the Company's directors from one to four years. While there were valid reasons behind these reforms, both in terms of providing stability of management and enabling strategic planning in such a long-distance trade, they also reduced the accountability of directors to their constituents and disenfranchised some 1,200 stockholders.[98] The opposition at the time accused Lord North's government of reducing the number of voting proprietors in order to make the Company easier to manipulate.[99] Although there is strong evidence that North did try to manage the Company after 1773, his efforts were stymied by the fact that there remained a sufficiently independent spirit among the stockholders opposed to government encroachment. Efforts to impose further reform were repeatedly blocked by the general court. Increasingly, as government and the stockholders squabbled over control of the Company, the title of 'old', 'real' or 'independent' proprietors shifted. Initially it had differentiated the long-term investors from those created by stock-splitting. During the 1770s it came to distinguish between those who supported or opposed government intervention in the Company's affairs.

By 1783–4 both Charles James Fox's and William Pitt the Younger's rival India legislation sought to diminish the power of the stockholders, who had been widely blamed for the failure of North's reform legislation. Fox's failed India Bill would have replaced the directors with a group of commissioners, all of whom were to be parliamentarians and were named in the legislation itself. They were to be supported by nine assistant commissioners, who would be composed of individuals holding £2,000 or more of East India stock, the same

[97] Woolf, 'Joseph Salvador', 111.

[98] BL, Egerton MS 250, ff. 121–2: speech of William Dowdeswell, 10 June 1773; *LJ*, xxxiii, 681–2.

[99] BL, IOR/D/28, f. 11: minutes of the committee of correspondence, 27 May 1773.

amount required to serve as one of the Company's directors. Future vacancies among the assistant commissioners would be filled up by election among the stockholders. However, the authority of the assistant commissioners only extended to the Company's commercial activities and, even then, remained subject to the supervision of the parliamentary commissioners. Pitt's India Act of 1784, on the other hand, also sought to limit the power of the general court, but more subtly. The Company's constitution was altered so that the stockholders could no longer overrule the decisions of directors, although they still retained the right to elect them. The directors, however, were placed under the supervision of the newly created crown-appointed board of control. As a result, Pitt's act allowed government to overrule any decisions by the stockholders or their elected directors, all the while maintaining the façade of the Company's independence if no issue was in dispute. Pitt's India reforms therefore drew the curtain over what was a unique period of politicisation of the Company's governing institutions, which, while they were in some ways admirably democratic, were ultimately found to be wholly inappropriate for the governance of an empire.

Tracing the participation of Mary Barwell, William Bolts and Joseph Salvador in the East India Company's governing institutions provides a window into a variety of ways that the Company offered an alternative venue for political activity for groups often otherwise excluded from the formal politics at Westminster. Each of the three individuals discussed, remarkable as they were, exhibit a range of ways that people could participate in the Company's politics, despite certain customary or legal barriers to full political participation. Mary Barwell could invest, vote, lobby and even create votes with her family's wealth, but she could not partake in the Company's debates; Bolts, whose fortune was tied up in Bengal amid tedious legal proceedings, invested only £5 in stock but his impact as a whistle-blower can hardly be overstated; and Salvador, as a well-connected financier, utilised his connections with government for the benefit of both the Company and his private trade in diamonds. Each of them had a substantial impact on the development of the East India Company at various points during its most political decades between 1757 and 1784. Barwell facilitated the elevation of her brother to the supreme council in Bengal and maintained his position there with significant consequences for the longevity of Warren Hastings's governor-generalship. Bolts's revelatory publications paved the way for parliamentary inquiries that resulted in the government's unprecedented intervention to reform the Company in 1773. Salvador was a crucial figure in initiating the process of government intervention in the Company's affairs, facilitating the loans that kept it afloat in pressing times and encouraging government to throw its weight behind Lord Clive and his designs of territorial expansion on the Indian subcontinent.

Index

Packham, Kendra 5
Paine, Thomas 108, 124
Parliamentary Elections Act (1695/6) 18
Parliament, Scottish
  Burgh and shire commissioners 54, 59
  Composition of 53–4
  Committee for controverted elections 56–9, 67, 71
Patronage 11, 21, 22, 44, 46, 49, 50, 67, 69, 71, 76, 79,
  89, 91, 95, 104, 105, 116, 132, 144
Pelham, Henry 26, 27, 29, 30, 143
Pelham, Thomas 26, 31
Phillips, John 117
Phipps, Constantine 17
Pitt, George 45–7, 51
Pitt, William (the Elder), 1st earl of Chatham 96, 145
Pitt, William (the Younger) 91, 94, 96–111, 118, 142,
  146–7
Poll books 5, 7, 12–18, 20–3, 26–7, 34–35, 36, 38,
  40–1, 91, 93–4
Plumb, J. H. 21
Plumptre, Anne 126
Plumptre, Robert 104
Presbyterians 54, 62, 65–6
Price, Richard 126
Prichard, Dr James Cowles 120
Priestley, Joseph 123
Privy council, Scottish 53–71
  Abolition of (1708) 64
Protheroe, Edward 112, 117–19, 121–2, 124,
  127, 128
Protheroe, Sir Henry 127

Quakers 65
Queensberry, James Douglas, 2nd duke of 64
Queen's College, Oxford 83, 85, 89

Reading 112–16, 122, 123, 124–6, 128
Renfrewshire 60, 69
Ridley, Matthew White 17
Rogers, Colin 13
Romilly, Sir Samuel 112, 117, 118, 119, 121,
  125, 127

Salvador, Joseph 142–7
Sancho, Ignatius 14
Sandilands, John 64–5
Sandwich, John Montagu, 4th earl of 145
Schism Act (1714) 29, 32
Schofield, Tom 5, 11
Schoneboom, John 5
Scott, Walter, of Jedburgh 67
Scott, Sir Walter 124
Septennial Act (1716) 7, 72, 75, 79
Sergison, Thomas 26
Seyer, Samuel 124
Shaftesbury, Anthony Ashley Cooper, 1st earl of 41,
  48, 50
Shelley, Lady Margaret 29
Shippen, Robert 82, 87
Shippen, William 82, 83

Sims, John 13
Smith, Adam 126
Smith, Joshua 16
Smith (Smythe, etc.), John 23
Smith, Richard 124
Society of Merchant Venturers 116
Somerset, Charles Seymour, 6th duke of 28–9, 31
Southey, Robert 127
Speck, W. A. 16
Sperrey, John 18
Squadrone volante 53, 57
St John's College, Oxford 86
St Mary Hall, Oxford 78, 82, 86
Stanhope, James, 1st earl 75, 77, 79
Steadfast Society 116, 117, 119, 122
Sterne, Jacques 14
Sterne, Laurence 14
Stockholder-democracy 144
Strangways, Colonel Giles 46, 47, 50
Stuart, Daniel 123
Subscriber-democracy 115
Sulivan, Laurence 133, 135, 144
Sunderland, Charles Spencer, 3rd earl of 75, 77, 79–81,
  83, 87

Tobin, James 122
Townshend, Charles, 2nd viscount 77, 87
Townshend, John 96–103, 105–7, 110
Triennial Act (1694) 7, 75
Trinity College, Oxford 86
Tuffnell, Kevin 14
Turner, Cholmley 14
Turner, William 18

Union, Scottish (1707) 57, 64
Universities 8–10, 92, 108

Verelst, Harry 139, 140
Vincent, Sir Francis 24–5
Voltaire (François-Marie Arouet) 26
Voters
  Black 14
  Floating 38, 40
  Jewish 14, 142–3
  Minors 18, 19, 132
  Non-resident 17, 72–4, 88
  Outvoters 16–17, 72–3
  Resident 9, 18, 32, 40, 61, 62, 70, 72–3, 84–6
Voting age 18
Voting practices and behaviours 14–18
  Clergy, voting behaviour of 36, 46, 92, 101,
    108
  Deference model 36, 38, 39
  Dissenters, voting behaviour of 36, 46, 50–2
  Participatory model 36, 28
  Plumping 14, 17, 100, 107, 121
  Split voting 14, 17, 24, 28–29, 30, 42, 46, 51, 99,
    103, 107, 121
  Straight voting 14, 25, 46
  Tallies 17